GAME
DESIGN
FOR TEENS

AND ALPINE STUDIOS

ISBN: 1-59200-496-2
Library of Congress Catalog Card Number: 2004108017
Printed in the United States of America
04 05 06 07 08 BH 10 9 8 7 6 5 4 3 2 1

COURSE TECHNOLOGY
Professional ■ Trade ■ Reference

Thomson Course Technology PTR, a division of
Thomson Course Technology
25 Thomson Place
Boston, MA 02210
http://www.courseptr.com

SVP, Thomson Course Technology PTR: Andy Shafran

Publisher:
Stacy L. Hiquet

Senior Marketing Manager:
Sarah O'Donnell

Marketing Manager:
Heather Hurley

Manager of Editorial Services:
Heather Talbot

Acquisitions Editor:
Mitzi Koontz

Senior Editor:
Mark Garvey

Associate Marketing Managers:
Kristin Eisenzopf and Sarah Dubois

Project Editor:
Jenny Davidson

Technical Reviewer:
Greg Costikyan

Course Technology PTR Market Coordinator:
Elizabeth Furbish

Copy Editor:
Gene Redding

Interior Layout Tech:
Susan Honeywell, LJ Graphics

Cover Designer:
Mike Tanamachi

Indexer:
Katherine Stimson

Proofreader:
Laura Gabler

For Kim, Jeanne, Susan, Sue, and Corinne—we simply couldn't do what we do without you!

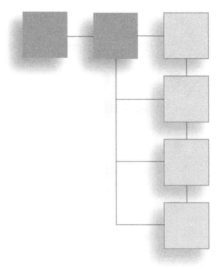

Acknowledgments

This has been a fun book to write. Each of the authors was able to write about the part of game design in which he is an expert. The benefit is that the reader will receive great guidance from a variety of directions. Les is a great artist; Eric is a great audio/sound director; Scott and Brent are great programmers; and Ross rounds out the group with his legal and business background.

Additionally, Jenny Davidson, Mitzi Koontz, and many others have provided significant help with the book. It has been a real pleasure working with each of them and their help has been greatly appreciated. Our biggest thanks go to our families for their continued support. To all who have contributed to our writing this book, we express our deepest appreciation and gratitude.

ABOUT THE AUTHORS

In the fall of 2000, Les Pardew and Ross Wolfley founded Alpine Studios, a game development company focusing on family-friendly games. Eric Nunamaker, Scott Pugh, and Brent Iverson joined the company shortly thereafter.

LES PARDEW started his career in the game industry in 1987 by creating animation for *Magic Johnson Fast Break Basketball* on the Commodore 64. His work in the years since encompasses more that 100 video game titles, including some major titles such as *Super Star Wars, NCAA Basketball, Starcraft: Brood Wars, James Bond 007, Robin Hood: Prince of Thieves,* and *CyberTiger.*

ROSS WOLFLEY began his career in the game industry when he and Les founded Alpine Studios. An attorney by education, Ross is a former US Air Force pilot, having flown and instructed in the F-111 and T-37. He began his business career with WordPerfect Corporation in 1986 and was responsible for marketing, customer support, sales, and business development in the PC, VAX/VMS divisions. At Alpine Studios, he focuses on quality control of the products and the business side of the company.

ERIC NUNAMAKER has been in audio/sound production for game development for over 14 years. He is a musician himself, performing with various groups, and is currently a member of the Utah National Guard 23rd Army Band. As Audio Director, he oversees all audio requirements for Alpine Studios projects, from management to production. Some of the major titles that Eric has worked on include *Starcraft: Brood Wars, Tom Clancy's Rainbow 6, Tom Clancy's Rogue Spear,* and *Oddworld Adventures.*

SCOTT PUGH has been programming games for nearly 20 years as the only programmer, lead programmer, or senior programmer. He has also developed extensive software tools for getting artwork, models, and motion into the games. A few of the major titles that Scott has worked on include *Hardball!, WWF Wrestlemania, Space Jam, WWF War Zone,* and *WWF Attitude.*

BRENT IVERSON graduated cum laude from Weber State University with a BS in mathematics and a French minor and then further pursued his education in the masters of mathematics department at Brigham Young University (Algebraic Topology, Adv. Linear Algebra, Adv. Ord. Differential Equation), with an emphasis in 3D computer graphics (graduate coursework). He joined Alpine Studios in 2001 as a programmer. He has enjoyed working on games on his own time since the first 8086s. Brent has worked on *Kublox, Motocross Mania II, Ford Truck Mania, Combat Medic, Broken World,* and *Silent Run.*

Alpine Studios is a dynamic company made up of industry veterans who have come together to build better games through a better understanding of the development process. Their mission is to create the very best games, while maintaining the highest moral and ethical standards in their products. Alpine Studios' products include *Kublox, Combat Medic, Motocross Mania II,* and *Ford Truck Mania.*

CONTENTS AT A GLANCE

CONTENTS

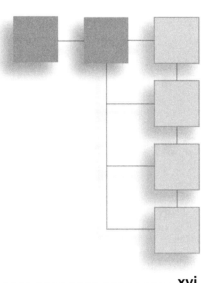

INTRODUCTION

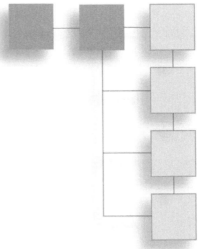

Now that you've come up with a great idea for a game, what do you do? We hope that this book will help you answer that question. Game design is a challenging task because it requires the understanding of art, programming, audio/sound, and business. And, even with all those bases covered, you need to be able to put it all down on paper in a way that the reader will understand it and become enthusiastic about the game. Hopefully, the following chapters will help you understand what is needed to create a solid game design document.

Each chapter is written to help you better understand the elements that will generally be included in a game design document. You should also understand that design documents vary significantly because there are lots of different kinds of games and because authors are different. That is great! It means that you will have to adapt the game design document to fit the needs of your game. After reading and studying the materials provided, we hope you will be better prepared to create your own game design document.

The examples used throughout the book are real-world examples. We hope they will be useful to you. In a few cases, we have altered the examples used in the book to be for PC-based games instead of the original console platforms. As a result, don't scrutinize the details too closely!

We hope that you will enjoy reading and learning from this book. Above all, we wish you great success in your game designing. The game industry is an exciting place to be. We truly hope that this book will aid you in your path to becoming a great game designer. If you need help or you would like to discuss anything contained herein, you may certainly e-mail us at info@alpine-studios.com. We'll route the question to the right person and get back to you.

CHAPTER 1

WHAT IS GAME DESIGN?

If you are interested in how games are created, you have probably wondered how games are designed. What is game design? The word *design* is a verb that means to plan out, devise, or contrive something. Let's say you want to go to a concert with your friends. It is going to take some time and effort to make sure you have a way to get to and from the concert, money to pay for the concert, permission from parents, and a way to meet your friends. Planning all of these details is in essence designing your concert trip. When you have all the details of your concert trip planned, you have just designed your trip. Game design is much the same thing with the exception that instead of designing a simple concert trip, the plan is to create a video game.

Games are very complex productions. Even simple games take a considerable amount of time and effort. This book should help you to understand how games are designed and how you can design games. By studying this book, you should gain an understanding of what it takes to be a game designer.

A professional game design takes a significant amount of effort from a team of very talented individuals. Publishing companies spend thousands of dollars to create game designs. If your dream is to become a game designer, this book should help you on your way.

What's in the Book?

If you picked up this book, you probably have a great idea for a game and are looking for some direction in getting that idea turned into a great game. If that is what you are looking for, then you have come to the right place. This book is designed for you, the beginning game designer. Its objective is to help you learn how to create a game design document that is ready to submit to a publisher.

1

Game Design for Teens takes a realistic approach to helping the beginner learn about designing games. It teaches the designer the important design elements that publishers look for in a game design. It is based on real-world knowledge from professional game developers of all aspects of creating a game design document. It then shows the designer how to create his own design document. Included in Appendix A, "Design Document," is a sample document derived from an actual game design.

If you have dreamed of becoming a game designer, stop dreaming and start designing your own games!

How Are Games Designed?

Before we get into designing games, we should take some time to explain how games are designed. Unlike other forms of entertainment, games are *interactive*. Interactive means that the player has a say in the outcome of the game. In a movie or a TV show, the view is just that; a viewer has no say in the outcome of the show other than turning it off or walking out of the theater. This fundamental design difference makes designing for games infinitely more complex than other, passive media.

Most beginning game designers think that the critical part of coming up with a great game is the idea for a good premise or story. Unfortunately, the story is only part of the total game design. In a later chapter we will cover in detail all the major features of creating a game design document. For now, let's take a quick look at the major parts of a game concept.

- Gameplay
- Story
- Characters
- Environments
- Audio
- Interface
- Fun

As you can see from the list, there are many facets to creating a good game design. In fact, it is rare that one person is skilled enough in all the necessary areas to complete a game design by himself. Many game designs are the joint efforts of a team of people with expertise in the different areas of game design.

In larger companies and most smaller development studios, a team develops a game design. The team usually consists of the following members:

- Designer
- Writer
- Programmer
- Artist
- Musician

Sometimes a person who is talented in more than one area will fill more than one role on a design team. For example, a designer may also be a good writer and therefore will fill the role of both designer and writer. This is not to say that you can't come up with a good game design working alone. It is just important to note that your design is competing with other designs that were created by teams of experts. If you can find some talented people to work with, your design will usually improve.

When designing a game, the team collaborates on the design. The word *collaboration* means that the team talks about the design and listens to everyone's ideas. Then the team works together to create a great design document, with members contributing in their own areas of expertise. The collaboration process often leads to significant contributions to the design if the team is able to come up with a common vision.

Vision of the Game

Building a common vision is sometimes difficult. It is the first thing a design team needs to accomplish before anything else. Every game needs to have a core concept. The core concept of a game is the underlying premise that drives the game. For example, if the underlying premise of the game is to build the most realistic racing game ever, a discussion of fantasy course design is inappropriate. It is the designer's job with the help of the team to come up with the core concept that will drive the game design. Core concepts are one-sentence statements that express exactly what the game will be. A clear, easy-to-understand core concept will be the first step in creating a common vision for the game within the design team and later within the development team.

The game design team needs to have a common vision for the game. Reaching a common vision takes leadership on the part of the team leader and the willingness of all members of the team to work together for the good of the game. No one member of the team should push the design in a direction that benefits only him or her. For example, the artist should not push so hard on the number of polygons for characters that it causes the game to exceed the technology. The result will be that the game may look beautiful but only run at one frame per second. On the other hand, the programmer should not put artificial art restrictions on the art team that make the graphics of the game uncompetitive. Team members need to learn to work together in a spirit of mutual desire for the best combination of game attributes.

In game design, the designer typically is the team leader and is responsible for keeping the team on track. Here are some suggestions for the team leader to help him or her with running a game design team.

- Be organized but flexible. Design meetings can get out of hand very quickly. The team leader needs to have an agenda for every meeting so that all members understand the items that will be covered in the meeting. There needs to be ample time to fully cover the topics on the agenda. At times there will be moments of inspiration where some great progress is made. The team leader needs to learn to recognize these moments and not stifle creativity by calling a discussion short just to get on to other topics. This balance of organization and flexibility is sometimes difficult to reach, but it is a sign of a good leader.

- During meetings where ideas are generated, the leader needs to remember not to criticize the ideas. Criticism will discourage team members from expressing their own ideas. Remember that the next idea a team member comes up with may be the one that will be pivotal for the game. Criticism will often cause the team to keep their ideas to themselves.

- Make sure everyone on the team participates fully. There is nothing worse than to have one or more team members who are not fully committed to the game. If for whatever reason a team member holds back or is too involved in other things, the whole team will suffer. The team leader needs to get a commitment from each team member to support the effort completely and then hold the members accountable for their assigned parts of the design.

- Build a spirit of cooperation. Game design teams often come from differing backgrounds. Programmers and artists may have difficulty understanding each other. The same thing is true for musicians and other team members. Take time in the meetings to help build understanding for the issues that each team member feels are important. Don't proceed with the meeting if there is a basic conflict of opinions. Try to encourage open-mindedness among team members.

- Keep track of ground covered. Make sure that someone is taking notes during the design meeting so that the team doesn't have to cover ground that has already been covered. After the meeting, have the notes printed and distributed to all team members so that everyone can keep track of what was discussed. Make sure all team members have a list of specific assignments. In subsequent meetings, make sure the notes and assignments from the previous meeting are reviewed.

- Keep the core concept of the game foremost in everyone's mind. It is real easy to get sidetracked in a design session. The best way to avoid derailing the design is to constantly remember the game's core concept.

This list should help the team leader work effectively with the rest of the design team. Running a creative team is more of an art than it is a science, and game design is definitely a creative endeavor.

The Game Layout Chart

The game layout chart is the first step in defining the game's design. The chart works as a blueprint of the game, defining what the game will be and how the game will work. It should be a simple and clear diagram. The chart should show how the game will work and all of the areas in the game. It should also show how the player navigates through the game. Figure 1.1 is an example of a simple game layout chart.

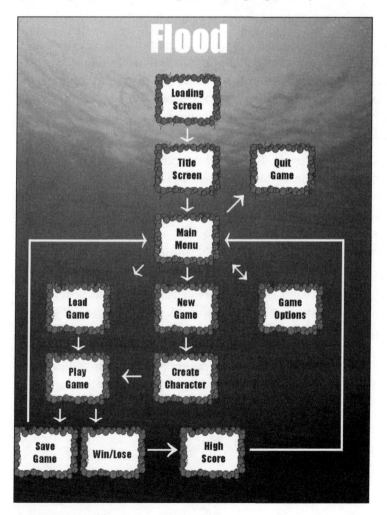

Figure 1.1
An example of a simple game layout chart

The advantage of creating a game layout chart is that it forces the designer to fully explore how the game will work. As a designer works on the chart, game elements often will change because the designer is getting a better picture of how the game will work. For this reason, it is important to make the chart in such a way that things can be moved around.

Charts can be as complex as needed to explain the game but should be as simple as possible so that the reader can quickly tell how the game will work.

Designing Gameplay

Gameplay is an industry term not found in most dictionaries. It refers to the process of playing a game. A game that is fun to play, has controls that are easy to use and understand, and has objectives that make sense is often said to have "good gameplay."

Designing good gameplay into a game is not easy because so many factors influence good gameplay. However, visualizing how the game will play is a critical first step in starting the game design. A good exercise is to imagine playing the game and then think about all the different aspects of the game that go into the game experience. How is the game controlled? What do you see on the screen? What does the game sound like? How do you progress through the game?

Often when I am trying to visualize a game, I will hold the game controller in my hands and pretend that I am playing the game. If the game is on a PC, I will use the mouse and keyboard with the system turned off just to get a feel for how to control the game. I find that the control system for a game is one of the most overlooked aspects of game design yet one of the most important. A game is supposed to be fun. When visualizing the game control system, I ask myself, "Is this fun?" If it isn't fun to control, it is not going to be fun to play.

Next I think of how the game looks. Game graphics are getting better and better all the time. To be competitive, a game has to have great graphics. A good thing to ask yourself when you begin a game design is, "What will we do to make our game stand out from other games in graphics?" We will cover designing art later, but it is important to get some kind of a feel for the graphics at the beginning of the design process. This will help give the team member responsible for designing the graphics some initial direction.

In addition to the graphics, you also need to visualize the game navigation. How does the player get started? How many screens does the player have to go through before he or she can start playing the game? What do the menu screens look like?

Like game graphics, games have sound as well. Think about the audio experience of the game as you pretend to play the game. What kind of music do you need in the game? Don't just think of the music that you like to listen to, but rather think of the music that really embodies the mood of the game. A good practice is to watch some movies that have a theme similar to your game. Listen to the music in those movies.

Another aspect of gameplay is a player's progress in the game. As a rule, games should increase in challenge level as a player progresses through the game. The designer needs to think about how a game will become more challenging and how that will affect the other aspects of the game experience. Will the game become harder to control? Will the game become faster? Will the obstacles or enemies become stronger?

As the game design progresses, you will have to continue to reevaluate the gameplay. In fact, the gameplay design isn't truly done until the game is finished.

Designing the Story

I remember a peer of mine once telling me that a game doesn't need a story, it just needs an excuse. While there is much to what he said, I don't agree with him completely. Games are different than other media in that the player creates the story or at least has a hand in the creation of the story. A game is a series of possibilities that becomes a story when it is played. Therefore, writing a story for a game is different and in some ways more demanding than writing for other media.

In designing the story for a game, the designer or writer needs to take into account the many possibilities that result from player choices. In some ways it is more like writing a spreadsheet than writing a story. For example, a game has a player enter a room with three possible exits; the writer must account for each exit in the story. What happens when the player uses exit one versus exit two? How does it affect the game? Can the player re-enter the room? Does anything happen according to *when* the player exits? What other conditions apply? Is there someone or something chasing the player? What happens if the player stays in the room for an extended period of time? Figure 1.2 shows an excerpt from an adventure game.

Location	Items in room	Characters in room	Events	Exits
Living Room	couch, lamp, desk, recliner, TV, Matchbook, magazines, knife	Old man on recliner watching TV	Talk with old man	door to hall=F11
			Find knife	Window to porch=F7
			Find matchbook	door to kitchen=F16
Porch	porch swing, Railing, shovel	dog	dog attacks	Front steps=F21
			use shovel on dog	jump rail=F29
				window to living room=F3
Hall	phone, coat rack	maid	talk to maid	door to living room=F3
			use phone	door to dining room=F33
				door to restroom=F39
				stairs to second floor=F45
Kitchen	stove, refrigerator, counter, table, two chairs, sink, cabinets, pot of soup, meat cleaver, dishes, broom	cook	talk to cook	door to living room=F3
			eat soup	door to hall=F11
			take cleaver	door to dining room=F51
			take broom	back door=F57

Figure 1.2
The spreadsheet shows the organization of the possible story outcomes.

As you can see in Figure 1.2, a story for a game can become very complex with branching events and situations.

The complexity of the story will depend in large part on the type of game you wish to create. A puzzle or racing game may have very little story to it, while an adventure game may have a very complex story.

Two parts of the story are written in a normal story fashion. Those story elements are the *back-story* and the *post-story*. The back-story is the events that lead up to the game. For example, if the game is a racing game, the back-story will be the events that lead up to the first race. The story may be about a young driver who enters his first race on a dare from his buddies. The post-story of the game is the events that happen if the player wins or the events that happen if the player loses. In the case of a racing game, the winning event may be a major endorsement for the player, while losing results in ridicule from his friends.

Designing Characters

In almost every game—with the exception of puzzle games—the player has a character or vehicle to control. This character or vehicle is called the *player character* or *player vehicle*. In some games, the player will have both a player character and a player vehicle. In addition, many games will have what is called non-player characters, or NPCs for short. With almost every game the designer has the task of designing characters.

Character design entails two parts: a written description and a character sketch.

Character Description

A character description is a short explanation of the character. It is usually the first step in creating a character design. The following is an example of a character description.

> Malden Stonebridge—Malden is a guard in the queen's palace. He is large for a dwarf and was chosen as a guard for his strength and skill with pole arms. He never leaves his post and is very dedicated to the queen. Malden wears a red uniform (similar to the English Beefeaters' uniform) with a white neck ruffle and gloves. Atop his head he wears a dragon-crested helmet. He carries an ornate spear as a weapon. A creature that looks like an overgrown rodent with large luminous eyes accompanies Malden on his rounds.

The idea of the character description is to give everyone a clear picture of the character. In some cases a character description will also include a breakdown of the character's attributes as they are applicable in the game. For example, a vehicle in a racing game may have a number of attributes, such as top speed, cornering, suspension, weight, and frame strength. These attributes may play a significant role in the game. A human character may have attributes like strength, speed, dexterity, and intelligence.

Character Sketch

A character sketch usually accompanies a character description in a game design. The character sketch is a detailed picture of the character. It is usually derived from the character description. Figure 1.3 is a character sketch of Malden Stonebridge.

Figure 1.3
Character sketches are usually derived from the character description.

The amount of time and effort put into the character design is dependent on how important the character is to the game. Some character sketches are done in black and white as a simple pencil sketch. Figure 1.4 is an example of a more simple character sketch.

The designer should designate to the artist the time and effort for a character sketch. Central characters like player characters or important NPCs should take priority over minor characters unless the minor character is very unique. Unique characters should be drawn with detail because the artist creating the 3D models for those characters will need greater direction in building those models once the game is in development.

Not only are character sketches used in the design of the game, they also are often used in the promotion of the game. Sometimes a good character sketch will do more for a game getting picked up by a publisher than the written document. To promote the game to the public, the publisher may also use the sketches. It is very important that the design contain the very best art possible.

Figure 1.4
Some sketches are done as a simple pencil sketch.

Designing Environments

An environment is the setting for the game or, in other words, the world of the game. The environment for a dark horror game may be an old abandoned mansion, while the environment for a racing game may be a crowded speedway. The environment of the game is important because it is the stage upon which the game takes place, and it should be designed carefully. Like character designs, environments have both a written description and a drawing or photo of the location.

Written Description

The written description of an environment is a brief outline of the location, with any important gameplay features. A gameplay feature is anything in the environment that the player can interact with. For example, a computer console that allows the player to move to a new level is an important feature. The following is a written description of a dungeon hallway:

The hall extends for about 40 feet from the foot of the stairway to a massive door at the far end. Along either side of the hallway about every 10 feet are doorways cut into the solid rock walls. Each doorway is fitted with a rusty ironbound wooden door about 4 inches thick. The doors have no windows and only a small slot at the base to pass through a meal tray. The walls are damp with slime. The floor is covered with slime water about 1 inch deep. The massive door at the far end of the hall looks about the same as the other doors except that it is larger by half with a painted shield on the center of the door. The painted shield is of a hangman's noose.

The better the description of the environment, the better readers of the design document will be able to get a feel for the world of the game. Care should be taken to describe the world in detail, so that when the game is in production, the development team will be able to create the game world accurately.

Environment Pictures

In some instances the game will take place in a real-world setting, or the game may take place in a setting that is very similar to a real-world location. In those situations, the designer just needs to take pictures of the location. Figure 1.5 and Figure 1.6 are location pictures.

Figure 1.5
A European city location photo is used for an environment picture.

Figure 1.6
A photo of an alley sets the stage for the game.

More often than not, a photo of the desired location will not be available to the design team. In those situations, the design team will need to create sketches of the environment. The sketches can be in either color or black and white, depending on the importance or complexity of the area. Figure 1.7 is a sketch of a game setting, with the main character done as a pencil sketch.

Figure 1.7
The main character stands in the center of an environment sketch.

Like the character sketches, environment sketches are sometimes used to promote the game.

Designing Audio

Audio is an ever-increasingly important part of game design. Game audio is the combination of all the sound effects, voice, and music used in a game. Many games have a signature audio feel to them. You know how you often can tell what game your buddy is playing just by listening to the game without even seeing it onscreen? The game designer needs to think about the audio experience of the game. What kinds of music will the game have? What kind of sound effects will the game need? Will the game have character dialogue or narration? What will the volume of each audio component be during the course of the game? Should the sound effects be louder in some areas or should the music?

Unlike characters and environments, a paper document can't contain audio files. However, it can contain a description of the audio. If the document will be delivered on a CD-ROM or other form of media that supports audio files, samples of the game audio can accompany the document. The following is a description of the audio in a particular location in a strategy game:

> The initial base is established on the barren hillside. In the background the lonely moan of a desert breeze is heard. Mechanical noises come from the machinery used to extract raw materials from the ground. The whine of hovercraft is heard as units transport refined metals to the manufacturing plant. Banging and construction noises are heard from the manufacturing plant. The sound effects are kept low to create the feeling of a busy colony just starting out on a desert planet. Over the background noise, the music plays an inspiring march song. The highest level of sound is the command center giving the player audio updates on the progress of the colony and its defenses.

This example is a vivid description of the audio for a scene in a game. In this case the example is a combination of sound effects and music, with voice as the loudest feature of the scene. For practical purposes, the designer may wish to divide the three audio elements into separate categories and create a spreadsheet to organize all the audio design.

Interface Design

Game interface is an overall term that describes all the elements used in the game to give the player control over the game or information. The interface is both the physical controls, such as the mouse and keyboard for a computer game, or a game controller for a console game, and the visual elements on the screen that are used for information and control. Game designs should include descriptions of both elements of the interface.

In most games, with the only possible exception being custom-built game systems such as arcade machines, the physical interface controls are set, and the designer has little say in what they are. A computer game must be designed to be played with a mouse or a keyboard or a combination of both. A console game system has its own controller that the designer must use. If the designer does not use the standard control devices, he runs the risk of having the majority of players unable to play the game.

Even with a standard input device, the game designer has some leeway in configuring the device. In other words, you may not be able to change the input device, but you can design how it will be used.

The best way to show how an input device will be used in the game is to draw a diagram of the device, with call-outs indicating the uses for each button.

Onscreen Interface Graphics

A game often will include an onscreen system for control and information. In other words, the interface is not always just in the controller or the mouse. In many games there is a system of displayed graphics like buttons or a health meter. These items are included in the overall term *interface*. These onscreen elements can be menu windows or screens, or they can be game components that are displayed during the game. Menu windows or screens are interface elements that help the player navigate through a game or make choices during a game. For example, a fantasy role playing game may have an inventory for the main character. The player can choose to look at the inventory by clicking with the mouse on an icon at the bottom of the screen. When the player clicks on the icon, a window fills the screen with pictures of all the items the player is carrying. Menus can also be used to help the player set up a game. Figure 1.8 is a mock-up of a Game Options menu.

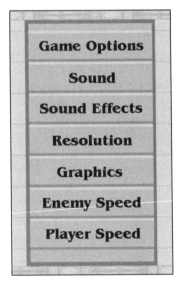

Figure 1.8
Menus are used for setting up game options.

Interface elements displayed during gameplay are sometimes referred to as the HUD, which stands for *heads up display*, a term taken from the aviation industry. This display is primarily for giving the player critical game information such as health status or current score. In many games it is on display constantly and is updated in real time. HUDs are tricky to design because they need to look nice while staying unobtrusive to the rest of the game. They usually occupy the edges of the screens to allow the main play action to take the center. Figure 1.9 shows a HUD design for a racing game.

Figure 1.9
A HUD design for a racing game

We will cover more about interface design in another chapter.

Designing Fun

Designing fun is the most elusive element of any game design. It is also the hardest to define. There is no concrete way to describe how a game will be fun. Fun is something that has to be shown rather than something that is described. In fact, many game designs don't even include it as part of the design. I have found, however, that attempting to describe how a game is fun helps everyone working on the game to have a better vision of the goals of the game.

The best way I have found to describe the fun of a game is to narrate a small sample walk-through of the game. The following is a brief excerpt from a fantasy game:

The wind moans softly over the grassy hillside as the player looks down into the village below. A dog howls in the background. There is something wrong with the village that the player notices right away. There are no people in the streets. In fact, other than a few stray chickens pecking in the street, there is nothing moving. As the player steps forward, three figures appear before him. One moment there is nothing between him and the village, and the next he is confronted by three death mask warriors who had hidden themselves from his view. Each is carrying a long curved sword and a spiked shield. The three warriors spread out for an attack, with the largest taking the center and the two smaller figures flanking the player on either side.

Choosing to attack the warrior on his right, the player sprays the other two warriors with a blast of magic wind, knocking them over for a moment. With a somersaulting leap, he then clears the sword swing of the right-hand warrior, coming down hard with both feet planted on his chest. A quick binding spell fastens the warrior to the ground with vines as the player rolls to his feet a few yards away.

The smaller of the two remaining warriors has regained his feet and is charging the player. The player quickly casts a magical fist of super-hardened air full in the face of the oncoming warrior, knocking him senseless.

The last warrior has regained his feet and with a roar swings a flail over his head. The warrior releases the flail, sending it toward the player and hitting him in the chest. As the player regains his feet, the third warrior is full upon him with sword raised. Only a quick dodge to the side saves the player from a splitting headache.

The player raises his staff and begins to twirl it, creating a magical shield, which stops the blows of his opponent. Then with another spell the player fastens the third warrior in place with vines crawling up his legs. He then drops the magical shield and sends another magical fist to cold-cock the trapped warrior. With a smile he turns and walks to the village. He has defeated his three opponents without killing, keeping the covenants of the higher magic.

The above example is more of a story narrative of a game encounter. The idea is to help readers of the design visualize the possibilities of the game and help them see how the game can be fun.

Fun is a hard term to define. What is fun to one person is boring to another. Some people like action games where the object of the game is control, while others like turn-based games where strategy is more important. It is important to let the reader of the design document understand the type of player that your game will appeal to. For example, you can say, "My game will appeal to racing fans who are looking for a truly realistic racing experience." You have just stated the type of people who will find your game appealing. Now you can describe your game to that audience.

Game Demo

In addition to a design document, which is the focus of this book, design teams may want to consider creating a playable demo of their game. A playable demo is a working version of the game that shows basically how the game will play. The closer the demo is to a finished look and feel, the better chance it has of attracting the attention of a publisher.

Demos are expensive to create and generally take a larger team because there is much more work to be done. A good demo will show the publisher that your team understands not only how to design a game but how to build one as well. The problem with creating a demo is that if the demo doesn't look as good and play as well as the final game, it can actually hurt your chances of landing a publishing deal. Regardless of whether you feel your design and demo are good enough to compete with professional games, creating a demo is a good way to test your game ideas. Even a simple demo can help you explore concepts.

The idea here is to learn how to design games so that you can develop your skills to a professional level. At some point, if you stick with it, you will have something you will want to show a publisher. It may be when you are looking for a job as a game designer or when you are putting together a young development team, looking for that first professional game. Whenever it is, understanding how your designs work because you created a demo and tested them will give you a clearer picture of good game design.

Demos usually take precedence over a game design document in the eyes of a publisher. If you decide to create a demo of your game, don't send it to a publisher until the demo is a good version of your game idea. Make sure all the art and the sound in the demo are of professional quality. It is also important to refine the game controls so that they behave as closely as possible to the final version of the game.

Creating good demos of a game takes money unless you can convince your team to work for free until the game is picked up for publication. In any case, it is a good idea to limit a demo to a small portion of your game. A smaller, well-done demo is much more impressive than a massive, poorly made demo.

Game Engines

One of the easiest ways to create a game demo is to use an existing game engine. Game engines are software programs that development teams use to run their games. A number of game engines are available for beginning teams to use to create demos of their games. A quick search on the Internet will show that there are many engines available. Some have very impressive credentials, with hundreds of games completed using their software. Others may be just as good but not as high profile or with as many completed games.

The best way to choose an engine for your demo is to look at the games that have already been created with the engine. If you can find a game that is similar to yours and plays the way you want your game to play, you can put that engine on your short list of possible technologies.

Game engines usually have a licensing fee; however, sometimes you can use the software free or at very little cost to create demos. Contact the individual engine developer to get information on programs for new developers.

Art for Demos

It is usually best to create your own art for a demo because the publisher will want to see what you can create. If you have a problem getting art, there are a few other things you can do. The Internet is filled with free or inexpensive 3D models. Many of those models can be downloaded and used right off the Internet. Generic things like trees, buildings, and vehicles are the easiest items to find, but there are even a few characters. The benefit of using these models is that you can get moving right away. The drawbacks, however, are many. Many of the models on the Internet are recognizable, so your game may look like many others out there. The quality of the models varies greatly. Some are very good, and others are unusable. While some of the models may look good, they may not render well in your game because of texture size or number of polygons.

A better way to get art for your demo is to make a deal with an artist or a group of artists. Some may like your game idea and be willing to supply the art for a demo in return for a small fee and an agreement to have them create the final game. Some may even join your team and invest time and effort in the design as a partner with you. Some of your friends may just like the idea of having their art in a game and donate the art just for the fun of it.

Sound for Demos

As with art, there are many sound libraries available for both sound effects and music. Some of these libraries are very good and work great with games. Many game development houses routinely license sound effects libraries. Some also license music libraries. The problem with sound libraries is the same as it is with art. Many of the sound effects are recognizable. Some are very expensive. Sometimes libraries don't have the right sound. All-in-all, sound libraries are generally more effective than art libraries for game demos.

The best way to get the right sound for a game demo is to have someone write it. Like artists, musicians may want to help you with your game and be willing to work on it. Before you bring a musician on your team, take some time to listen to his work. Has he created music similar to your game before? Does he just write music or can he do sound effects as well? What experience does he have in voice recordings? Check with your friends to see what talents they have. It may surprise you what you find.

Non-Playable Demo

Another solution to the demo issue is to make a non-playable demo. A non-playable demo is a movie of your game. The movie shows how the game will look and how it will be played but does not have any controls that the player can use. The advantage of the movie is that it can be created with less time and money than a playable demo, and you might even be able to build it with just you and some talented friends.

A non-playable demo is created in the same way as a movie is created. The designer comes up with a script of the demo. The artist then creates a series of storyboards. From the script and the storyboards, the team then builds the demo using an art package such as a 3D modeling animation software program. Each scene is built and rendered to look just like the final game. Once the graphics are finished, the sound can be laid in, and the demo is ready.

Summary

This chapter has been a very quick overview of game design. Hopefully it has given you an idea of what goes into a design and what you need to learn to be a game designer. The rest of this book will go into greater detail concerning concepts of game design.

In this chapter, the following concepts were covered:

- Designing games is a complex process involving many skills. Designs usually are created by teams of professionals who have expertise in fields such as programming, writing, art, and sound.
- Beginners can form teams to create game designs.
- The designer is usually the leader of a game design team. A game designer needs to use good leadership skills to manage a design team.
- Designing gameplay is a process that continues even after the design is completed and the game is in production.
- Many elements of a game design are artwork. Great artwork can help a design grab the publisher's attention, while poor artwork can doom a design.
- A demo is a valuable part of a game design if the demo is as good as the final game. A bad demo can kill the chances of a good design getting published.

Chapter 2

What Is a Game Designer?

So you want to be a game designer. What exactly is a game designer, and what does a game designer do? This chapter will explain what game designers are, what they do, and what you have to learn to become one. It will also give you some step-by-step projects to help you get started designing games.

The Game Designer

Let's start by defining what a game designer is. A game designer is the person responsible for developing a game concept into a plan of development for a game. The plan is called a game design document. This plan is the blueprint of the game and is used by the development team to create the game.

In a lot of ways, the game designer can be compared to an architect. An architect defines every aspect of a building, from the way it looks to how it is wired. Likewise, the game designer defines every aspect of a game, from how it looks to how it will be created.

Crafting a great game takes dedicated work and a passion for games. The best game designers are those who not only love to play games but love to study them as well. A good game designer should have the following attributes:

- Loves to play games
- Is a creative thinker
- Understands the game development process
- Is good at solving problems
- Knows how to have fun
- Knows how to work
- Is dedicated to creating great games

This list may not contain every attribute of a good game designer, but it does contain the most important ones. If you don't have every attribute on the list, don't worry—you can work on it as you go. Just look at the list as a goal for aspiring game designers. As you read this book and gain experience in designing games, you will soon find you are becoming competent in most areas of the list. Let's take a closer look at each attribute.

Love to Play Games

Gamers can generally tell if the designer loves playing games by playing the games that he creates. A good game designer needs to have love for his work. He needs to spend time playing games, because he needs to understand the game-playing experience. It is the game experience that you are designing for when you design a game.

Games are different from many other types of entertainment in that they are active. When a person plays a game, that person is involved in the entertainment. This involvement is what makes games so interesting for so many people. The more the designer can get the player involved in the game, the better the game experience will become.

The best way to learn about the game experience is to experience it. But don't just limit yourself to one type of game. You might like to play shooters or fantasy role playing games, but limiting your playing time to just those types of games will not give you a very broad base of game experiences. I have often found that playing games outside of the ones I really enjoy can give me ideas for making better games.

Creative Thinker

Game design is a creative process. Without creativity, games can become stale and boring. The game designer must be a creative thinker. Creative thinking means that the game designer is able to solve problems creatively. The designer is also able to make connections between seemingly unrelated topics or subjects to come up with something new and innovative.

Creativity is the essential in game design, but it needs to be tempered with good game sense. Some game designers get so involved in doing something no one has done before that they forget that the game needs to be fun for the player. There may be good reason that no one already created that game. It may not be any fun. The best way to work with creative thought is to channel it toward something useful.

Creative thought channeled by knowledge and good game sense can become a powerful tool in the hands of a game designer. The process kind of works like this:

1. The designer is presented with a problem.
2. The designer studies the problem to gather as much information as possible.

3. When the designer feels that the problem is understood, then she or he goes into a free form creative exploration. The exploration is where the designer searches for ideas from any and every source imaginable.

4. The ideas are written down as they come, without any judgment. That will come later. The exploration stage may take some time.

After creative exploration, the next phase is to channel the creativity. All of the creative ideas are organized. During the organization phase, the designer will have a chance to evaluate the ideas and categorize them into different levels of usefulness. This is the analysis phase, which is important because it puts the creative ideas into perspective based on practicality. The best ideas are those that are both creative and practical.

After the analysis phase, the designer should have a list of ideas to solve the problem, but the work is not done yet. The last step is to choose the best idea and convert it to use in the game. This step may take more creativity and analysis. The idea will need polishing and refining to get it to work in the best way possible. Figure 2.1 shows the creative progression chart.

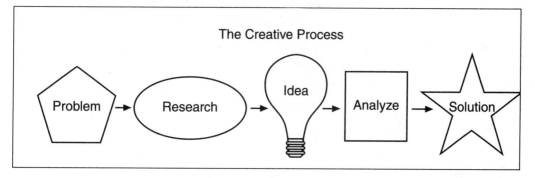

Figure 2.1
Creative thinking needs to have structure to be effective.

This chart should be viewed as a guide, not as a rigid system. The point is that the best ideas are those that combine great creativity with solid practicality. You should practice the concept. Think of some problems you see in games. Go through the creative process defined by the chart in Figure 2.1 and see what kind of solutions you come up with. You just might be able to solve some problems and in the process come up with some good ideas for future games.

The Game Development Process

To be a good designer you have to understand how games are made. You might have the greatest idea ever conceived for a game, but with no solid knowledge of game development the idea can't progress. Progression of the game idea to a game comes only when the designer understands the process and knows how to get to the next step.

Game development requires the skills of a number of highly talented people working together for months, if not years. Some development teams are as large as 100 people, but most are smaller and number around 20 individuals. Each person brings a certain skill set to the group. The designer needs to understand the role each person plays in creating the game. It is a little like the composer of a symphony. The composer needs to understand each instrument, even if he or she doesn't play each one. Like the composer, the game designer needs to understand each facet of development, such as programming, art, animation, sound, and so on

After the game is developed, the work is still not done. The game has to get to the players, which requires extensive work from another team of specialized people. These people create the packaging, do the marketing, get the game to the retail outlets, and then sell the game to the players. Figure 2.2 shows the basic process for creating and selling games. It is broken down into four major categories: concept, pre-production, production, and product.

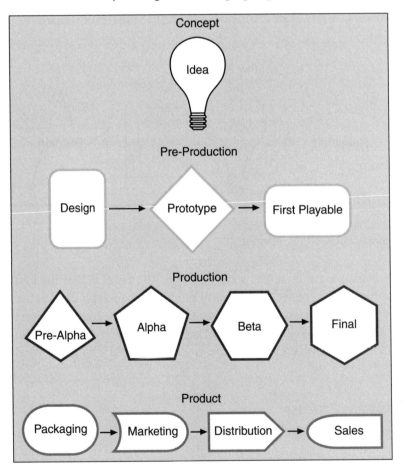

Figure 2.2
The process for creating and selling games includes four major categories.

Concept

The concept phase of game development is the idea phase. It is where the designer jots down the idea for the game. It usually results in a basic concept document of anywhere from 1 to 10 pages of game information. It is not a full design document but rather a brief explanation of the game.

Most aspiring game designers have got this stage under control. They have one if not several game concepts. Some are well defined and documented with drawings and charts. The problem is that they can't get past this stage to the next one.

Pre-Production

The pre-production phase is the foundation of the game. It is where the game design document is created. During the pre-production phase of the game development, the designer takes a leading role in day-to-day operations.

The pre-production phase generally has three distinct stages: design, prototype, and first playable. Each stage has a purpose. The design stage is where the design document is created and the production plan for the game is generated. The prototype is where the development team takes the design and creates a rapid prototype of the game. The purpose of the prototype is to give everyone an idea of how the game will look and function, but it generally has very limited playability. The last stage is the first playable. The first playable stage is a limited playable version of the game. The purpose of the first playable version is to be a proof-of-concept of the game. In other words, the first playable version shows how the game plays.

Production

The production phase is where the game is developed. It is in this stage that the game is built, tested, and brought to a final product. This is the longest and most costly of all stages of development. It includes the development of all the game assets, implementation of the assets into the game, programming the game, and testing the game.

During the pre-production phase of the game development, the designer takes a leading role in day-to-day operations. During the production phase, the leading role is that of the producer, who manages the day-to-day affairs based on the production plan. The designer's role during the production phase is more of a problem solver. When unforeseen problems with the design occur, the designer works out those problems with the development team and updates the production plan with the producer.

Product

The product phase is not always considered to be part of game development, but it is important for the designer to understand the whole picture, so it is included in this section. The designer is not as involved in the product phase because there are new games that need to be designed. However, the designer often will be consulted on things such as packaging and marketing. It is also important that the designer understand how the game will be sold to the consumer. All of these things affect the sales of the game, which affect the budget for the game.

Solving Problems

Earlier we went over the creative process, which is related to solving problems. Solving problems is a specific skill that designers need to have in abundance. The creative process is a good way to approach the solving of problems, but it is not the only way. Many problems require more than creative thought. They may also require research, experimentation, and compromise.

Many problems in games have already been solved in other games. If it is a problem in your game, chances are it is also a problem for other games. Research is a great tool for solving problems. Once you have a well-defined problem, do some research to see if that problem was solved in other games. Find out what they did to solve the problem and see if their solution will work with your game.

Games are usually at the forefront of technology. The designer often has to go out into uncharted territory when developing a game concept because of the constant pressure to always find something new and unique. Therefore, as a designer you also have to be a bit of a scientist. Many times the solution to solving the problem of finding something new is unknown, and the only way to find out if a solution will work is to experiment with it.

Sometimes there is no adequate solution to a problem. Either the technology is just not robust enough to handle the game as designed or the planned solution just isn't fun. In those cases, the designer has to find a viable compromise. In other words, if what you thought would work just doesn't, what else will?

A big area of compromise in games is between graphics and technology. Ever since the beginning of game development, there has always been pressure to have the best game graphics possible. It is easy for the artist to create great-looking models and scenes, but if the game technology can't support them, they might as well not even try. The compromise is in doing the best possible graphics within the technology limitations of the game.

Is It Fun?

The key ingredient for any successful game is what is called the fun factor. The fun factor is very hard to pin down. What is fun for one person is not for another. Some people love to sit for hours doing matching games, while matching games drive other people crazy. Some people love a fast-paced first-person shooter, and others find that the first-person perspective makes them sick. About the best a designer can do is to make the game fun for its intended audience.

The intended audience for a game is the basic group of people that the game is targeted toward. For example, if the game is targeted toward business travelers waiting at airports, a fun game may be an interesting puzzle game. On the other hand, if the game is targeted to young teenage boys who love head-to-head competition, a fun game might be a sports game that they can play over the Internet.

By defining the intended audience, the designer can narrow the requirements for fun to a specific group of people who have common traits. Once the group is narrowed down, the designer then can start to work on understanding what that group feels is fun. Some of the best game ideas come not from professional designers but rather from the people who play the games. The designer should listen to the audience, much the same way a comedian listens to them in a monologue. The comedian listens for the laughter. When the audience is laughing, the joke was a success with the audience. When the audience is not laughing, the joke didn't work. The designer needs to watch the target audience playing games to see what they enjoy.

Often a game designer will get stuck in the trap of designing games that are fun for himself. The industry is riddled with what I call nerd games. These are games that are very fun for a very small group of people, namely the guys who develop games. The game designer needs to remember that in most instances what is fun for a sophisticated game professional is not fun for the average consumer. And likewise, what is fun for the average consumer may be very boring for someone who plays games all the time.

Some of the biggest problems occur in designing games for children. Children often have limited motor skills (the ability to control fine small movements of the body), causing them to have problems with sensitive game controls. They also have differences in their attention span. A six-year-old child is very different from a nine-year-old child. Designing a game for a three-year-old is a lot different from designing a game for a twelve-year-old. For one thing, most three-year-olds don't know how to read. The designer needs to study the intended audience as much as she or he studies games.

Do You Like to Work?

The aspiring game designer will soon find that designing games requires a lot of work. The good news is that most of the work is fun, so it is not as hard to do as let's say digging ditches or washing cars. Although, some people may like digging ditches and washing cars so that may not be the best example. Aspiring game designers tend to like working on games more than almost anything else.

Even if you like the work involved in designing games, you will find that it can get tedious at times. Some of the work can get downright boring. I have yet to find the creation of asset lists to be an inspiring event.

Just to give you an idea of what I mean by game design being a lot of work, let's take a look at some of the jobs a game designer has to do.

Writer

A game designer is a writer. Designing games means writing a design document, some of which can be very extensive, with several hundred pages of information.

Artist

Although being an artist is not necessary, the game designer must be able to sketch well enough to give the concept artist direction on creating the art for the design document. Even non-artists can learn to sketch. If you don't draw well, try taking a couple drawing classes.

Graphic Designer

The game designer is responsible for the look of the game design document. The concept artist may do the actual graphic design, but the game designer is the one who has to come up with the direction for that design.

Programmer

Game designers are not necessarily programmers, but they do have to design how the game works, which is the basis for the programming of the game. They also have to design the game within the limitations of the hardware and software, which also takes technical knowledge.

Manager

Designers manage the design team. The game designer is the leader of everyone involved in the creation of the design document. This means that the designer is in charge of several individuals and has to manage their work, including things such as budgeting, work schedules, and team relations.

Salesperson

Game designers have to sell their ideas to a number of people. They are responsible for presenting the game idea to everyone involved in the game. Most of the time, the people who are funding the development of the game need to have the game idea explained to them. The designer is the person who has to do the explanation. In larger game companies, upper management requires reviews of the games. The designer is the one who has to convince management that the game is good and progressing on schedule.

Researcher

Games are always trying to push technology in some way. The designer needs to stay abreast of the latest technology. This usually requires extensive research. The designer also needs to be current with the latest trends in the market.

Game Tester

A good game designer is a good game tester. Every aspect of the game design has to be tested to make sure the game is good. The only way to know if a game design is good is to test it.

Communicator

Good game designers are good communicators. The whole idea of creating a game design document is to help everyone involved in the game understand what the game is and what to expect when it is finished. The designer will find that he or she will often have to explain the game to any number of people. The more high profile the game, the more the designer will have to communicate.

Needless to say, there is a lot to do as a game designer. These are just a few of the many jobs a game designer has to do when creating a game. There are probably more, but this will do for now.

Dedication to Games

A good game designer is dedicated to the craft of making games. He spends countless hours studying games and game development. It is a passion for great games that drives the designer to create better and better games.

A dedication to games means that games are important in your life. If you enjoy games but don't really think of them other than as a form of entertainment, then game design is probably not for you. Games are very complex. Understanding them to the point where you can successfully create them is a job that takes more than just an interest; it takes years of dedicated work to master the media.

The game designer should do more than just play games. Playing games is a great way to learn more about them, but it doesn't give the designer the understanding that is necessary for coming up with great game designs. The designer should study and analyze games. The designer should spend time just thinking about games. The designer should imagine new games and play them in his or her mind.

A good practice is to keep a game design journal. The journal is kind of like an artist's sketchbook. In the journal, the designer writes and sketches game ideas. If you plan on being a designer, keeping the journal with you is important because you never know when a great idea will come around.

Getting Started

I am sure you are anxious to get started, so let's get going on some game design. We are going to start on something simple and then move on to a few more complex exercises. Okay, here is your first assignment.

Assignment

A hardware company is looking for a fun puzzle game for its Web site. They have asked you to design something that is simple yet fun. They want the game to use products found in a hardware store, such as tools, bolts, nails, and so on. The game should be easy to play and learn.

There's the assignment. Short, sweet, and to the point. Now what do you do?

Research

The first thing that you need to do is learn about hardware stores. Get a pad and a pencil and go down to your local hardware store. Wander around and see what is inside. Think about the items and write down some game ideas. You might not get any good ideas right away, but keep working at it until you have at least five game ideas. You need at least that many to start narrowing down your options. Make sure that there are some significant differences between your ideas. You need to put some thought into this. If all your game ideas are basically the same game with only minor differences, you really only have come up with one idea.

When you get back from the hardware store, set your ideas aside and do some research into puzzle games. You may have some already on your computer or on some of your game systems. Take some time and play a few puzzle games to refresh your memory. In your notepad, write down an entry for each game you play and why you found it fun or why it wasn't fun. Don't worry yet about your game—just spend some time analyzing some games.

If you don't have any puzzle games around the house, try looking on the Internet. There are several places that have puzzle games. Many of them will let you play them for free. Try some of these games and see if there are any that you like. Write down an entry for each game.

Another good source for information on games is to look at the game review Web sites. These reviews are helpful because they have information on many games that you might not be able to find and play. Look up puzzle games and read the reviewer's impression of the game. You can also find game reviews in game magazines, if you have any.

Create

You should be ready to start the creative task of coming up with a game idea. If you have done the work in researching as outlined above, your mind should be filled with information on puzzle games and hardware stores. Now you can apply some of the knowledge you have gained creatively thinking of some games.

Get out your trusty game design journal and start working on some ideas. Give each idea about a page in the journal. Write short game descriptions and make some sketches of how you think the game will look and how it will be played. Don't worry about feasibility yet. You need to get the ideas coming. You will go through an analysis phase later, so it is better to just think of ideas. If you start to analyze your ideas now, you will slow the creative process and may not get the one good idea that will be the winner you are looking for.

It might be a good idea for you to return to the hardware store. Putting yourself in the environment is often a great way to spark some innovative new game ideas. While at the store, you should take the opportunity to talk to the people who work there. Get some insight from them on what customers do while in the store. It might also be a good idea to just spend some time observing people.

Okay, this next step may sound a little crazy, but try it anyway. It is time to do some creative combinations. Sometimes to be creative, you have to stretch things a little bit. Thinking outside the box is what some people call it.

Start thinking of places and things that are seemingly unrelated to a hardware store. Say, as for instance a city park or a bakery. Try putting the two seemingly unrelated things together to see if any new ideas come up. Sometimes the most amazing things happen when we take a look at unrelated things. The formal wear store has hardware in it. In fact, they probably couldn't do business without it. The bakery uses items from a hardware store as well.

Now here is the real fun part of the process. Think of things people do. Puzzle games are repetitious activities. Think about the activities that people do every day. Think about work, sports, school, entertainment, and so on. Apply each activity you think of to a hardware store. What would it be like to play golf with items found in a hardware store? What would it be like to play volleyball inside a hardware store? What about eating out with items from a hardware store? Would it be interesting to try to use items from a hardware store to build something?

I hope you are having fun with this project. If this is hard for you, try loosening up and not putting so much pressure on yourself. Games are supposed to be fun. Creating them should be fun, too.

By now you should have several pages in your game design journal filled with game ideas. It is now time to move to the next step and sort your ideas.

Analyze

Now it is time to really get to work. You need to take your game ideas and start working with them to see which ones are good and which ones you need to discard.

Just because you discard a game idea for this project does not mean that it is not a good idea. It may just not work for this game. That is why it is a good idea to keep the journal. There may be a game in the future that will be perfect for something that you discarded on this project.

It is often useful to rank your ideas in the important areas of the game to see which ones are better suited to the project than others. Figure 2.3 is a screen shot of how the game ideas might be ranked using a spreadsheet. The ideas are listed in the leftmost column, and the ranking categories are listed across the top. In this example, only five categories are chosen to keep this process simple. Some games may have many more categories.

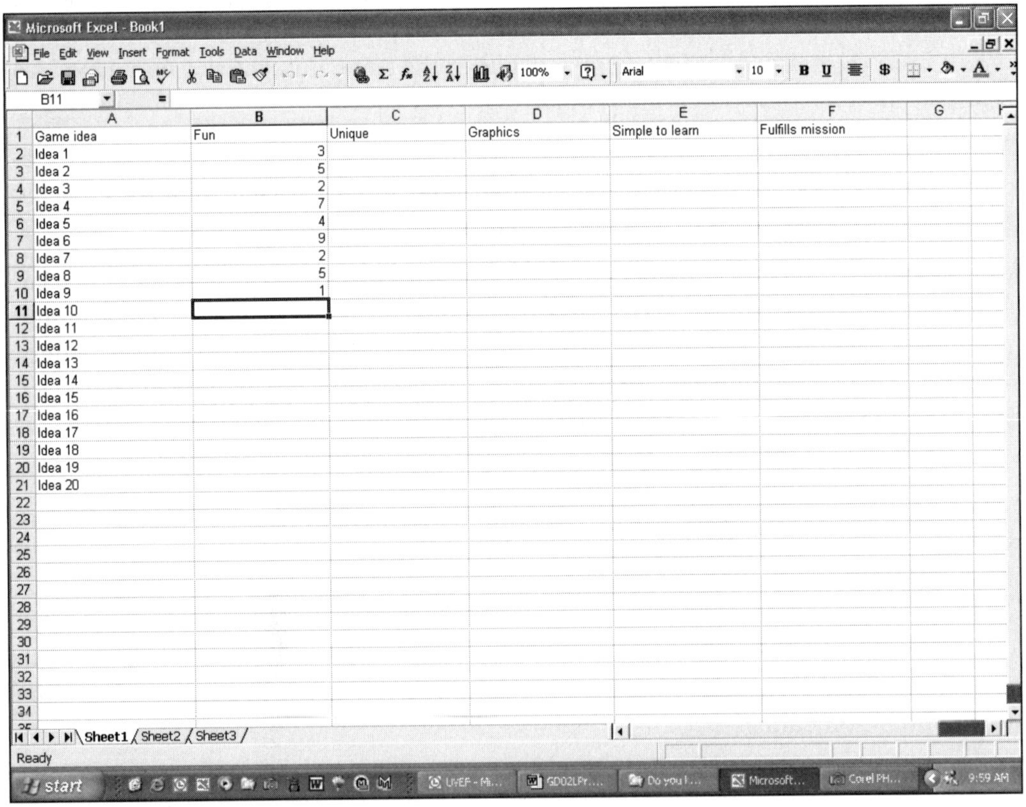

Figure 2.3
Use a spreadsheet to rank the game ideas.

The categories chosen for rankings are fun, unique, graphics, simple to learn, and fulfills mission. The designer, projecting as best as possible how they will turn out in a finished game should rank each one.

Fun

Fun is a measure of how much fun the designer feels the game will be when finished. You have to imagine playing the game. Does the game seem to be fun?

Unique

How unique is the idea? You need to rank the game based on whether the game is doing something that other games don't do.

Graphics

Will the game look good? This one is a little harder to judge, but it is still important. You have to imagine how the game will look on screen. Will it be attractive? Can you think of a way to make this game look good?

Simple to Learn

How complex is the game? Will it be easy for the player to pick up and play, or will it need to have extensive instructions?

Fulfills Mission

Does the game fulfill the mission of a puzzle game that uses things found in a hardware store? How well does it fulfill that mission?

In Figure 2.4 the rankings are filled out for each category.

Microsoft Excel - Book1

File Edit View Insert Format Tools Data Window Help

E38

	A	B	C	D	E	F	G	H
1	Game idea	Fun	Unique	Graphics	Simple to learn	Fulfills mission	Totals	
2	Idea 1	3	2	7	1	9	22	
3	Idea 2	5	3	5	2	8	23	
4	Idea 3	2	1	6	3	3	15	
5	Idea 4	7	5	4	2	6	24	
6	Idea 5	4	3	3	4	3	17	
7	Idea 6	9	4	6	5	7	31	
8	Idea 7	2	2	7	3	5	19	
9	Idea 8	5	3	5	7	8	28	
10	Idea 9	1	1	4	8	7	21	
11	Idea 10	0	5	5	4	7	21	
12	Idea 11	9	3	3	6	4	25	
13	Idea 12	5	2	2	7	8	24	
14	Idea 13	8	5	1	3	9	26	
15	Idea 14	3	3	4	5	1	16	
16	Idea 15	8	4	3	6	2	23	
17	Idea 16	2	2	6	5	5	20	
18	Idea 17	7	2	4	7	3	23	
19	Idea 18	3	3	5	3	7	21	
20	Idea 19	8	2	7	6	3	26	
21	Idea 20	4	5	3	4	7	23	
22								
23								
24								
25								
26								
27								
28								
29								

Figure 2.4
Fill out the rankings for each idea.

These are only a few of the considerations a designer might have for creating a game. Others are cost, difficulty to develop, available technology, available resources, and file size, to name just a few.

The rankings should be weighted by the importance of the category to the success of the game. Weighting a category means that more points are possible for items that are more important. In this case, a new line is added to the spreadsheet to show how the categories are weighted. Notice in Figure 2.5 that fun and fulfills mission are both equal in importance and are weighted the highest, followed by simple to learn, graphics, and unique. This is a subjective call. Every game will be different in what is most important and what is least important. Figure 2.5 shows the ranking line with the possible points for each category.

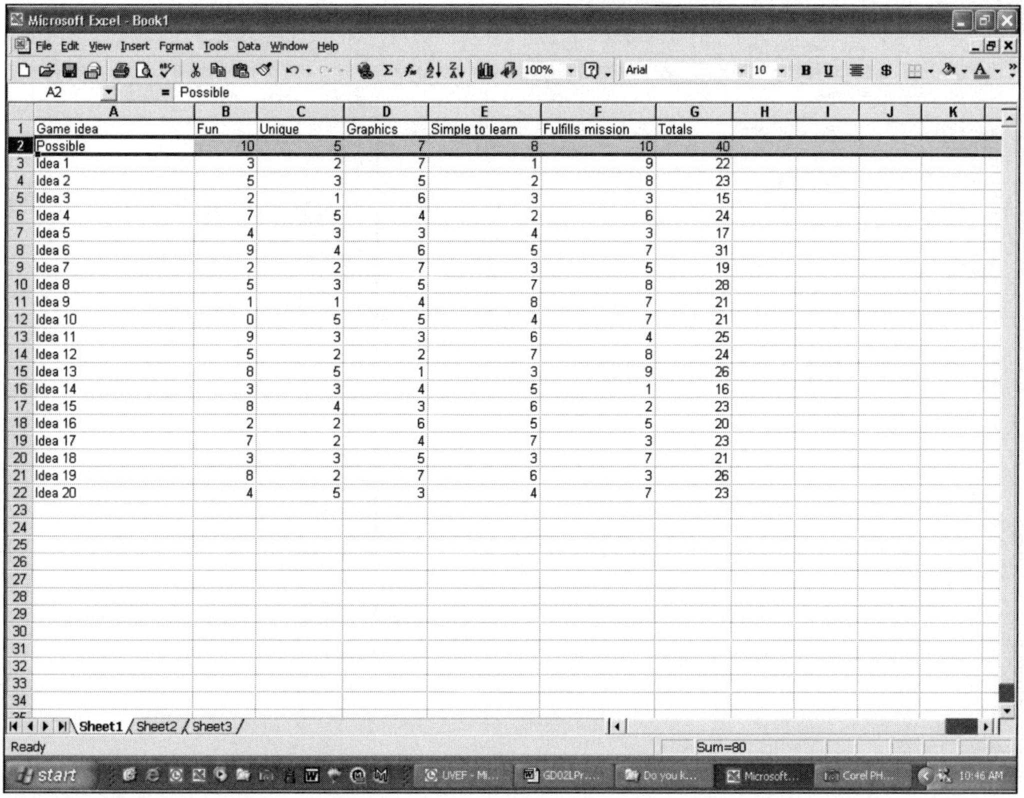

Game idea	Fun	Unique	Graphics	Simple to learn	Fulfills mission	Totals
Possible	10	5	7	8	10	40
Idea 1	3	2	7	1	9	22
Idea 2	5	3	5	2	8	23
Idea 3	2	1	6	3	3	15
Idea 4	7	5	4	2	6	24
Idea 5	4	3	3	4	3	17
Idea 6	9	4	6	5	7	31
Idea 7	2	2	7	3	5	19
Idea 8	5	3	5	7	8	28
Idea 9	1	1	4	8	7	21
Idea 10	0	5	5	4	7	21
Idea 11	9	3	3	6	4	25
Idea 12	5	2	2	7	8	24
Idea 13	8	5	1	3	9	26
Idea 14	3	3	4	5	1	16
Idea 15	8	4	3	6	2	23
Idea 16	2	2	6	5	5	20
Idea 17	7	2	4	7	3	23
Idea 18	3	3	5	3	7	21
Idea 19	8	2	7	6	3	26
Idea 20	4	5	3	4	7	23

Figure 2.5
Along the top are the possible points for each category.

Using a spreadsheet is helpful because you can easily total and compare ideas with it. The column on the right of the spreadsheet is the total number of points for each game idea. Figure 2.6 highlights the totals column.

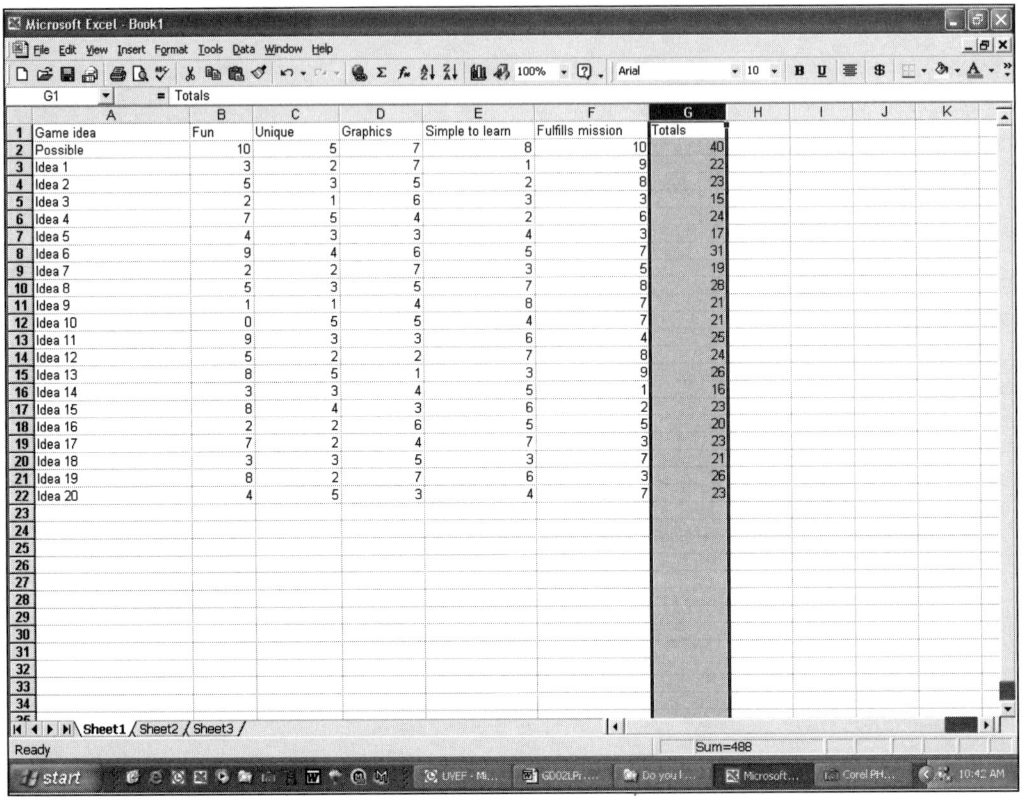

Figure 2.6
The right-hand column contains the totals for each game idea.

It should be very easy to see which games have the most potential. Figure 2.7 shows the game idea with the highest total and the one with the second highest total.

Using this method, you should be able to select two or three game ideas to analyze further. The idea here is not to make the final decision, but rather to get the list down to two or three ideas that can be developed into game concepts.

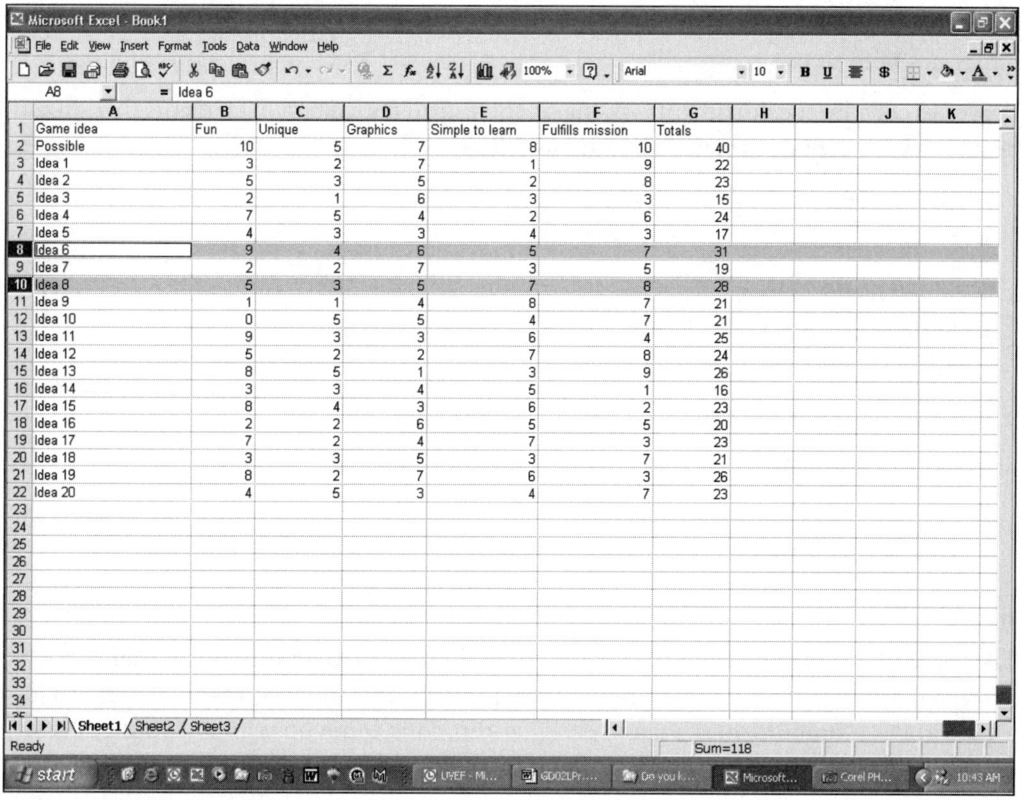

	A	B	C	D	E	F	G
1	Game idea	Fun	Unique	Graphics	Simple to learn	Fulfills mission	Totals
2	Possible	10	5	7	8	10	40
3	Idea 1	3	2	7	1	9	22
4	Idea 2	5	3	5	2	8	23
5	Idea 3	2	1	6	3	3	15
6	Idea 4	7	5	4	2	6	24
7	Idea 5	4	3	3	4	3	17
8	Idea 6	9	4	6	5	7	31
9	Idea 7	2	2	7	3	5	19
10	Idea 8	5	3	5	7	8	28
11	Idea 9	1	1	4	8	7	21
12	Idea 10	0	5	5	4	7	21
13	Idea 11	9	3	3	6	4	25
14	Idea 12	5	2	2	7	8	24
15	Idea 13	8	5	1	3	9	26
16	Idea 14	3	3	4	5	1	16
17	Idea 15	8	4	3	6	2	23
18	Idea 16	2	2	6	5	5	20
19	Idea 17	7	2	4	7	3	23
20	Idea 18	3	3	5	3	7	21
21	Idea 19	8	2	7	6	3	26
22	Idea 20	4	5	3	4	7	23

Figure 2.7
Two games with the highest point totals

In most cases the designer is not the person who chooses the final game idea. Most of the time the person or persons who make that decision are the ones who are paying for the game. In this case that would be the hardware store executive. The designer should present two or three game ideas to the hardware executive, who then will make the choice based on the concept document.

The Concept Document

The concept document is a 1–10-page document that briefly states the basic game concept. It will usually have a few pieces of concept art to help the readers better visualize the game. It may also have some charts or graphs to explain parts of the game that might be hard to express in written form.

Every concept document is different because the game and the purpose of the document are different. If the document is going to a major publisher for review, it should be a formal document with extensive work on its design and appearance. If it is an internal document, it may not need so much formality.

Regardless of who the document is going to, there are a few common elements that should be in every concept document. They are as follows:

- Game title
- Game platform
- Game genre
- Basic gameplay
- Basic premise
- Main characters (if any)
- Cost to develop
- Time to develop
- Development team

Game Title

The game title is the working title for the game. A title has to go through a legal check to make sure it is free to use. Most companies want to trademark a game's title. This is a job for attorneys. About the best a game designer can do is come up with a working title for a game concept.

Game Platform

The game platform is the machine the end user will be playing the game on. For example, the assignment for the puzzle game project is an online game. Its platform is online PC systems.

Game Genre

Game genre means the type of game. In this case, the game is a puzzle game. There are several common names for genre in the industry, such as RTS (real-time strategy), FRP (fantasy role playing), RPG (role playing game), racing, fighting, FPS (first-person shooter), sports, adventure, simulation, puzzle, and hunting/fishing.

note

Sometimes it is useful to give the reader of the concept document a point of reference. Some games may not fit nicely into any specific genre. It is often helpful when dealing with these types of games to find existing games that have similarities to the game being designed. In the concept document, the designer can mention the existing games and then explain why the new game is similar and how it is different.

Basic Gameplay

It is important to explain in the concept document exactly how the game will be played. What will the game view be? Will it be first person or third person? What does the player do in the game? How will the player control the game? How does the player advance through the game? How does the player win the game? Is there more than one play mode? All of these questions and more need to be answered in the basic gameplay section of the concept document.

The basic gameplay section of the concept document is usually the longest. It is often accompanied with artwork and charts.

Basic Premise

The basic premise of a game is the underlying story as it relates to the game. Some games, like adventure games for instance, may have an elaborate premise, whereas others, like puzzle games for example, might be very simple. The premise is the reason for the game, or in other words, it answers the why question about the game.

Main Characters

If the game has any characters, they should be explained in the concept document. Most documents will also include a sketch of the main characters. If the game does not have any characters, this section can be left out of the document.

Cost to Develop

The concept document should have some estimates of the cost of development for the game. At this stage the exact cost for development is hard to define. The designer needs to take into account as many factors as possible and come up with a range that the development costs will fall into. For example, a game might work out to cost in the range of $1.2 to $1.5 million dollars.

Time to Develop

Related to cost of development is the time it will take to create the game. This is critical for some projects because there may be a specific date by which the game needs to ship. To come up with an estimated time to develop the game, the designer has to do a preliminary production plan. We will talk about production plans later in the book.

Development Team

A very important consideration for anyone looking at a concept document is the development team. The development team needs to have the ability to complete the game. It is one thing to come up with a great game idea. It is another to actually be able to create the game. The designer needs to include in the concept document information on each of the key team members, including their education and relevant game development experience.

Writing the Document

Now that you understand what a concept document is, try writing one for the puzzle game ideas that you just created. Do the best job you can. If you are not a good artist, see if you can get a friend to help you with the art. You should be able to handle the rest on your own.

Start by taking the list of topics in the concept document section of this chapter as your table of contents. You may need some subsections under the basic gameplay and the basic premise. Do the best you can. It will be a good practice for you as you work your way through the rest of this book.

Try to make the document look as professional as possible. If you can, make the document's appearance similar to the game concept. At a bare minimum, give the document a nice title page that includes a picture from the game.

Once you have completed the concept document, you are finished with the first exercise. How do you feel you did? Did you enjoy the work? What was fun and what was hard?

Character Design

For the next exercise, you will be designing a character for a game. This is a little different process from designing a full game. Some games are so large that several people have to work on the design. A typical assignment for a designer on a large game might be to design a character for the game.

Exercise

Design a character for a fantasy game. The character should be the female heroine. She should be beautiful and strong. She will be one of several characters that the players can choose from in the game.

The process for designing characters is both a visual and a written exercise. In a design document there is both a written description of the character and a graphic to show what the character will look like.

Research

As in the previous exercise, start by doing some research. One of the toughest jobs of the designer is getting ideas for good characters. Designing a good character takes a lot of work. Sometimes you might have several ideas, go through dozens of sketches, and still not have just the right character. So where can an artist look for inspiration for characters?

One of the best sources for human characters is to observe your surroundings. Sometimes the best inspiration comes from normal day-to-day observance of people. A good practice is to go to a public place with a sketchbook in hand and draw. Figure 2.8 shows a page from a sketchbook dealing with everyday people in a public place. The sketches are done very quickly with very little emphasis on detail. Most people don't hold a pose for very long, so the object is to get some quick general impressions.

Figure 2.8
Quick character studies from everyday life

Another great source for inspiration for characters is to look at the work of other artists. There are many great examples of characters in great masterpieces of art, comic books, movies, and other media. All of these media have great examples of character design. One of the best ways to be the best is to learn from the best. Study how other artists dealt with and solved the problem of designing a character.

Copying great masterpieces is a long-standing tradition in art that goes back to the Middle Ages. However, the copying should be done only as a study and never as an original piece of artwork that the artist uses for a commercial purpose.

Creativity

Once you have gathered the information from the research stage, you can start work on creating some characters. The idea here is to get just the right character for the game. Use the clues in the exercise assignment to break down what you need. Now take a look at the reference material you have gathered. Write some quick descriptions of some characters that might work for the design. Do about 12 different descriptions. Try coming at the problem from several different angles.

Each description should be about one paragraph long. The following is an example.

Description

Aloena is a princess of the forest kingdom Fairwood. She is tall and athletic. She has long hair that she typically keeps tied back behind her head. She is a spell caster and carries no physical weapons because they just get in her way. She practices forest magic, which is a school of nature magic. Her skin is fair, and her eyes are green.

Aloena is about 22 years old and has been trained in woods lore by the best trackers in the kingdom. She is proud of her accomplishments, yet she is pleasant to be around. She loves to sing and play the flute.

Does the description give you a pretty good feeling for the character? Can you picture her in your mind? Each of your descriptions should give enough information that if you gave it to an artist, she or he would be able to create a good looking character just from what you have written.

Create a quick sketch of each character to go with the description.

Analyze

Once you have your character descriptions, it is time to select the one you feel will be the best for the game. Set out each description and pick the one you like the most. Ask a few of your friends to give you their opinions. If you want to create a selection grid similar to what you did for the first exercise, go ahead and give it a try.

Selecting characters is often a very subjective process, and there are no hard rules for what you do. Just eliminate each character one by one until you have only one left.

The Character Design

The character design is usually a one-page document that has your brief character description and a rendering of the character. If you don't draw well, have an artist friend draw the character picture. Figure 2.9 shows the character from the description.

The character shows confidence and strength by her stance, with her legs braced apart and her arms at a ready position. Her jewelry shows her to be a woman of substance, as does her embroidered tunic. She has an athletic, elongated build.

Now just put the character description and picture together and you have completed another exercise. Are you starting to get the hang of how to design games?

Summary

So what do you think of being a game designer so far? I hope you are having fun.

In this chapter, several important aspects of being a designer were covered. You should now have a good idea of what a game designer does and what a game designer is. You should also have a good understanding of the attributes of a good game designer.

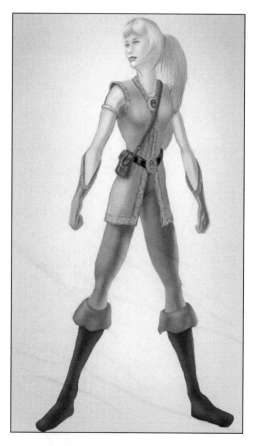

Figure 2.9
The character sketch should match the character description.

Hopefully you followed the exercises in the chapter. If you did, you will have learned about designing games and designing characters.

In the next few chapters you will be learning about creating a game design document of your own. Each chapter will cover a specific aspect of creating a game design document. In this chapter we covered the game concept document. I suggest you take some time and create a game concept document for the game you will be designing as you go through the book.

CHAPTER 3

THE DESIGN DOCUMENT

Now that you have designed your game conceptually, it's time to put that design down on paper. The result will be the design document. This document will be revised multiple times. Even after the game is in development, there will be revisions to it. Keep in mind that you'll be working with the design document for a long time.

A well thought out design document is crucial to developing a good game. You need it so that anyone reading the document will know what the game is all about. It will help you, the developers, and the publisher understand what is being developed. You will describe the game's story, how levels are played through, development of the characters, possible marketing and distribution, and so on.

A good design document should be readable. While you may need to use some sophisticated or technical language to explain certain aspects of the game development, it is important not to make it difficult to read or understand. The language should be persuasive and excite the reader to want to play the game. Of course, to make it more readable, use a spell-checker, check your grammar, and make it look good! Make the reading of the document as enjoyable as possible. Most people do not enjoy poorly written material full of misspelled words. Making it look good is a sign of your professional abilities.

In the design document, you will want to prioritize the elements of the game development. This is important for the publisher as well as the members of the development team. Sometimes there are financial or time restraints that require that the project be reduced. If it becomes necessary to limit the project, this prioritization of the game is a great place to look first. With the elements prioritized, it should be clear to everyone what elements are most important and which ones are of lesser importance. If you have to make a decision to cut something, generally you will want to cut those things of lesser importance to the game.

If you are wise, you will use the design document during the development phase of the game. As with all game development, lots of great ideas for the game aren't conceived until during the actual development phase. After reviewing these great ideas, you then have to make the decision as to whether or not they should be implemented. If the schedule has already been created in such a way as to allow for some change, it is easy to implement some of the small changes. However, some ideas cause significant changes to the development schedule, and a continuous barrage of small changes will ultimately cause problems as well. The design document should include how changes are reviewed during the development cycle and how they might be implemented.

tip

When you enter into an agreement with a publisher to develop the game, it is important that the contract between you and the publisher provide very specific language as to how changes in the development of the game will be implemented. It doesn't matter whether changes come from the development team or the publisher. There must be a procedure put into place that will protect you if changes are implemented that increase your development time or costs. This is a great time to use an attorney.

The rest of this chapter will describe elements that are often included in a design document. Because there are many types of games, your design document may include elements that we haven't described, and you may decide not to include some of the elements that are described here. You may also decide to completely change the order from what is presented here. Hey, that's perfectly okay. The design document is your opportunity to explain and describe your game, and you should certainly create it to fit your needs. To further help you in developing your design document, we have provided a sample design document in Appendix A, "Design Document." The original design document is for a motocross game that was developed for a popular game console. We have modified the document by changing the game platform to the PC. As a result, don't look at the technical details too closely.

Again, remember that the design document is a fluid document!

Layout of the Design Document

Throughout the writing of the design document and especially during the final preparation of the document before sending it to the publisher, you should be giving significant thought to how to make the document look good. You should use fonts, graphics, color, layout, and so on to create a mood in your design document to match the game you are describing. If you are creating a game of mining gnomes, you might consider using whimsical fonts for your section headings and include some fun graphics (see Figure 3.1). The cover page should draw the reader into the document. Remember to indicate on the cover page that the document is copyrighted. If your word processor has a Header/Footer feature, use a continuous footer and include your name, page number, and "Confidential" throughout the rest of the document. You will have spent a considerable amount of time designing the game and putting it down on paper, so take the time to clearly indicate that it is copyrighted and confidential.

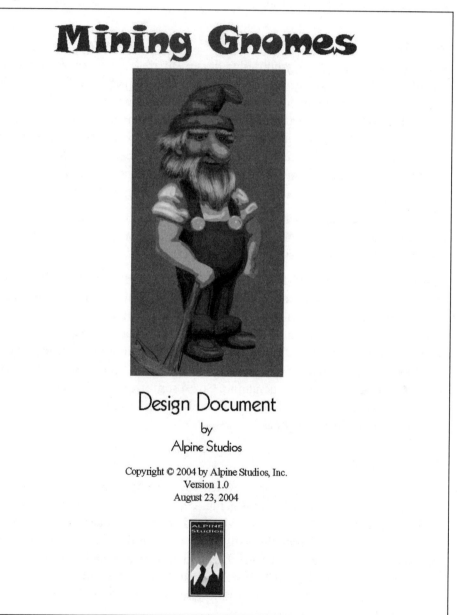

Figure 3.1
Use graphics, fonts, and layout to draw the reader into the document.

Design Document Elements

Now it's time to start writing the document. The following sections will give you some good ideas of what to include in your design document. Remember that you should write the design document to explain your game. If you need to add or remove any of the suggested sections, feel free to do so.

Introduction

The first few paragraphs of your design document are a summary of the rest of the document. Essentially, it is an executive summary. The introduction will be one of the last elements of the design document to be finalized. After writing the rest of the document, pick out the highlights that give a brief overview of the document and place them at the beginning of the design document in the introduction. This serves two functions. Those individuals who don't take the time to read the entire document will at least get a reasonably accurate overview of what the game is about. And the ones who continue to read the document to the end will have an overview of what's coming in the rest of the document.

In just a few paragraphs, describe what you envision as the game. Build excitement into the document, and since some of your readers may not get past the introduction, you want that excitement to start in the first paragraph.

Clearly state the goals of the game in the introduction portion of the document. Obviously, this means that you must have decided what those goals are. Tell the reader up front what it is you are trying to accomplish. Are you developing a brand new type of game, or are you developing a complete knock-off of an already popular game? It doesn't matter; just tell what it is that you want to accomplish. This is the place to give an overview of the explanation and description of what the game is all about. Start by telling the reader what type of game you are designing. Give a summary description of the game world. Describe what and how the player will control. You will want to answer the obvious questions that the publisher might ask.

Game Overview

You are now entering the section in which you flesh out the substance and detail of the game and the philosophy behind the game. This is where you lay out in detail your vision for the game that your design team has decided upon. Give a reasonably complete description of the game and include the goals of the game in this area as well. You have already created at least a simple game layout chart and have determined how the game will work. Now you need to describe that on paper so that the reader can understand the game. This isn't the section to include any real technical information, but it should be descriptive and very readable.

At the end of this section, follow up with the game requirements. There is a delicate trade-off that you must address when you are designing a PC game. If you want the broadest possible market penetration, then you need to develop a game that will run on some pretty old hardware. Unfortunately, those restrictions will stop your game from being on the cutting edge of technology with all the neat bells and whistles that the artists and programmers will want to put into the game. On the other hand, if you develop the game for only the latest technology, you won't be able to sell very many copies of the game. When you establish the hardware parameters, you are doing two things. You are setting the limitations within which the artists and programmers must work, and you are setting the level of expectation for the publisher.

If you are anticipating that the game will be localized, indicate that multiple languages will be supported as part of the game requirements. Knowing that the game is going to be made available in other languages is something that the programmers should know about right up front. The ultimate decision, of course, will be made by the publisher, but your consideration of the matter at this point is a sign of a good designer.

Follow up with the anticipated completion date for the game. The completion date is generally the month or quarter when you will give a gold master of the completed game to the publisher. Understand that the completion date and street date are two different dates. The street date is when the publisher will release the product for sale. The publisher has to have sufficient time to test, replicate, and package the product and then move it into the distribution channel. If you are developing a console game, then you may need to increase your development period sufficiently to include the approval process by the console maker.

An example of the game and hardware requirements might be these:

- Game Genre—Arcade strategy.
- Target Audience—12 years and older. (List the primary demographic. If there is a strong secondary demographic, feel free to list it as well. A demographic is a statistic which describes segments of human populations broken down by age or sex or income and so on.)
- Minimum Platform Hardware Requirements:
  - 1.4 GHz Pentium 4
  - 256 MB RAM
  - High color/16-bit capable 8 MB video card
  - 48x CD-ROM drive
  - Sound card
  - 250 Meg available hard disk space

- Languages to Be Supported—English, French, German, and Spanish
- Street Date—The anticipated time that the game will be available for purchase by a customer, for example, Q3 2005 (July–September of 2005)

Position the Game

An important part of the design document is "selling" the game concept and your design of it. After you have given the overview of the game and established the premise for the game, you need to sell your design. Now is the time for you to *position the game*. The title of this section would generally not be "Position the Game." Rather, you will use titles such as "Key Features" or "Unique Selling Points." You could easily view this as the marketing portion of the design document, and it is very useful. Positioning the game will force you as the designer to answer these important questions:

- Who is the target customer?
- What are the key benefits of the game?
- Who is your competition?
- What is the key difference between your game and the competition?

Answering these questions will help you to better define the game's design and to make a better, more cohesive presentation in your design document. A common problem in the development world is developing a "cool" product, assuming that once it's developed, there will surely be a market for it! While this happens occasionally, it is very rare. The more sensible approach is to assess the marketplace and develop a product that fills a need. In this regard, developing a great game for an established market segment often is more appealing than developing for a "new" market. In any event, you need to answer these questions in your design document.

Your Target Customer

You have partially answered this question earlier when you identified the target age group. However, is this game for 12-year-old boys, 15-year-old girls and boys, middle-aged housewives, or 16- to 24-year-old hardcore gamers? You should know for whom you are designing the game. Knowing whom you are developing for will help you during the development phase when the creative juices are coursing through the veins of the team members. It will help you stay focused and on track so that the team doesn't wander away from the group you are trying to develop for.

Key Benefits of the Game

In this section you will list the "cool" aspects of the game. This is where you differentiate your game from everyone else's. Don't go overboard and list page after page of points. You should focus on a few of the elements of the game that make it special.

The Competition

Unless you are creating a new genre, there will be competition. Identify the other games, either announced or on the market, that directly compete with you in your genre. Tell the reader enough about these other games that he will be able to understand why your game is different and, hopefully, better.

Key Differentiation

Okay, now it's time for you to take the key benefits you listed and combine them with the competition section to define the key difference between your game and the others. This should be a short section. In fact, you should try and make it just one sentence. And, you might as well memorize it! You are going to be asked more times than you want to count what your game is all about. When you combine this sentence with a one-sentence overview of the game, you will have a great answer.

Succinctly stating the key differentiation will help the publisher better understand the game. It also means that you have thought this out, which builds the publisher's confidence in you as a designer.

Game Features

The Game Features section is the meaty part of the design document. Here is where you are going to give significant detail so the reader can visualize the game as you see it. Spend as much time as you need to make sure that this section is very readable and understandable.

Game Flow

Game flow describes how the game is played from a decision-making tree. You should work closely with the programming member of your design team in developing this section.

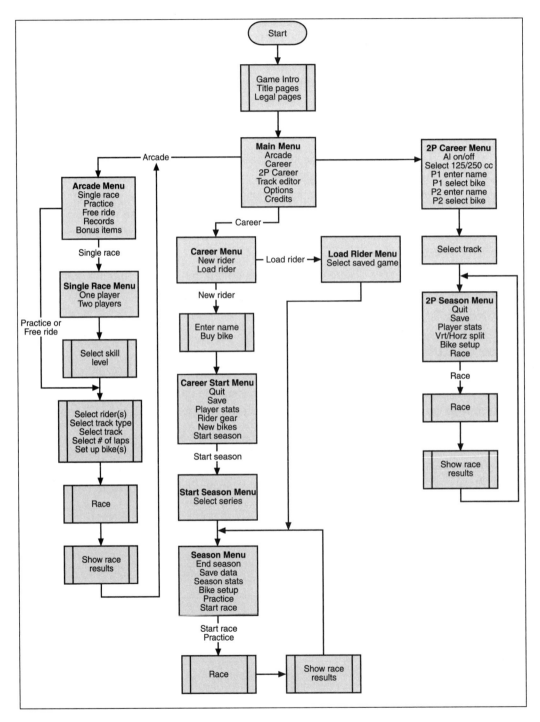

Figure 3.2
An example of a simple game flowchart

The Game World

The game world is the overall game environment. Within the game world there usually will be multiple levels. Provide a summary overview of the game world. For example, the game world for the *Motocross* game was the 16 levels, with each level having three tracks. Each level included a track for each level of difficulty. This resulted in the game having 48 different tracks for the players to race on.

Game World Features

In game world features, you should break down the game world environment into major components and describe each of them in its own subsection of the design document. For example, in the motocross design document, the features broken out as major sections are these:

- Camera
- Modes of Play
- Trick Mode or Free Ride
- Motion
- Racing Level Overview
- In-Game Progress, Timers, and Clocks
- Race Replay
- Report Card
- Reward or Trophy Screens

Each major section is then briefly described so that the reader understands how that element fits into the game. As previously stated, there were actually 16 racing levels in the original design document for the *Motocross* game. For convenience sake, the document in Appendix A has been modified to include only four levels. A graphic for each level that indicates all three tracks in the level is included in the design document. You will want to include enough graphics to give the reader a good vision of the game.

You should describe any objects that will be included in the game. If weather and time of day options will be part of the game, then describe them. For example, if the *Motocross* game includes racing in day, dusk, and night conditions, this should be stated and described. If you will be racing in rain, snow, sleet, or sunny conditions, then describe these conditions.

Character and Model Development

Now is the time to describe the models and characters that will be used in the game. Include as many graphics as necessary. In the *Motocross* game, the motorcycles are the important elements, not necessarily the riders. On the other hand, if the game were highlighting specific riders on the motocross circuit, then the riders would be the more important characters in the game. In that case, you would include more graphics of the riders.

Explain how the player will personalize the character. In the *Motocross* game, the player has the ability to choose whether the rider is male or female. The player then selects from four different motorcycles and has the ability to change several of the bike's handling characteristics, as well as the paint scheme.

Graphics Rendering System

In this section you will describe how the game will be rendered and indicate the 2D/3D rendering engine to be used, if relevant.

Figure 3.3
Sample female character drawing

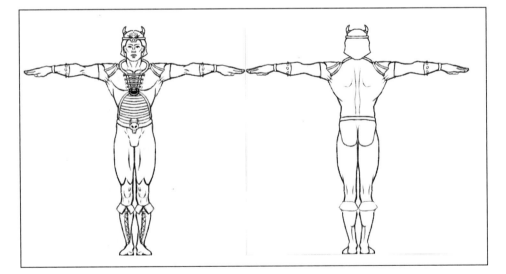

Figure 3.4
Sample male character drawing

Figure 3.5
Sample character art

Figure 3.6
More sample character art

Figure 3.7
Sample motorcycle art

Figure 3.8
More sample motorcycle art

Game Engine

A game engine is a software program that a development team uses to run the game. You will probably be able to create your game much more quickly and efficiently if you use an existing game engine. After you have determined which engine you are going to use, give an overview of it and describe its primary attributes. For example, explain how the engine handles collision detection, particle effects, water, and so forth.

Camera

The placement of the camera is an important issue in gameplay in 3D games. In this section, you will want to explain how the camera will be used in the game. If this section is very sophisticated or changes throughout the game, then break it down into subsections.

For example, *Motocross PC* offers three different camera positions while racing. The default is a third-person follow camera with the camera positioned just behind and above the motorcycle. The player may select from two other camera positions: a first-person view with the camera located just above the handlebars or a more distant third-person follow camera with the camera located farther behind and above the motorcycle. However, the replay mode provides only a fixed camera view in which cameras are positioned throughout the track in such a manner that the player is always in view. When the player begins to move out of view of one camera, the onscreen view is switched to the next camera.

User Interface

The user interface section includes all the information that is provided to the player to help him play the game and includes the player controls. Break down the components of your user interface and provide a detailed section on each component.

Player Controls

For a PC game, the considerations for player controls are generally greater than for console games. The reason for this is that the PC has so many more potential control options when compared to the console. You will need to decide how many ways the player will be able to play the game. Will the player use the keyboard only or will the mouse be used as well? Will other PC input controllers be supported? The better you can describe how the player will experience the game, the better. Explain how the player moves characters, vehicles, and so on. If keyboard control is allowed, explain the keys that will be used in the game. If you are supporting a controller, insert a graphic of the controller into your design document. Then use text boxes and arrows pointing to the various parts of the controller as you describe how the player controls the game. You might also consider using a table to list the elements of the game that can be controlled by the player and the keystrokes or controller button presses necessary to execute it. For example, Table 3.1 is a list of the tricks that can be performed by a player in the *Motocross* game and the keystrokes necessary to perform each trick.

Table 3.1 How Tricks Are Performed

Trick Name	Keystroke(s)
Nac-Nac	D
Cliffhanger	S
Surfer Seat Stand	E
Recliner	F
Pummel Bar Spin	C
Can-Can	Shift + C
Cordova	Shift + F
Double Can-Can	Shift + S
Seat Grab Indian Air	Shift + D
Nothing	Shift + E
Rodeo Heel Clicker	Alt + C

Gameplay

In this section you will describe the stuff that is key to the gameplay experience. If the game will be both single- and multi player playable, this section will generally be broken down into Single-Player and Multi-Player sections. This section should be bigger rather than smaller because this is where you are describing in great detail what the player or players will be doing during the game. Remember, in a game, you want the player to be able to do lots of fun things. Describe as many of them as you can so the reader will more fully understand why the game will be fun to play.

Single-Player Mode and Features

Here you will explain and describe how the game is played by a single player. Provide the key points of the single-player game.

Describe what the player can do to customize his character or vehicle.

Explain how the player will be able to win and what the rewards are for the player when he finally wins the game. After the player has won the game, what does the player do? For example, in the *Motocross* game, a player can choose to race in the Arcade or Career mode. The Arcade mode allows the player to choose the level of difficulty to race, such as amateur, semi-pro, or professional. However, at the beginning of the game, the player has only a few amateur race tracks from which to choose. The player must "unlock" additional tracks or levels by progressing through the Career mode. In the Career mode, the player will race through a specific set of races, beginning with the Amateur level, and will progress level to level. As the player completes each level of difficulty by finishing in the top three positions, additional tracks are unlocked for play in the Arcade mode. After the player has "won" the game by completing the Career mode, there are still many hours of playing left in the Arcade mode. The player will be able to race against the artificial intelligence (AI) racers provided, or he may play against another player in the two-player mode.

A key element in developing a game is to understand and plan for the amount of time that a player will spend playing the game. You should indicate how many hours you think a player will spend playing the game as a single-player game.

Multiplayer Modes and Features

If your game is a multiplayer game, then you will devote a section of the design document to this particular area. You will develop this section in the same manner as you did the single-player section. You should indicate clearly the maximum number of players who can play the game simultaneously. Describe how the game will be presented to the players. For example, if two or more players are playing simultaneously, will there be a split screen? If players are using the same keyboard, which keys will each player use? Also, you should indicate if players will be able to play over the Internet or a network.

Elements of the Game

Describe the elements of the game. For example, in *Motocross* the motorcycles are described in great detail. Additionally, the Track Editor is an important element that is also described. If you were developing a first-person shooter, you would describe the weapons to be used in the game.

Audio

Generally, you will be working with an audio designer to complete this section. At the very least, you need to have the input of someone who knows and understands the audio issues that will be involved in the game.

The audio effects are often the unsung hero in a game, adding a sparkle that gives a sense of fulfillment to the player. Take the time to give a good overview of the voice, music, and sound effects that will be used in the game.

Technical Considerations

In this section you are going to discuss the known technical issues. While the technical issues of the game are discussed in the design document, it is a mistake to include the technical design document within the design document. The technical design document is written after the design document is done. A good technical design document will significantly cut the development cycle. Unfortunately, many programmers don't create a technical design document. The time spent in preparing well thought out design and technical documents will pay off significantly during the development phase of the game. The technical design document should include the requirements of the game; overviews of how objects, functions, and data interact; and coding conventions such as variable naming and comments. The document will describe and explain all the technologies that will be used in the game development. It should include the projected system requirements and dependencies, file types, and data layout.

In the design document, however, you will include a summary of known technical issues. For example, in the *Motocross* game, all motorcycles not controlled by players are controlled by AI. How is the AI going to be implemented?

Artificial Intelligence

If the game will need artificial intelligence (AI) in the game, include a section on how it will be implemented. Where will it be used, and what are the issues involved? You may need only a brief description if it will be covered in more detail in the technical design document. Otherwise cover it more fully in the design document.

Give an overview of the code architecture. If the game is a multiplayer game, address the issues that will arise. For example, if your game may be played over the Internet, then you need a section briefly describing how this will work. If the game may be played over a network, provide a section briefly describing how and what type of networks will be supported and how the player will experience the game.

The key in this section is to let the publisher or whoever is reading the design document know that you recognize the technical issues that the development team will have to address and overcome. You aren't expected to address the issues as completely as they will be addressed in the technical design document.

Development Team and Approach

In this section, you should identify the leading members of the development team. We like to include pictures and a short biography of each team member. It is nice for the publisher to have a face to match with the name and voice that he speaks to frequently over the telephone or through e-mail.

Schedule and Budget

A fairly well-described development cycle should also be put into the design document even if you are not working with a publisher. Typically, this development cycle is broken up into "milestones." Generally, the milestone chart is determined before the agreement with the publisher is signed. The publisher has only a certain number of dollars to spend on the project. Obviously, that can be a limiting factor. If this is a development project in which you hope to make money, it is important that you budget the project carefully.

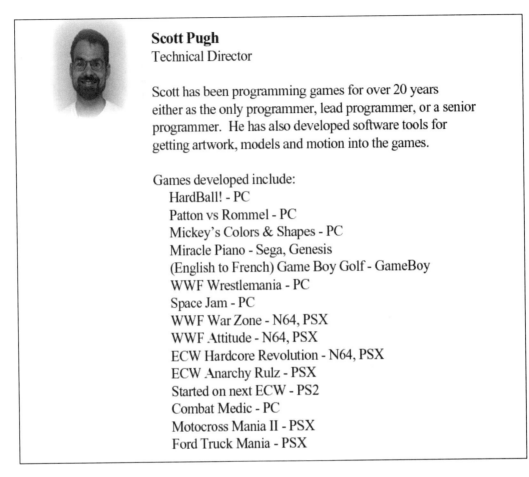

Scott Pugh
Technical Director

Scott has been programming games for over 20 years either as the only programmer, lead programmer, or a senior programmer. He has also developed software tools for getting artwork, models and motion into the games.

Games developed include:
HardBall! - PC
Patton vs Rommel - PC
Mickey's Colors & Shapes - PC
Miracle Piano - Sega, Genesis
(English to French) Game Boy Golf - GameBoy
WWF Wrestlemania - PC
Space Jam - PC
WWF War Zone - N64, PSX
WWF Attitude - N64, PSX
ECW Hardcore Revolution - N64, PSX
ECW Anarchy Rulz - PSX
Started on next ECW - PS2
Combat Medic - PC
Motocross Mania II - PSX
Ford Truck Mania - PSX

Figure 3.9
Sample development team member bio

At least three elements are contained in a milestone if you are being paid to build the game. If you aren't being paid to complete a milestone, then there will only be two elements in each milestone. First, you have to decide what level of development will be accomplished at a particular milestone. Then you have to decide by what date that milestone will be finished. Finally, since most people like to be paid for their efforts, you need to attach a payment to each milestone. Each milestone then includes a reasonable description of the game development that will be completed, the date by which that development work will be accomplished, and the amount that the publisher will pay for that milestone. Table 3.2 is an example of what a Milestone Chart might look like.

tip

While we're on the subject of being paid for your efforts, you should fully understand the lag time between when you have completed a milestone and when you will actually be paid for it. There is generally a lag time of 2–4 weeks between when you complete the milestone and when you get the check in your hands.

Table 3.2 Portion of a Sample Milestone Chart

#	Milestone Description	Date	Amount
1	Contract signing	10/4/0_	$xx,xxx
2	Design document approval by publisher	10/15/0_	$yy,yyy
3	Technical design document approval by publisher	10/31/0_	$yy,yyy
4	Pre-production:	11/22/0_	$zz,zzz
	Early prototype/preliminary play mechanics		
	Game prototype—Because a licensed engine will be used, this milestone will be a process of defining the look and feel of the game, using the engine's current physics and AI routines. The prototype will include:		
	A. One controllable motorcycle		
	B. One race track		
	C. Initial sounds		
	D. Initial interface screen		
5	Production 1—Construction	12/20/0_	$zz,zzz
	Putting in the assets, race up and running, getting on a motorcycle, and riding it. This milestone will include:		
	A. Two complete tracks		
	B. Ability to race against other motorcycles		
	C. Scoring		
	D. Ability to make modifications to motorcycle such as color scheme, shocks, and brakes		

This is an extremely important section. You must be accurate and realistic in building the milestones. First, it is from this section that you will be paid. You must accurately determine how much time and work it will take to accomplish what you have described in the milestone requirement section. Additionally, you must hit your milestones on time. You don't want to discover until after you're in the development cycle that your programmers take twice as long to complete their work as you budgeted for. Virtually all publisher development agreements include a termination clause by which the publisher can cancel the agreement if the developer is not producing the game in accordance with the milestones listed. While such a clause is there to protect the publisher, the result is also helpful to you as a developer. You probably need to keep the project on a sound financial basis! Following the schedule and budget that you put together is a great step in the right direction. In putting the milestone chart together, you should use all the help you can get from the other members of the design team.

As stated above, you should seriously plan on having at least one milestone per month. This will allow you to pay your employees, overhead, and even yourself on a regular basis. However, there is another equally important reason. Communication between the publisher and the developer can be less than desirable during the development cycle. Submitting and gaining approval for milestones forces the two parties to communicate. You don't want to be going in a direction other than the one the publisher thinks you are going in. The earlier a problem can be detected, the quicker it can be addressed and corrected. Frequent milestones help in this area.

If you are submitting the design document to a publisher in hope of obtaining a development agreement with a publisher, you should include proposed completion incentives and royalties for the game. If you have already entered into an agreement, and the design document is one of the milestones, then leave that information out because it will already have been covered in the publisher's development contract. For example, if you finish the development project on schedule, the development team will receive a cash bonus of $xzy.

Summary

Now that you understand what is involved in putting your game design on paper, there are just a couple of things to remember.

- The design document is the culmination of a lot of work by you and the rest of the design team. If you haven't done a great job, there probably won't be any additional work done on the game you've designed. As a result, there are a lot of good reasons why you should do your very best in putting the document together.

- It requires that you not only think the game through from the beginning to end of gameplay but to accurately describe it on paper. The outline used in this chapter is representative of how a design document can be laid out. However, remember that this is your document. Feel free to rearrange the sections of the document to describe your game accurately. Add more if you need to and remove what isn't applicable to your game design.

CHAPTER 4

THE GAME IDEA

Ideas are a dime a dozen. It's the really good ideas that count. Surely, you will want to share this idea with your friends and others, but half-baked ideas won't interest them. It may seem easy to just sit down and say "this idea might be fun," but there must be some thought put into it for you to take the idea and make it a good game. You need to focus on this part for some time to really flesh it out. But too much time is not a good thing. First, you won't be able to write the document consistently, making it sound good from beginning to end. Secondly, you have to get it down on paper so that you can present it to your friends or a group that will actually help you develop it. So let's get started.

Where Can I Find an Idea?

Ideas come from everywhere, from the basketball game out on the curb to television to the movies to the computer game you played till 3 am last night. When looking for an idea, you should look everywhere. Even if you have a pretty good idea of what you want your game to be, you are still going to need to be able to flesh it out with things you see around you. Tying your game to the real world, even if it is set in fantasy or outer space, will help others identify with those elements you've added to the game. This will bring the player into the game and make him want to play more, and this makes it a hit.

Where are the best places to find game ideas? If you have Internet access, you can find a plethora of information that will lead you to your idea. The ideas found on the Internet are copyrighted, so you will want to use these only as a launching point for your own idea. You can also find ideas in books and stories you've heard. TV in general can spur many ideas and can help you find things to add to an underdeveloped idea. The news—yes, the news—is also an interesting source for games. Other family members might be surprised to find you watching the news instead of cartoons, but the ideas are there. Everyday activities like going to the mall to hang out can inspire a new game. Oh, sorry—that one is taken with *Mall Tycoon* from Take Two. But that doesn't mean that you can't top it and make something better.

note

Remember when you start working on an idea to make sure there is not something too similar already done. Copyright laws could keep you from making it to the big time. Be sure when you use an idea that it is different enough from where you got it. Making a game with orcs and humans at war and calling it *Battlingcraft* instead of *Warcraft* would not be enough of a change to overcome that copyright holder's rights.

Examples

You may want to find something that is in fashion and will stay in fashion for a while. At least it will need to stick around until after you have developed the game. Or you may want to create the fashion or trend with your game. Many games try to set the fashion or trend for a time. *Warcraft* by Blizzard Entertainment set a standard for real-time strategy games, but now there are so many people trying to copy and change that genre that the games seem to be the same old thing. If you choose to follow this path, you must find a unique quality of the game that will change how others view the game. It could be as simple as changing the story, but it will usually mean finding a gameplay element that has not been seen before. Blizzard decided that more depth was needed. They took the game from a 2D sprite-driven game and added a missing key component, the third dimension. The change took the old game and made it into a great hit, not that it needed much to become one. This was not the only change that was needed for their next generation of gameplay, for they also added a role playing aspect

Others create and keep a good trend going, like *Castlevania* by Konami. But they do have to reinvent the game for the new console or the better PC. More power means that more can be done. If you look back to the 1990s and see a game that might have been popular back then, and if it has good gameplay, then making that game come to life with the new power of the console or PC could be a great idea. Or vice versa, find a game you like now and remake it into a board game. There are many groups that love to play role playing card games and war board games that are still looking for other ways to play and more variety.

Castlevania started as a simple 2D side-scroller that built up a following by releasing several new storylines and new time periods. These games with their new stories caused a change in the gameplay. But later the designers reverted back to the original gameplay, as they saw that the followers liked the older style of play. While the general idea was still the same, a lot of the goals and what was required to win had to be updated and modified.

The next step in its evolution had to be 3D, and it worked. The zealots (or the following) thronged to see the new incarnation of Count Dracula. A fun aspect brought into this game is the flow of being able to trek through the castle without having to worry about which way to go. This aspect draws many players to spend more time playing the game because they can better their skills and better their character.

This form of the role playing game (RPG) was really striking. It added something new to the way an RPG could be played. When looking for your idea, you'll probably select a genre and find that you have some new element to add to it. You will have an idea worth putting down on paper.

It doesn't have to be an RPG. There are many different types of games out there, and when you find a game that you like to play, you probably want to make a game that fits in that genre. You will be more passionate about your work. You will want to devote your time and effort to your masterpiece. If you really don't love the type of game, you might not put as much energy into it, even though the idea may be a great one.

Read

One of the best things you can do for yourself if you want to be a good game designer is read. Reading will stimulate your mind and help you find solutions to holes in your design. In addition, there are great ideas out there waiting to be picked up and read. If you read before going to bed, there is a good chance you'll dream something similar to what you have read. There's an even better chance you'll remember the dream, ready to be written when you wake up. There are many topics and information available at your local library that you can use as a starting point. The legends of Robin Hood have initiated many good games and titles, for example.

Any Questions?

There are many questions that you can ask yourself to help find and identify your ideas. Below is a list of a few questions that you must ask yourself and answer. In the rest of this chapter, there are probing questions and thoughts that can help you find these answers. Think of this part as the brainstorming session.

- What is the game?
- What will the game do?
- How does the game play?
- What will the player do?
- What are the goals of the game?
- How does the player win the game?
- How big will the game be?
- What is my story?

What Will the Game Do?

This is the general idea or overview. Some people call this the philosophical point; there are usually several points. This general idea is what determines the genre or style of the game; for example, is it first-person shooter or strategy? You may have such a good new idea that it doesn't fit the current set of genres but is a style all its own, but you need to define what the game is going to do or how it plays. This part of the game design should be about two paragraphs, describing briefly the genre or style and the goals of the game.

This is that part of your idea that says how the game is going to play. Will it be first-person, like *Quake* by Id or *Half Life* by Sierra? Will it be third-person, like *Dark Alliance of Interplay* and the *Warcraft* series? What other major features have you seen in other games that you want to emulate? What are the player's objectives? What other goals will the game try to achieve?

What Are the Goals of the Game?

Up to now we have just thought about what kind of game you might want to design. You also have to determine what the player is going to do and what needs to be accomplished to win the game. This means that you have to define what you want the player to do. You have to come up with the main goal or objective, which defines how the game is won. How will the player win? What must he do? What challenges are set to keep the player from winning too easily? How will the player overcome these obstacles?

Let's look at this example. The overall goal of the game might be to achieve the top professional status in motocross. The player will have to win several races in order to meet this goal. The other racers will not be easily beat, but the player will get upgrades to his bikes as he wins races.

Some of the goals of the game will include the player's objectives. How will the player play the game and win? How does the player learn to play? This is a goal you set for the beginning player. The player will need to be able to accomplish each task and understand how to control the game.

This should include levels of the game.

note

In the creation of your document, you must consider the main point of your design document: What will the player do? This question must be answered before you will be able to get a design document to flow. A good first step or first rough draft consists of a short one-page description of what the player must do or accomplish, either for gameplay or to win. The next section of this chapter will help you with a general idea, but after reading it you should have a good idea of what that first step will be. As you read through the next section, remember to consider these two things: You need to enjoy the type of game, and you need to know the player's goal.

Pick Your Genre, Any Genre

When you start working on the idea, you need to settle down to a type of game or genre that really fits your style of gameplay. You need to like to play the genre—no, you need to love to play the genre. It needs to be a passion or the genre that you spend most of your game time playing.

Each of the following sections discusses some of the major points that define the genre, but each has questions that you might ask yourself regardless of the genre. The sections briefly present information such as inventory or camera movement to help you find the right genre and to flesh out your idea. Be sure at least to peruse the information; it will help you, and it may inspire you to select a genre that you passed by before.

These genres are presented in alphabetical order, not best to worst. Remember that you will really need to play the genre you choose.

Action-Adventure and Bears, Oh My!

These two genres overlap so much that we will discuss both of them together here. These are the games that collect items in an elaborate story to obtain a happy ending. Along the way, the character has to overcome great obstacles to gather the items necessary to progress through the game. As the character finds the next item, he is rewarded with a cutscene or movie that explains the next goal. As the player is led in this manner, the story unfolds, and hopefully the player gets better at fighting the enemies, jumping to new heights, and obtaining the next item.

Some of these games are also known as platformers because of the way the levels are designed. The levels have raised areas to explore that are reached by jumping or traversing narrow bridges to overcome great chasms. If the player falls, it's lights out. For example, an in-game character might fall off a cliff into water and be swallowed up by a whale or shark. Or the character could fall off a really high cliff into a mist of oblivion and can't return. You can play these levels over and over to try and gather all of the hidden items, such as gold or other forms of money. Many times you have to break boxes, crates, barrels, or pipes or knock out enemies to find the items. This is the replay quality of the game: having a reason to play again to beat your score and finish in less time than your first try.

Is There a Difference?

There is a difference between action and adventure, albeit a small one. Action tends to have more fighting, and adventure titles let the player collect more items and use them in the story. Both have what is usually a single-player story. The player will probably be required to traverse many different areas or levels in exploring the world to accomplish the final goal. Along the way, the player should learn of the character's abilities and the best way to use them. This gives the player a mode of progression, making the game better and more fun to play.

What is in the world that needs to be fixed so that there is a happy ending? What will the player collect? Can the player use the stuff that he collects? Will the player automatically pick up the items, or will there be a key or button to use to collect the items? Usually the player will have a health meter of some sort; will the items heal or help the player stay alive or keep from fainting? To win, how much stuff or what percentage of stuff will the player need to collect? Think about the items that you will want to pick up. What will they be? What use do they have?

Inventory—You Said I Had to Pick Up Your What?!

As the player collects items, some sort of display will be used to indicate what was gathered and how much has already been gathered, usually called an *inventory*. Some games use a HUD that shows onscreen what the player has earned, picked up, gained, or collected with a small picture or numbers. Other games use a display somewhat like a backpack, where the items are displayed on a separate screen all laid out with details of their use and their worth to the player. Either way, some form of an inventory exists to keep track of the collection of items, though it is not always visible.

Suppose you have to collect a flying insect to increase your health. Only a certain amount would be useful. To collect too many would be a waste of time and effort because you have only a certain number of health points and cannot exceed that number. Maybe by collecting too many you would get an extra life. That would add more to this form of collection, more gameplay. You would need to see that you have collected 10 flying insects and that your health is full. When you collect the eleventh flying insect, you would need to see a symbol letting you know you earned a life.

Power-Ups

One type of item you can have in your game for collection is a *power-up*, which increases a character's skills or abilities. They are usually used to help the player progress in the game. Power-ups add to the gameplay and sometimes are critical to getting through some parts of the game.

You have a deep chasm in front of you and the princess is on the other side; how do you get to her? How are you going to save her? Then you notice a small object. What does it do? You collect the object, and now you can jump fives times farther.

Having special abilities can make the player more empowered. The player can become more immersed in the game if he can do something better, if it is done in the flavor of the game. Too many power-ups can make them seem bland. Be careful as you design to think this part through.

Fighting

Mano-a-mano, hand-to-hand, foot-to-foot, and other appropriate body parts can be thrown together. Using more confined areas or arenas, you must outmaneuver the competition and literally kick its butt. Fast finger movements and quick reflexes are the king and queen here. To stay alive, you have to fight your way up the list of contenders.

Below is a list of things to consider when choosing this genre:

- Location. Location. Location.
- Special movement for the camera—fixed or following.
- Fighting combinations and reactions.
- Controls.
- Special effects.

What Is Your Location?

From the Swiss Alps to the French Mediterranean, from the shores of Hawaii to the deserts of Africa, the player will need a variety of locations. You can pick the most interesting of places. These battles could take place deep in the heat and magma under the earth's crust or under the ocean in a pod arena specially designed to broadcast the fight throughout the universe. How many locales or arenas will you generate for the player?

You circle left around your opponent. He executes a great uppercut; luckily, you put yourself in your block stance and take very minor damage. You respond with a flying leap of Dodulus Destruction and send him flying through the wall. Yes, through the wall. Many of these types of games use destructible worlds and objects, walls being among them.

Lights, Camera, Fight!

When designing the game, think about what flavor you would like the game to have. The flavor of your game will determine the camera movement style. A fixed or somewhat stationary camera is more like a cinematic fight scene from *Maxetor, the Rabid vs. Thela, the Not So Bold Part III*. The moving, floating camera that follows all contestants keeps all characters visible. Both are used in this genre.

A fixed camera will point at the player's character and try to keep the action in view. It rotates a little but does not move from its position, as if mounted to a wall or under a table. The camera may zoom to accentuate the action or dramatic area. If the camera does not have a good view of the scene for the player, it will switch to another camera or location so that the best or closest shots are made. This method relies heavily on the game content designer, as he must place the locations for each scene.

The follow camera tags behind the player's character. This camera tries to keep the area just in front of the character's movement visible at all times. If the player is moving around, the camera will swing around to stay behind a little for a better view. If the player stops and turns around, the camera might wait for further movement before it will swing around. This motion requires camera controls that the player can use to swivel it into position. To some players, this can be disconcerting and annoying at the very least. Keep the camera in a good position behind the player's character.

Combo #5

A combo is a sequence of moves that deals more damage when performed together rather than separately. The sequence can also produce a new movement for the character, for example, pressing left moves left but left, left, then up might produce a roll to the left jumping at the end of the roll. A small list of the really good combos and how you can pull them off will help with the next section. Also, this helps you come up with one of the selling points, a point that marketing directors want to see. Think about the takedown maneuvers and what can knock down a character in the game. Will the characters get thrown very far, or will it be more realistic? Make the character's actions fit your location. What are the best moves? How hard is it to realize or complete these actions?

Stay in Control

The controls that define movement and attacks are critical in making a serious fighting game. The player will need to move easily and pull off the sequence that will perform an attack. If the controls are not separated well enough from the left and right hands, the player might find it confusing and hard to play. Keep the controls simple.

You're Special

In thinking about your custom moves and controls, ponder a moment about what these actions will look like. The special effects of actions are the eye candy that keeps the player interested. If you want the character to make a great swing, then there should be an arc that is shown behind the arm doing the swinging. The custom moves or actions will need to have custom or special effects associated with them. You will want to lay out a few ideas of what they might be like in your design document.

First-Person Shooter

This is a very common genre found among young adults and older kids piqued by interest in historical battles and war. If you like to sneak around and spy on others, this is your kind of genre. If you like to run around with a water gun and don't care if you get wet as long as you get everyone else wet, then this is your genre. There are many activities that can draw a parallel with this genre. It includes games from sneak and spy to seek and destroy, from small foam ball or paint ball weaponry to large weapons of mass destruction.

Down On the Lines

Battlefield 1942 by Electronic Arts has a bit of it all. You can be a sniper from the second story of a downtown apartment building, a foot soldier charging up the beaches of Normandy, an engineer rushing forward to set up mines to take out advancing tanks, a tank driver advancing on the front, a jet pilot laying out bomb after bomb over land and sea. With some of the modifications, you can even play with a lightsaber, thus showing how one idea can branch into many others.

Battlefield 1942 has many great points that have given it great success and acclaim. They include points that you may want to include in your game idea:

- The Machines of War allow you to battle on land and sea. You can choose from tanks, rocket launchers, jet fighters, bombers, ship's captain, or gunner, to name a few.
- Battle with or against your friends online or via a LAN network.
- You can choose your side, from American to Russian.
- The selectable weapons are authentic for the time period.
- Play multiplayer (up to 64 players) game types such as *Team Deathmatch*, *Capture the Flag*, or *Conquest* through many large maps, even user-defined maps.

What Else?

This list is not exhaustive and is small compared to the overall game design document you are preparing. These are just the high points of a successful game. A very good practice while making your designs is to visit Web sites that display such highlights. These points are those that will be made by the marketing team when your game is published.

This genre almost requires that there be a multiplayer experience along with the single-player story mode. There have been a few games in this genre that have succeeded without a multiplayer mode but not many. The whole idea is to blast something, with or against your friends. The player uses the single-player mode to get better at the game so that when he does battle with friends, the player will be the best. Be sure to remember that. The single-player mode is for training in this genre.

Weapons

Will your weapons be the latest in technology? Will they be authentic for the time period? Will they be futuristic and advanced? This helps define the storyline and gameplay. The player able to use only a knife while the enemies have superpowered laser-guided missile launchers probably won't have fun. Will the player be able to pick up anything or use anything in the game as a weapon? The player could find rocks at first and then after beating an animal use the hide to make a sling and then beating a larger animal use the sinew as a bow string, and so on. Will the player be able to destroy the world? Can the player make a hole in a wall to get a better shot at the enemy?

Answering these questions makes changes in gameplay and in the story for the player, including the final goal. As you think about the weapons and what the world is like, remember to keep the winning objective in mind. Will the player be able to accomplish the tasks necessary to win? Be sure that your goal matches the gameplay.

Hunting

Similar to first-person shooters, hunting games use weapons and the techniques of that kind of fighting. Hunting games pit the player against animals or other, supposedly less intelligent, creatures. These games usually stay realistic in nature, with vast expanses of territory that can be covered. Current high-powered rifles allow you to shoot your prey from quite a distance. Will your weapons resemble antiques or be more modern? Review the previous "Weapons" section.

Crawling through grass, nesting atop the branches, sighting in the prey, making sure the right deodorant was used, and the wind blows the right way. You are now ready to shoot, but you left your gun in the truck. You miss the opportunity of a lifetime as a brilliantly crowned stag runs off as you begin your trek back to the truck. Remember the vast terrain that you just hiked through. That way you can find your place again, just in case that stag comes back.

Terrain

In order to stalk prey, the player will need to have varied terrain that includes some sort of cover: hills, buildings, rocks, grass, trees, or cactus, for example. What will the environment look like? The Jurassic period has received some acclaim. Off-world locations might be interesting as well.

Maybe you can play as a Native American on the Central Plains and follow the buffalo trail. You might find yourself on an extraterrestrial landscape hunting the worabog. Wherever you choose to wander and stalk, you need to keep the weapons and tools functional in the given terrain. The world may also be used to set and lay traps as the fur traders did. It might also be fun to make the world deformable, so that you can make your own hideout or dig your own lion trap.

Weather You've Been Bad or Good

The player may be told that he must make a living or survive for a given period of time through all conditions, so weather will affect gameplay as well. Can the player survive during the weather conditions? The player may have to seek shelter during certain conditions. In this case, you may want time to be able to lapse more quickly. Maybe storms should last only until the player has taken shelter. Will the player play as though he will have to survive on an island with nothing more than a few shots left?

In targeting and shooting, weather will have an impact on the player's ability to acquire the actual creature accurately. Weather hinders the visibility and detection of creatures. But rain, snow, sleet, and even pouring golf ball-size hailstones will not stop the hunter from bagging his prey.

Puzzle

Many sub-genres or types fit into the puzzle genre. If you have browsed the Internet, chances are you have run into puzzle games, at least the advertisements for them. These games use strategy, as is true for any puzzle. The range of these games includes fast-clicking action, slow-moving jigsaw, card and board, letters and words. The Web is full of puzzle games, with many sites dedicated to just that.

Letters and Words

From day one at school, kids are taught that letters are important and that letters make up words when mixed together. This is so impressed upon those minds that when faced with a letter or word puzzle, it is hard not to try to solve it. When you see one of these puzzles, you might see a jumble of letters, and you want to make sense out of those letters. You want to understand what is being portrayed, so this is a type of game that is very addicting. Even if someone doesn't or didn't like English class, he still can enjoy playing with letters.

Making combinations of letters to spell words or picking words out of a mess of letters can create a game worth many hours of playtime. Letters on tiles, letters on balls, letters almost anywhere, words upside-down, and words all around have given gamers the chance to work on their vocabulary. If you haven't tried a word puzzle game, you are missing out.

Royal Flush Down the Tube

Card games might seem a little out of place, but trying to lay down just the right cards at the right time is a puzzle. Any Solitaire game, for instance, requires you to solve the puzzle—where should you go next? There are many different styles of play and new playing fields to create, especially those in 3D. You could create realistic reactive opponents for classic games like Canasta or Spades that animate and deliver good old bluffing chatter.

Cards don't have to have the usual faces like the queen and jack. The cards could have aliens with different powers that are used to protect your cards and destroy the opponent's. The cards might represent soldiers in battle in a life-and-death struggle for two people trying to capture all the cards. Use the cards as land, magic, creatures, warriors, countries, principalities, or just plain old numbers.

Board games play as puzzles: You must solve something to win. Some of the time it's the best path from beginning to end, but games like chess, Mah Jong, murder mysteries, and shape placement or inlays use quite a bit more thinking. Chess still does well on the market. Mah Jong or tile collection games keep players interested by allowing them to create their own tiles and layouts for collection. Murder mysteries get new twists with more rooms, more objects, and more suspects. Shape inlays build on mathematics skills or problem-solving skills without the player knowing.

Do you want to use more strategy working out a solution? Find out who did in Mr. Nobody in the root cellar with the rat poison. You must correctly remove items from eyewitnesses or find clues in the creepy old house to solve the mystery. Would you like more random roll-the-dice kind of play? Little snakes are chasing our little lizard hero. Roll the dice and help the little lizard make it to his hole and into cover before the snake gets him. If a snake lands on him, he has to start all over again.

Jigsaw

One type of puzzle is a jigsaw puzzle. There are many different ways to approach a jigsaw game. There are pieces that lock once they are placed, and there are free-floating pieces that allow the puzzle to be finished anywhere on the playing field. Some have borders to show where the edge of the puzzle must go. A timer for counting up or down can be used to keep the player placing pieces as fast as he can. Before starting, you see the picture that you are trying to make for only 15 seconds, and then you must re-create it.

Fastest Fingered Clicking

Keeping track of the changing scenario and clicking as fast as you can stimulate the mind and body. Well, maybe at least your clicking finger. This type of game might use a mouse to show where the next ball, egg, or square should go, and clicking shoots it off the location. This type of game might use the clicking to help navigate through a maze. This type of game can drive you crazy because you can't finish the level to progress to the next. In any case, these games try to get your adrenaline pumping and your heart rate up.

Many say these are games of skill. You have to find the right time to launch the right ball into the right place so that the whole level comes crashing down or cracks open and lets you move on and get the highest score. Will there be a time limit? Will the player have to remove objects or place them? Will the game play on without any limit to how many levels you complete? The player might be able to rack up any score, given great skill for the game. Of course, the game should present some training in the form of simple levels and make early advancement easy so that the player gets hooked. Then throw the big stuff at him, continually making it harder with higher levels. Then maybe time won't matter. The players will eliminate themselves.

Putting 'Em Together

For new diversity, the next logical step is to combine several puzzle types into one game. Take a classic card game and add fast-action clicking while making patterns and dropping in new cards. Put a time limit to the puzzle and slowly change parts. Make levels that need to be cleared. Use ducks to bring things onto the screen. When you mix and match game types, you can stumble onto a great hit.

Some game providers and publishers have turned these simple games into cashcows by allowing players to compete for cash. You might be able to find a publisher that would like to use your idea as a compete-for-cash game. This can get you started. But you won't be able to play them until you turn 18.

Role Playing Games

You are Thrug. You see a door to the north. What action do you take? Open door. You now face an 80-foot fire-breathing dragon. He has not noticed you yet. What action do you take? Draw sword. The sound you make startles the dragon into looking your way, but it does not react yet. What action do you take? Strike dragon with sword. You do 37 points of damage. The dragon opens its huge jaws and...

Apprentice Mark, you have been given the assignment to pursue and gather information for the Light Side. Let no one discover your presence. You have your power sword; go and seek. You enter the docking bay area, with only one door leading out. The door seems to lead to the control area. You move into position beside the door. Opening the door, you find two soldiers dressed in white plastic body armor. They do not look up at first. You use this and quickly dispatch them with your power sword. The console provides you with some information about this facility, but you need more...

You get the picture. A role playing game (RPG) places you, the player, in the role of a character that you are trying to enhance, improve, or develop. You gain experience and understanding as you venture through the country, the world, the universe, or even time. Through the experience that you gain, you are able to upgrade your skills and abilities. You will almost undoubtedly fight, cast spells, and talk, as is common in such games. Part of the game requires you to fulfill certain tasks or quests, which are used to progress the storyline. Your inventory grows as you explore, giving you items that enhance your powers, strengths, and abilities. They may also complete quests or harm you.

Universe

Sit back now and contemplate your universe. I'll wait.

Where will the character go? What requirements will you place upon the player's character (PC)? To what lengths will the PC go to win the game? Will the PC be able to roam and fight and keep on going without any end in sight? You can make the game respawn enemies every so often so that the world is always populated with them. This gives the player something to do at any time and can help him improve the PC. The game may be played on many different planets and allow the player to move from one destination to another through portals or space ships or whatever. From mountains to valleys, Earth to Venus, our solar system to Sigma Prime, wherever you wish to roam, you need to think about your player's ultimate goal. What is the player supposed to do?

Sometimes it is nice to contemplate that you will create the largest universe or playing area this world has ever known. Remember that if the character has to wander too far without anything to do, the player will get bored pretty quickly and think he didn't get what he paid for. You must also think of the logistics. How big can the universe really be? The game has to run on your chosen platform. Memory restriction, loading speed, number of disks, and disk space in general can preclude you from being able to realize your game.

RPGs have varied universes: underwater, underground, magma, fantasy or medieval earth, different planets, space vehicles, and space itself. They may contain anything in between and any combination. If you can imagine it, you can put it in. Just remember not to imagine too grandly. It can be unique and large, just not too large.

Quests

Marketing directors like to show that their RPG contains a vast number of quests and quests that evolve. This feature allows the player to pick and choose between the quests and find the ones he would most like to tackle. If you are forced to play through a lame quest, you might find it difficult to stay focused on the game and lose interest in it altogether. Make sure you create several different types of quests, not just a lot of them. The number of quests will not make up for the quality.

You might include helping a young couple, Romano and Julia, get married, even though their families are feuding. Overcome the monsters destroying the peasants' fields and their only source of food. Win the heart of some forlorn lass or lad. Destroy the giant beast that guards the bridge in order to make passage safe. Find your long lost brother or other relative that he might join your quest. Find the treasure rumored to be buried in the Tomb of Unforgetfulness. Help the town idiot find employment. Stop the cause of the plague.

Ready to Rumble

You will need to decide whether to include close-quarters fighting such as hand-to-hand and ranged fighting with a bow or some other distance weapon. Ranged attacks might include the use of spells or magic. In a futuristic or space title, a fighter would use more ranged attacks and weapons that fire energy pulses or whatnot. Designing this part will require you to think about the style of play and what the player must overcome. What kind of enemies and their weapons become part of the game? Will the fighting be real time or turn based?

The enemies will carry the same kind of weapons the player carries. They will use the same fighting techniques as the player uses. Will the player confront one major enemy or boss at the end of the game or will he face a boss during every quest?

Real-time fights require the player to attack, dodge, and move to stay alive. The player will move and dodge to keep from getting hit by his opponents and attack when he can. A turn-based fight makes the player wait for his turn to attack; then all other opponents will attack. Dodging is calculated during an attack on a defender.

Abilities, Strengths, and Powers

Certain attributes, abilities, strengths, or powers of a character will improve with experience gained with venturing. In fighting, the character may develop strength or magic. The character might sneak, hide, run, or jump, each a skill or ability that increases through use. Health, stamina, agility, knowledge, resistance, charisma, ingenuity, intelligence, speech, wisdom, and speed all fit well into the possible upgradeable attributes.

You are not required to list all the attributes that will be used in the game, but you should include the attributes that play a key role in the character's development. Many new forms of RPGs continue to emerge. Social gathering RPGs use a character's speech and charisma attributes to help define interactions with other characters. Space has become a new frontier for RPGs, with technology playing a major role in a character's progression. When you list attributes, refer to your universe.

Inventory

The inventory will hold many things, such as quest items, equipment, armor, magical devices, weapons, food, drink, potion ingredients, potions, and much more. What types of items will increase your abilities, strengths, and powers? What types will be wearable? What will be reusable?

You will not need to list all of the items that will be a part of the game, but you should have an idea of the items that will be required for the player to collect. Will the overall goal include an item? Will the player have to pass through many obstacles to find a single piece of the entire puzzle that will end the game?

MMORPG

A massively multiplayer online role playing game (MMORPG) contains the previously described features except that it is massively multiplayer. Many RPGs use a multiplayer capability and are online, but MMORPGs bring hundreds or thousands together to play at the same time. Some MMORPGs spread the players across several servers around the world, but evolving technology brings players back to one server. Worlds are large and expansive. The numerous quests must change often. These features require a team to continually monitor, update, fix, and enhance the games.

Players' characters gather for hunting parties, to fight together, to work together, to form guilds, and even to get married. MMORPGs use the concept of a social gathering to increase sales and playability. Social gatherings can make a big difference in a game's success.

Simulation

Pretend to be a railroad transit authority, a city planner, an island kingpin, a supreme entity governing life on a planet, or just an average Jane building your own moon base. Simulations imitate life situations past, present, or future. This genre includes a very diverse assortment of titles. Choose from Life, Business, Building, Flight, or Racing.

Life

Covering almost every form of living organism, including fantastical creatures, these simulations put you in control of their activities. Help people with their lives by giving them food, shelter, or work; host a hot tub party or other social event. Take charge of a medical facility, making sure the patients are cared for, keeping the place clean, and helping doctors and nurses maintain their bedside manners. Direct a colony of ants; infest a kitchen with your legions of cockroaches; teach a creature to feed itself and not eat the neighboring population.

Business

Business simulations put you in control of an empire, from local trash collection to airline services. These simulations depend upon you to manage the economic state of affairs. They often coincide with Building, as you may need to build your own transportation for goods. Manage a lemonade stand, a hospital, a city's power supply, a country, a coalition, a spy network, or other body. Open star lanes using space ships for transport and trade with alien races. Supervise a zoo or dinosaur park.

Money, that's what it boils down to. How much money can the player earn or raise to become a tycoon or political celebrity? What technology is needed to build the structures in the game? The player may need to spend money on science or technology in order to make better buildings, boats, trains, planes, or space ships. The game could require the player to provide citizens with law or some form of crime prevention. Protect your growing civilization from intruders with soldiers, borders, shields, or devices of destruction.

Building

Plan, design, lay out, dig, construct, and build your city. It doesn't even have to be a city. It could be a base on Mars, a space station, or a transit system on Earth, or go to the past and build Rome in a day, or an hour for that matter. Charge taxes to pay for future expansion and current costs for maintenance. Sell or rent retail and business space to help raise more funds. Beautify the location to increase your population's growth rate. Build parks, stadiums, libraries, and universities. Entertain your people. Make sure your transit transfers your goods off to market.

The scale of the project will need to be defined in the design. What architecture will be used, what might be animated, and what is the location? Will there be levels of complexity? How many? How much money does the player have to generate to complete the game? Will you have natural disasters that can destroy some of the player's structures?

Flight

From a Cessna 172 loaded with luggage to an Apache attack helicopter loaded with the latest air-to-ground laser guided missiles, take the yoke of your favorite flying contraption. Navigate a Boeing 747 via IFR through clouds and nasty, stormy weather to land at your favorite destination. Take off from Midway before your fighter plane is destroyed on the taxiway and then dogfight the enemy.

Whatever the flying machine, make sure that you have a firm understanding of the controls because these simulations must be accurate. From weather patterns to crosswinds, from updrafts to the jetstream, all the physics and motion need to be realistic. As you design, you must show that you know what you're talking about, especially when you get to the technical design phase.

Don't forget space. Movies have been made from space flight and attack simulations that have sold well. You can add futuristic weapons and destroy your enemy. The physics in space is quite different, but it's easier to implement because of less weather.

Racing

Whether it's Formula One at Monaco, NASCAR season, or underground downtown street racing, there is plenty of action waiting to be designed. You could race with dirt bikes, tricycles, or people with wheels on their hands and feet. You could design new vehicles and specialized terrain for the races. Give the player a good choice of vehicles and varied areas to race in. Racing simulations rate better if they contain a multiplayer aspect.

Physics plays a very important part in these simulations as well. If your design calls for racing on the moon or at the bottom of the ocean, you can bet these environments will affect the physics. Be sure to specify how your vehicles operate if they are not the standard four-wheel kind.

Sports

Basketball, baseball, football, soccer, rugby, and volleyball all belong to this genre. What can be done differently to make a splash? Some of the games available have clunky control settings, so you could enhance them or make them ergonomic. New characters, including fantastic creatures or alien lifeforms, could be used as players. The sport terrain could also be found in new locations.

You may want to include a simulation side to the game where the player will be required to manage his team as well as play. Build a team, fill the roster, trade players, sign contracts, build a stadium in which you will sell tickets and raise money for your team—and yourself, of course. Make draft choices, hire coaches, plan training, and get out there to win!

Don't forget that there are many sports to choose from. Racing is a sport, too. Golf is a sport, though to some it might not seem that way. Track and field events are favorites for many. Winter Olympic events such as the ski jump keep people busy for hours on end. Think about "backyard olympics," swimming in the neighbor's pool, racing across the yard, jumping the neighbor's fence, and so on.

Controls

One of the biggest drawbacks to a sports game is the controls. If you do not have easy-to-use controls, you don't have a game. Even though this holds true for any game, sports are the most demanding on the control system. The timing has to be just right in order to hit the ball with the bat or to make the high jump. Once you think you have this part down, have someone else check it. What works for you after you've studied it and tried it several times might not be natural for someone else. Get a second opinion.

Characters

Sports are played by all kinds of people, and a game should reflect that. Catch a pickup basketball game at the local gym in the morning before the sun rises or in the evening just before dark outside in the driveway. Playing soccer over at the schoolyard with a bunch of friends can be invigorating. But it's also fun to grab the controller and start running those touchdowns or striking out your friends on the latest sports title. In these competitions, the characters or in-game players should seem and look real.

There are times when real is not the way to go. Funny little kids running around trying to catch a fly ball, big-headed sports figures who slam the ball down in a mocking gesture, or creatures from mythology that fight opposing team members rather than actually carrying the ball to score can create the look you are going for. You can create a new game by mixing the rules of a few games and using strange characters to match. Animals that don't have hands can play soccer and kick the ball with all fours or maybe use their tails. Each animal might have a special ability that you would want on your side when picking a team.

Characters are very important to a title. What will the characters resemble, or what will they look like? When it comes to sports, you may want to model the in-game players after real players of the sport, or you might just have to come up with your own. Either way, this will be something to explain in your design document.

Terrain

In what kinds of places will the sport take place? The moon or some low-gravity planet would make a great place to run track or throw a javelin—somewhere you could throw something hard enough and it wouldn't come back down. There may even be a way to use the terrain as obstacles, or as other players—for example, kicking a soccer ball at a tree which then rebounds in to the goal. How about playing basketball on uneven terrain? Golf on the beach? Unusual locations create unusual possibilities for a sport, and backyard injuries from swing sets and trees might add a new dimension.

Strategy

The majority of strategy games are based on warfare of some kind. *Warcraft* comes from this genre and pits humans against orcs. Newer versions contain a few more races that join the battle. The general gist of such games starts the player with virtually nothing and expects him to build structures and with the structures build up a mighty army that can be used to destroy the enemy. Not all strategy games require battle or extreme force; some allow peaceful strategies and winning through alliance or other such means.

A large number of these games make the player ruler of a civilization and stipulate that the player has to keep control of the people while expanding his boundaries. The player will enlarge the economy and the population, will keep peace in the civilization, will defend and provide for the people, and will remain in power. To do this, the player will have to use resources gathered from the people or from the land.

A number of strategy games use a turn-based scenario, while others such as *Warcraft* are in real time. Strategy games that are turn based allow the player to think through each move or action, giving him deeper control over the management of the game. Real-time strategy games (RTSs) force the player to act and make decisions quickly. Both have their followings. Some people enjoy playing both forms.

Land

As it is with the world, power seems to be the root of the warfare or object of the game. The amount of land one owns measures the power one has. The land represents what resources and how much income are available and convertible to armies and people over which to govern. The amount of land that you control or can keep free from your enemies shows how much power you have.

What kind of land are you going to use? The terrain may be anywhere, and ownership of it can be assigned to anyone. Underwater, underground, space platforms, mountainous regions, entire continents, planetary surfaces, solar systems, and universes become battlegrounds for power.

Units

How will you defend your territory? What will be necessary to carry out your bidding? Men and women—human or not—soldiers, monsters, boats, frigates, buildings, workers, fighters, mercenaries, dwarves, elves, horses, deer, other animals, orcs, the undead, ghosts, hobbits, giants, rocs, ogres, trolls, goblins, knights, castles, bishops, popes, monks, peons, serfs, pawns, prawns, yetis, spiders, worms, mages, wizards, clerics, elementals, bombardiers, tanks, hummers, rocket launchers, missile towers, cannons, infantry, cavalry, musketeers, gunmen, bombers, strike fighters, helicopters, nuclear missiles, space ships, ion cannons, and lasers make a list from which you can start.

How will the people be governed? How will the player interact with the units? If the units are made from buildings, will the player need to provide for them? Where will the people come from? You may need to provide food and shelter.

Buildings

Where will the people live? Houses, farms, or space habitations could produce more people as they are built. Where will the people be led or governed from? Will a town hall suffice? Everyone loves a good castle or underground lair. The type of game will dictate this edifice. It could be a church or just a simple command post.

Some structures can be used as defensive devices. Cannon towers, missile turrets, and bunkers can provide for the safety of the people. Walls can be constructed. Proximity mine fields built in an otherwise unusable area can be a defensive measure. Create a star base with shield generators for your planet. Develop the technology to build arrow slits in your castle. Raise laser traps around your base.

Can the player destroy the buildings of the enemy? If the player is fighting to win, what constitutes a victory? Maybe total destruction of the enemy's units and buildings. Maybe the player has to destroy only one particular building to gain control of the enemy's people.

Gather Resources

The cost to keep land is high and needs to be offset with taxes or another method of resource generation. Gathering resources spread across the playing field helps the player continue to propagate his people and units. Another method requires the people to do the work by growing and harvesting. You can combine the methods: gather and sow. Machines and buildings may be required to do the gathering and processing of the raw materials.

What kind of resources will be available to the player? Will they be unique? Will they require a unique process? The gases venting close to the volcano are often toxic and will require a special extraction process with vehicles and buildings. The gold mine needs workers and a building. Trees can be chopped down and brought to a lumber mill where boards and other wood products can be extracted. Houses may be necessary for the population. Iron may be mined from the hillside with the use of a few miners. Of course coal may be necessary to use the iron. Upgrades can be made for each of these processes to speed them up and to better use the resources.

Technology Trees

Knowledge is power. The more you know, the better you can become. What kind of technology can you develop? How will it affect your civilization and its input and output? Will the technology tree depend upon which kind of unit is chosen? The skills and types of buildings that can be built depend on the technology you supply. The types of units available and what they can do depends on the technology. Before you can fight, the soldiers must be trained. Before you can have soldiers, you may need technology to change a person into a soldier. How much knowledge expansion will be possible? How long do you want the player to play before knowledge will be available? Will only certain buildings allow the upgrades? Will there be a group of scientists that under the player's employment search for the answers to problems facing his society?

Many elements exist that can be on your technology tree. What will you have on your tree? Increase wood collection. Upgrade ship engine design for further exploration. Cavalry units can be given flight through wing development or magical abilities. Will magic be part of the tree? Clerics can learn to raise the dead, which will serve their new owner. Learn how to construct a boat or ship. Remove the threat of cancer. Increase medical knowledge so that units can be healed more quickly. Develop more sophisticated weapons and defenses to better protect your claim to the land.

Multiplayer

Consider using a multiplayer feature for any genre. Publishers like to see multiplayer games, which sell well because of the social interaction. Players like multiplayer games because it gives them a chance to show off to their friends. They play the single-player mode to get better. When their friends come over, they flaunt their carefully honed skills.

People come together for parties just to play their favorite multiplayer games. This is a major selling point and cannot be overlooked. When you get to the technical phase of the design, you will need to think about connection or how multiplayer mode will be accomplished. Some of the options are LAN, Internet, or all on the same machine, whether turn based or simultaneous play. As was said previously, social gatherings can make a big difference in a game's success.

What's Your Story?

At this point, you will need to think about the overall story. What is this game about? The story should fit on a single page and describe the path the player will take to win the game. The quests and everything else are secondary to this. Reading the story should give anyone the full gist of what is supposed to happen from beginning to end. Do not include every detail, just the requirements for the player.

You might think of this as an exercise in drama. The story stands a good chance of becoming a theatrical masterpiece that unfolds as the player progresses through the game. Some stories come straight from movies, which are good material for games. But you would have to get the legal rights to use the material. Think of this as your chance to be the director.

How Big Can I Make It?

When you ask this question, you are really asking what platform or game system you are designing for. When you get to the technical phase you will need to flesh out this part a bit more. For now, you should try to keep things similar to other games made on the same platform. For example, a PC title will be allowed much more disk space than any console game, so you can put more into the PC game. It is best, though, to look at the genre you enjoy, find other games that fit that genre, and then design similarly sized material.

In games that you play, you might find something that makes you stop and say, "Wow, I want that in my game." The next thing you'll have to do is find a way to add it.

What to Keep

You'll have plenty of ideas come to you, so what should you keep? The general overview usually will dictate what can stay and what shouldn't. The game's goals will also help you determine the most important features that will make the game fun and what is just fluff that might not be needed.

After you have your general overview, you will need to consider the following:

- The general feature set
- Multiplayer features
- Gameplay
- Game world
- Editor
- Camera
- Special characters or general types of characters
- Pictures of the world and the characters
- Special items for collection
- Special weapons and armor

What to Throw Out

While searching for ideas, do not overdo it by imagining too many. Several games do not make it because the designers thought too big. Having too many elements can make the game cost too much to produce, and it won't have a chance before it even starts. Remember, someone must program and create the artwork for each idea, so try to keep only a few really cool ideas, with more simple ideas. That way the game is more likely to succeed.

Things you don't have to have in your game design:

- Every little detail
- Every simple single item
- Every simple weapon or armor
- Every special effect

Don't Keep It in Your Head

There are several reasons why you want to write things down as you come up with them, but the main thing that comes to mind is... Well, the thought just left me. You will forget more things about your game than you will remember, especially when you are ready to develop the game. Don't lose your great ideas just because you were lazy and didn't want to take the time to write them down.

Make notes when you think of something. Some designers keep a pad of paper and pencil always at hand. You might want to keep your writing utensils really close to the bedside, where dreams come quickly and leave quickly. Some great ideas have come from dreams. Lie in bed just before getting up, and try to remember your dreams or anything that might be useful from that night's sleep. Then write it down. You are trying to develop the ideas that will create the game and make your design consistent. If you fail to write things down, the worst thing is that you'll forget, but it also makes it difficult to create a flow from beginning to end. When you write down your ideas keep them together in a folder or binder. When you come to the full-blown writing of the design, you can refer back to the folder and be able to remove the stuff that doesn't flow. You should have a good idea by now; hopefully, you've written something down.

CHAPTER 5

THE HIGH CONCEPT

The *high concept* of a game design document is a summary of the important conceptual elements of the game. In many ways it is similar to an executive summary in other documents such as business plans. The high concept is different from a concept document, discussed in Chapter 2, "What Is a Game Designer?" because it is not a stand-alone document but rather part of a larger game design document.

The high concept is the first section of a game design document. It usually covers several headings, including introduction, overview, and executive summary to name a few. Some design documents will divide the high concept section from the rest of the document, and others will just incorporate it into the beginning of the document. The important issue is not as much how the document is formatted but rather that the designer knows the purpose of the high concept.

I remember reading a game design document not long ago that was really hard to understand. It had all the classic parts of a game design document, but it lacked anything that tied the document together into something that told me what the game was. I could see that great pains were taken to lay out how the game was being developed. The designer had good illustrations of the characters and vehicles. There was even an understandable game progress chart. But even with all those elements, it was still hard to understand what the game was. Reading the game design was a frustrating process, and even though the idea might have been a good one, I found myself very uninterested in it. My experience might have been different had the design contained a high concept.

In the previous chapter we talked about coming up with ideas for games. I hope you tried a few of the methods and have a list of video game ideas that you think will be cool to make. Some of those ideas may be very good, and some may not be so good. It is time to take a look at your ideas and choose the better ones to develop into a high concept.

The Purpose of the High Concept

The purpose of the high concept is to give the reader an overall feeling for the game quickly. The high concept part of a game design document condenses the important creative facts of the game into something that is easy to understand. Readers often don't have time to wade through lengthy documents and prefer to read something that is short and to the point. If the reader likes the high concept, there is a greater chance that he will read the rest of the document.

The high concept serves as a quick overview of the game. The rest of the design document then gives an in-depth detailed plan for creating the game. It is kind of similar to an architectural rendering of a building versus the blueprints of the building. The architectural rendering gives the viewer an immediate impression of the size, scope, and look of the project. The blueprints then give all the detail of how the building will be built.

It should be obvious that the high concept is easily the most looked at and important part of the design document. If the reader does not like the high concept, there is little chance that the rest of the document will get more than a passing glance. The high concept is the key to getting the reader to read the rest of the document.

If the high concept is so important, how do I write a great high concept for my game design document? I am glad you asked.

Writing the High Concept

Before you can write a good high concept for your game design document, you first need to understand what a high concept should contain to be effective. It does not contain extensive detail—just enough to make several key points.

- What the game is (the game statement).
- Why the game is important.
- Why the game is unique.
- Who will be interested in the game.
- Why the game should be published.

These five points are the foundation of the high concept. Figure 5.1 shows the five key points. Omitting any one of the points in the design document will weaken the document.

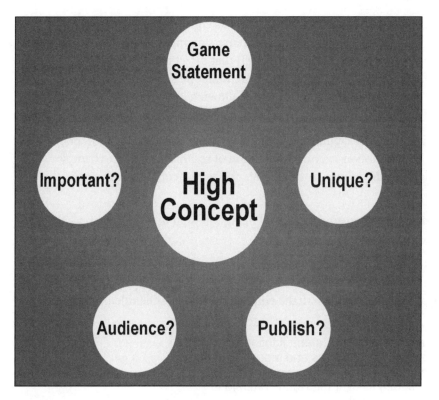

Figure 5.1
The high concept should include the five key points.

Before you write the design document, you should review the five key points to make sure you have addressed each one.

The Game Statement

A game statement is a one-sentence statement that defines the game so that if that one statement was all that anyone ever read of the design document, that person would still come away with a solid understanding of what the game is. It is a good way to see if you really understand the game you are designing. It will also help you to better communicate your game idea. If your game can't be described in a single sentence, it doesn't mean that it is a bad idea. However, getting the idea into a single sentence is something that will help you to focus on the core concept of the game.

A one-sentence statement is something that is used often in the motion picture and TV industries.

In those industries there are so many different projects competing for production money that most executives have resorted to the one-sentence statement to see if in one sentence a concept can be carried to the reader. The theory is that direct messages are easier to market than complex messages. If the game takes more than one sentence to explain, there is a good chance the game may be too complex. The following is an example of a game statement for a fighting game:

> *Martial Arts* is a cross-discipline arena fighting game for the PC with photo-realistic graphics and motion-captured animation of real masters, where champions of different fighting disciplines from all over the world compete to become the supreme martial artist.

This sentence covers a lot of ground while still being one statement. Let's break the sentence down and see how it works.

First of all, the title of the game is the very first few words in the sentence, as shown in Figure 5.2. *Martial Arts* is the game's title. The game statement should always state the title of the game clearly. Putting the title in italic emphasizes that it is the title of the game.

Martial Arts is a cross-discipline arena fighting game for the PC with photo-realistic graphics and motion captured animation of real masters where champions of different fighting disciplines from all over the world compete to become the supreme martial artist.

Figure 5.2
The statement starts with the title.

After the title is the word *is*, as shown in Figure 5.3. The word tells the reader that the next few words are connected to those before as a statement of equality. It is like the = sign in a math problem, indicating that one side is equal to the other. The reader knows that what comes after the word *is* will define the title. Okay, I know I am getting a little simple here but there is a point to this. The whole idea of a game statement is to tell the reader what the game is. Everything that follows should define the game.

Martial Arts **is** a cross-discipline arena fighting game for the PC with photo-realistic graphics and motion captured animation of real masters where champions of different fighting disciplines from all over the world compete to become the supreme martial artist.

Figure 5.3
The whole idea of a game statement is to tell the reader what the game is.

The next section of the sentence as shown in Figure 5.4, defines the game's type and genre. It says that the game is cross-discipline, meaning that several forms of martial arts are present in the game. Other words that might be used here are *technically accurate*, meaning the game uses accurate technique and physics, or *action-packed*, meaning that the game has action and drama. All these statements tell the reader what type of game it is.

Martial Arts is **a cross-discipline arena fighting game** for the PC with photo-realistic graphics and motion captured animation of real masters where champions of different fighting disciplines from all over the world compete to become the supreme martial artist.

Figure 5.4
The next section defines the type and genre of the game.

Arena fighting game is a statement of genre. Genre is important because it helps the reader to classify the game.

The word *for*, as shown in Figure 5.5, tells the reader that the next statement will further define the game. In other words, the game is targeted toward a specific platform or audience. Yes, I am getting simple here again but every game statement should include what the game is for. Is the game for a particular platform? Is the game for a particular audience? In this case the game is for a particular platform.

Martial Arts is a cross-discipline arena fighting game **for** the PC with photo-realistic graphics and motion captured animation of real masters where champions of different fighting disciplines from all over the world compete to become the supreme martial artist.

Figure 5.5
Every game statement should include what the game is for.

The next statement in the sentence is one of platform, as shown in Figure 5.6. The platform is an important element of any game statement because it tells the reader how to picture the game. The visual image of someone playing a game in front of a TV is very different from someone playing a game on a cell phone. It also gives the game a sense of residency—the game resides on a PC.

> *Martial Arts* is a cross-discipline arena fighting game for **the PC** with photo-realistic graphics and motion captured animation of real masters where champions of different fighting disciplines from all over the world compete to become the supreme martial artist.

Figure 5.6
The game resides on console and PC systems.

The next word, *with*, as shown in Figure 5.7, tells the reader that the game will contain something. *With* is a word used to show companionship or content. She is with him. The car with the leather upholstery was luxurious. Again simple but important. Having the word *with* gives you a chance to elaborate on some very unique aspects of your game.

> *Martial Arts* is a cross-discipline arena fighting game for the PC **with** photo-realistic graphics and motion captured animation of real masters where champions of different fighting disciplines from all over the world compete to become the supreme martial artist.

Figure 5.7
With tells the reader that the next statement will say something that the game contains.

Photo-realistic graphics and motion-captured animation of real masters, as shown in Figure 5.8, tells the reader that the game will look real and that the characters will move in a realistic way. This is a statement that further clarifies to the reader how to visualize the game. The more a game statement can project a positive image in the mind of the reader, the more likely the reader will be to continue to read the design document.

> *Martial Arts* is a cross-discipline arena fighting game for the PC with **photo-realistic graphics and motion captured animation of real masters** where champions of different fighting disciplines from all over the world compete to become the supreme martial artist.

Figure 5.8
The next statement tells the reader what the game has.

The word *where*, as shown in Figure 5.9, precedes a statement of place or function. It can place a game in a specific location such as a tropical island. It can also tell the reader how the game will work.

> *Martial Arts* is a cross-discipline arena fighting game for the PC with photo-realistic graphics and motion captured animation of real masters **where** champions of different fighting disciplines from all over the world compete to become the supreme martial artist.

Figure 5.9
The word *where* precedes a statement of place or function.

I am sure you have noticed by now that I have picked out four single word elements of the statement: *is, for, with,* and *where.* These four words are building block words that help the reader in very specific ways. A simple way to think of the game statement is as an is, for, with, and where statement. In fact, filling in the blanks between these four words is a good way to begin defining your game.

The last statement of the sentence as shown in Figure 5.10 is descriptive of what happens in the game. In this case it tells the reader about the characters and the game objective.

> *Martial Arts* is a cross-discipline arena fighting game for the PC with photo-realistic graphics and motion captured animation of real masters where **champions of different fighting disciplines from all over the world compete to become the supreme martial artist.**

Figure 5.10
The bold area tells the reader about the characters and the game objective.

Now that you understand the basic structure of the game statement sentence, you should try a few of your own. Take some of your favorite game ideas and see if you can create an effective game statement for each one. Use the formula below for a start. Once you get the hang of it, you will be able to adapt the sentence and change it to meet your needs.

_____ is a _____ for _____ with _____ where _____.

Why the Game Is Important

Publishers often will not pick up a game because the game idea is just another adaptation of some other game. There is nothing of importance about the game. In the current competitive game market, a game has to be important to get noticed.

If it is important for a game to be important, what is important about a video game?

That is a good question. What is important about a video game? The answer lies in what the audience for the design document values. The important issue for an investor looking to increase wealth is return on his investment. The important issue for a publisher might be market share of a genre in addition to individual game returns. The important thing to a potential team member might be a significant innovation to the game. The important issue to a marketing executive is the chance the game has to make an impact on the gaming press. This part of the document is a blatant sales piece, not a technical document. Every sentence needs to be geared to convincing your audience that your game is important.

Before you can define what is important, you have to determine who will be reading your document. For example, if you are looking to get a few of your friends to help you create a game, you will want to tell them why you think your game will be cooler than other games they have played. On the other hand, if you have a team and are looking for someone to publish your game, you will want to address why the game will sell better than other games in the same genre.

The best way to include why your game idea is important is to list all the potential readers along the side of a chart. Then list several important factors about your game across the top. Then rate as best you can the importance each potential reader may put on the individual elements of your game. Figure 5.11 shows an example of the chart. Notice that some things are more important to some readers than others. If you don't know how to rate something, ask the potential reader.

	A	Independent character AI	Improved rendering software	Recognizable license	Market through theaters
1					
2	Friends and associates	10	10	2	3
3	New team members	10	10	2	3
4	Potential employers	10	10	2	5
5	Potential investors	5	4	10	10
6	Potential publishers	5	5	10	5
7	The press	10	10	4	10
8					

Figure 5.11
Make a chart to see what is important to each potential reader.

The numbers in the chart represent a scale of 1 to 10 with 10 being very important and 1 being of no importance.

Hint

The idea of the chart is to help you focus your efforts in the high concept section of your document. You may want to have different high concept sections for different readers. That way you can match the design document to the reader.

You should be direct in defining to the reader the important aspects of your game. Use a sentence such as, "This game is important because _____." Make the sentence the first in a paragraph and then explain it further in a few more sentences. The following is an example of an importance statement:

> *Street Bike* is important because it will be the first game to depict the true physics of high-performance street motorcycles accurately. No other game has the total package of real-life physics combined with licensed motorcycles. These are the same motorcycles a player can buy at his local dealer.

The statement clearly shows an important aspect of a game with very little confusion. The reader may have questions about how you can back up your claim, but he will have no question about what you think is important. If he has questions, he can always read the document to see how you support the claim.

Why the Game Is Unique

In addition to why the game is important, you need to tell the reader why the game is unique. *Unique* means one of a kind or different from others of the same type. Your game might be important, but that doesn't mean other games aren't important in the same way. You have to tell why your game is different.

In business, many companies will apply for patents to protect the uniqueness of their products. A *patent* is a legal document that makes it illegal for anyone to duplicate a product without the permission of the patent owner. Patents are only one way to protect the uniqueness of a product. Other ways include copyrights, trademarks, trade secrets, licenses, and unique talent.

Copyrights

A copyright is legal protection for a document or any expression of an idea fixed in a tangible form.

If a document is copyrighted, no one but the copyright holder can legally copy the document. This book is copyrighted. It can be copied only by its publisher. Your game designs can also be copyrighted. In fact, by law, any document you create is automatically copyrighted, and you own the copyright. To enforce your copyright, however, you should do a couple of things. You should put a copyright notice on the document, stating who owns the copyright and the date the document was copyrighted. The following is an example of a copyright notice.

© Copyright (Your Name) 2004

The circle with the letter c inside is a universal symbol that means copyright.

You can also register your document with the U.S. Library of Congress for a small fee. If you want more information on registering copyrights, check out Ashley Salisbury's book *Game Development Business and Legal Guide.*

Trademarks

A trademark is legal protection for a specific design or phrase. The purpose of a trademark is to protect a brand or a symbol used to identify a product or company. The title of your game can be trademarked, as can the characters in your game.

Trademarks are more complex to obtain than copyrights. They are also more expensive. If you are interested in learning more about trademarks, you can find more information in Ashley Salisbury's book mentioned previously.

Patents

A patent provides legal protection of a specific technology or methodology. A patent protects an inventor from having someone else copy and sell his invention. If your game has unique technology, you may be able to patent that technology.

Patents are very costly and take some time to obtain. It is a good way to protect your game, but obtaining a patent is somewhat impractical for a beginner. If you want to learn more about patents, you can find some great information in Ashley Salisbury's book as well.

Trade Secrets

A trade secret is both legal protection and a practical method of protecting ideas, technology, and almost anything else that is part of your game idea. A trade secret means that you keep the ideas and technology secret and show them only to people who are willing to sign a special form called a non-disclosure form (NDA).

An NDA is a special form that binds the people or companies that sign it to secrecy concerning material that is designated confidential. It is often used in business, and more information on the document can be found in Ashley Salisbury's book.

Licenses

A license is a legal document that grants a person or company the right to use intellectual property owned by another person or company in defined ways. Many games have licenses. You have probably played a game that has characters from a movie or a pro sports league. You may have played games with other licenses, such as a brand name product or even an item such as a specific car.

When you license a property for a game, you are buying the rights to use the property in your game. The owner of the property is responsible for protecting the property through copyrights, trademarks, and other methods.

Licensing properties is expensive and usually not something a first-time game designer will deal with. It is not uncommon, however, that a publisher might take a game idea and add a license to it.

Unique Talent

Unique talent is not a legal protection but rather a practical protection. If you have someone on your team who can do something that no one else can duplicate, that is called a unique talent. Unique talents can be very valuable. Take for example a professional athlete. He is paid well because he can do something that few other people can duplicate. The more unique the talent in his given sport, the more he is paid.

You may be able to produce some part of a game better than anyone else. In that case, you can keep others from duplicating what you do by the sheer fact that they can't do it. For example, you may know an artist who has a very cool style for creating characters. Because no one can quite duplicate the artist's work, your game will be unique.

Now that you know a few ways of protecting the uniqueness of your game, you should take a look at what you need to protect. It is not safe to assume that your game idea is unique just because you have never heard of the idea before. You may think that your idea for creating a game about mashing potatoes is unique, but there may be a half dozen potato smashing games in production. You should do some research to see if there are any other games that are similar to your idea.

Once you feel comfortable about the uniqueness of certain aspects of your game, you should state to the reader what is unique about your game and why you feel it is unique. The statement might look like this:

> *Potato Smashers* is unique because there are no other potato smashing games on the market, and we have a new unique technology for flying potato parts.

This statement is direct in that it tells the reader what is unique about the game. It also tells the reader how the unique item is something that other game companies won't be able to duplicate.

Audience

Who will want to buy your game? This question is of paramount importance to many readers of your game design document. The high concept needs to include direct information on the game's audience. How are you going to find out who will want to buy your game?

There are many ways to define target audiences. These methods include direct research, comparisons, and design. Each method has its advantages, and even a new designer can successfully define the audience for his game.

Direct Research

Direct research is simply asking members of your target audience if they like the concept of your game idea. For example, if you want to make a game for teenage boys about back country dirt biking, you can just ask boys the age of your target audience if they are interested in the game. You will need to be specific and direct your questions in such a way that they understand what the game is. You can use the game statement discussed earlier in this chapter for a start.

When doing direct research, you will need to keep track of how many people you ask and what their responses are so that you can tabulate the results. You might want to classify the answers for easy tabulation, as in the following example:

> Very interested in playing____, interested in playing____, maybe interested in playing____, not very interested in playing____, not interested in playing____.

The more people you ask, the more accurate your survey is likely to be. If you want to do a scientific survey, you will need to take into account a lot of factors, including where you asked the question, the age and background of each respondent, and several other things relating to your audience. For the purposes of this book, all you are looking for is a general idea of how popular your game might be. For more information on this you should study the subject of statistics.

If you get direct research on your game, you should put it in your document to explain how you did the research and what your results were. The following is a sample statement that you could have in a game design document:

> In a survey of 50 boys in my high school, 23 of them indicated that they were either interested or very interested in playing a wilderness dirt biking game. The boys were randomly selected in the hall and range in age from 15 to 17 years of age.

Comparisons

Another great way to define a target audience is to compare your game idea to other games that are similar to it. For example, if your game is a racing game for golf carts, and there is another racing game that is similar, you can check with your local video game stores to see if the game is very popular. You can also sometimes get other useful information on who bought the game to try and narrow your audience. You can look at game sales charts in video game magazines to see if the other game sold well.

If you find a game that is similar to yours you should play the game to check out its strengths and weaknesses. Keep a notepad by you as you play so you can record what you like and dislike about the game. If your friends have played the game ask them what they liked and didn't like.

Another good method is to ask members of your target audience if they have played the comparison game and if they liked it. In your document you might put a statement such as the following:

> *Golf Cart Challenge* is similar to *Golf Cart Mayhem* but with licensed carts and larger courses. It will appeal to the same audience, which is primarily male and between the ages of 14 and 20.

Comparisons work well only if the game you are comparing to yours is a popular game. Comparing your game to a mediocre game may cause the reader to think your game will be mediocre as well unless you can make a good case for the validity of the concept despite the failure of the original game.

Design

Another good way to direct your game to a specific target audience is to purposely include things that are known to appeal to the audience. For example, a game directed to young girls between the ages of 6 and 10 might be designed in pastel colors, while a game designed for 14-year-old boys might have deep dark colors.

There are many elements that you can use to design your game for a specific audience. The use of things such as colors, art style, music, and a popular cartoon character might be good ways to target a specific audience. You will have to get the license for the character to make that one work, however.

A statement in a high concept that indicates an audience that the game is designed for might go as follows:

> *Clockwork Pinball* is designed to appeal to young children ages 8 to 10 because of the bright colors and the many moving parts on each table. The Clockwork license is also very popular among children of that age.

Establishing an audience for the game will help to put the game into perspective within the market. Readers will not only be able to visualize the game, but they will also be able to visualize someone specific playing the game.

Why Should the Game Be Published?

Even if you have covered all of the points so far, you still need to deal with the issue of why the game should be published. The game might be unique, important, and targeted to a great audience but still not be something that a publisher will want to pick up for publication.

Getting a game published is difficult because the competition is so high among developers. If this is your first game project, don't expect a major publisher to want to publish your game. The point of this section is to teach you about a section of a game design document. Learning why publishers make decisions will help you understand what you need to include in your document.

Publication is a big financial commitment for a publisher. There could be many reasons for publishing or not publishing a game. A publisher of sports games may not be interested in adventure games. A publisher may already have a game that is similar to yours and does not want to compete against itself. A publisher may have limited money for development and does not wish to invest any more money for the time being. A publisher might not publish on the target platform. A publisher may not like the current phase of the moon. Who knows what a publisher might consider when selecting games? As a designer you can't control everything about what a publisher might think about your design, but you can present a case for publishing your game.

A good high concept document will clearly spell out why the game deserves to be published. These reasons should be those that will benefit the publisher if the game is published. These benefits include financial gain, market share, publicity, industry prestige, and publishing deadlines.

Financial Gain

The most obvious question for most publishers is, "How will this game make money, and how much will it make?" Will the game sell 10,000 units or 1,000,000 units? How much profit will there be on each unit? While these questions may be important to the publisher, they are difficult for the designer to answer. Very few games will be able to guarantee that a set number of units will sell. Even publishers that have connections with retailers have trouble estimating how many units of any game will sell.

The designer can only give evidence of how many units a game might sell. A statement on financial gain for a publisher in the high concept might look like this:

Rock en Roll Kings should be published because there are 100 million fans of the groups included in the game. A survey of the fans showed that nearly 25% said that they would buy the game. That makes 25 million fans who are interested in purchasing the game.

The publisher might argue with how you came up with your numbers for this statement, but there is very little argument about the potential for the game.

Market Share

To some publishers, market share is even more important than financial gain on any individual product. The reason that market share is important is that the number one selling game in any market usually can control that market, and domination of a market can mean huge long-term financial rewards. Publishers who take a longer view on the market will sometimes sacrifice short-term gains for long-term results.

Market share is an issue of competition between publishers. If a publisher wishes to gain market share, it has to either attract customers from other publishers' games or find new customers and expand the market. If the high concept is going to show that the game will increase a publisher's market share in a given market, the designer has to show how the game will either attract customers of other games or attract new customers.

A statement on market share might look like this:

Hot Rodders should be published because the game has great potential for increasing market share in the home mechanic market. The game will license the brand *Hot Rodder*, which is the most popular magazine in the home mechanic market. *Hot Rodder* boasts a subscription base of 250,000 readers, of which 45% say they own a game system.

In this statement, the publisher is given evidence that the game will have a pull on current game system owners who also read *Hot Rodder* magazine. If the game does well, it could help increase the publisher's market share in the custom-built racecar game genre.

Publicity

Some games have a very high profile with consumers. A publisher may agree to publish a game based on the fact that the game will bring publicity.

Publicity is probably not a deciding factor to a publisher, but it is at least an influencing factor. Whether or not publicity will be helpful will depend on the publisher's position in the marketplace. A large, well-known publisher may not need any publicity, but a smaller publisher may be happy to get some publicity.

A statement in a high concept regarding publicity for the publisher might look like this:

> *Corn Grower* should be published because it is tied to one of the most popular trade magazines in the Midwest. The magazine has committed to running articles about the game for six months prior to the release.

Granted, *Corn Grower* magazine might not be a prime target for a game-playing market, but the statement works because it shows that the game will have publicity. There is a commitment on the duration and type of publicity, and there is a specific group of people who will read about the game.

Industry Prestige

Sometimes a game may not have potential to sell well, but it may be so innovative that the publisher will receive industry awards and recognition. It is hard to state the value of industry prestige, but it does have a positive effect on a publisher. Prestige helps a publisher in many intangible ways, such as recruiting employees, positive press, heightened product awareness, and increased public attention. By itself prestige is not a major factor for publishers, but it does play a role in their decision process.

Like publicity, industry prestige may not add directly to the publisher's bottom line, but it can have a long-term effect on company profits. If your game is highly innovative and something that will catch the attention of other industry professionals, you may be able to promote that aspect of your game to the publisher in the high concept.

A statement of possible industry prestige might look like this:

> *Dune Buggy* should be published because it has the most innovative approach to racing in deep sand ever conceived. Our highly tuned suspension system takes into account not only the tires, the speed, and the angle of the terrain but also the depth and consistency of the sand. Industry press has already hailed this driving innovation as the most important advance in off-road racing in years.

Of course, the above statement about industry press will have to be backed up in the design document, but the statement clearly indicates that the game has some possibilities of gaining recognition in the industry.

Meeting Publisher Deadlines

Many times publishers will have products that are delayed. A product delay can cause significant problems for a publisher, not the least of which is a loss of revenue. Some publishers are publicly traded on the stock market. If a public company does not maintain a reasonable quarterly profit, its stock can go down in price, causing an inability to raise money in the future. Because publishers need to maintain profits, they often will look for substitute products when planned products are delayed. If your game is nearly finished, a publisher might publish the game simply because it needs to fill a product slot.

A statement that will attract a publisher's attention in regard to delivery of your game might read as follows:

> *Duck Pond* is close to being finished. We are currently testing and should have a gold master of the game in about two months, in time for publication in the second quarter.

This statement lets the publisher know when the game will be finished and also reminds the publisher that it can fill a slot for the second quarter. The publisher may or may not have a need for a game for that quarter, but it doesn't hurt to bring it up.

Other Reasons

There could be any number of other factors that a publisher might think is important. Maybe your game is just so beautiful that the publisher can't pass it up. Maybe your dad knows the publisher and can call in a favor. Who knows? The important thing here is that you gain an understanding of how publishers look at a game design document.

Summary

This chapter was devoted to the opening part of the game design document, called the high concept. The high concept may not be a specific heading in a game design document but rather the opening section of the document. It is designed to catch the reader's interest so that the reader will read the rest of the design. Here are the highlights of this chapter:

- Different readers will have different priorities. Sometimes it is a good idea to have different high concepts for different audiences.
- The game statement should condense the important aspects of the game into a single sentence.
- The high concept sections should state why the game is important.
- Anything that makes the game unique should be included in the high concept area of the design document.
- The high concept should tell the reader the intended audience for the game. Knowing the intended audience will help the reader visualize someone playing the game.
- The high concept section should show the reader why the game should be published. The most obvious reason for publishing a game is for financial gain, but there are many other important factors, including market share, publicity, industry prestige, and meeting a publisher's deadline.

CHAPTER 6

VISUALIZING THE GAME

O ne of the most highly sought jobs in the game industry is that of *concept artist*. The concept artist is the person responsible for designing the visual aspects of the game. The concept artist works hand in hand with the game designer to create the foundation upon which the game will be created. A game design document without pictures is like ice cream without any sugar. It just doesn't have any appeal. Games are visual, and the game design needs to express how the finished game will look.

Graphics in a game design is usually the first thing a publisher or investor sees. The better the design's graphics, the more likely the publisher or investor is to have a favorable impression of the design. Great concept art often can mean the difference between a design being read or ignored.

This chapter uses a hands-on approach for the beginning artist to learn how to create concept art for game designs. It includes many step-by-step examples and a number of samples taken from game designs.

Art Used in Game Designs

Game designs include extensive amounts of art to help the game developers in creating the final game. Some of the art typically found in a game design is as follows:

- Storyboards
- Level layouts
- Environment illustrations
- Character designs
- Model sheets
- GUI designs

We will not be able to cover each area in detail in one chapter, but we can give some examples to help you see what a design needs to have in it to be competitive.

Storyboards

Storyboards are sketches that indicate how sequences of events are to take place. In many ways they are similar to cartoon panels in that they are pictures with captions explaining the scene and any possible dialogue. In games, storyboards are used to show how the game will work. When you build your game design, you will want to include storyboards wherever you need to show how an event or action will take place. Figure 6.1 shows an example of a storyboard where the character can go through several doors.

Figure 6.1
The storyboard shows possible events in a game.

Many forms of media like film and video are linear in that they relate a specific story that does not deviate from beginning to end. Unlike film and video productions, games are not linear in nature, and events seldom occur in exactly the same way each time the game is played. Camera angles, character positions, and even outcomes will differ because the player is in control of one or more elements in the game. Storyboards for games, therefore, are not used in the same way as they are for film and video. A storyboard in a game design will show a possible sequence of events. The development team uses it as a guide for setting up the event. Sometimes the storyboard will need to include several possible outcomes to an event, depending on how pivotal the event is in the overall scheme of the game. Figure 6.2 shows two possible outcomes of a game event.

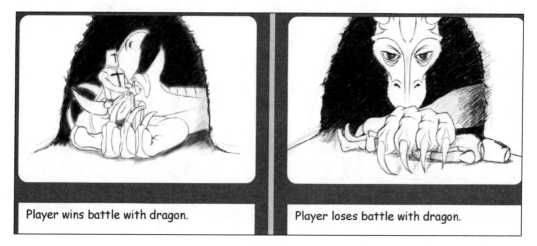

Player wins battle with dragon.   Player loses battle with dragon.

Figure 6.2
Game storyboards show possible outcomes of a game event.

Storyboards in game designs are also used to show *game navigation*, which is the process of moving through the game. It is usually accomplished with a *user interface*. User interfaces are all the elements that are used in controlling the game, including *input devices* such as a game controller or a mouse, and onscreen elements such as buttons, menus, windows, and such. User interfaces also include onscreen information elements such as score, health, time, or any other important information that a player needs to play a game effectively. Because games require player input in order to progress from one part of the game to another, the design team needs to communicate how this navigation will be accomplished. Storyboards are a great way to show how the navigation system in a game will work. Figure 6.3 shows a menu design for game navigation.

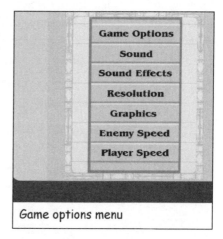

Game options menu

Figure 6.3
Storyboards are used to show game navigation.

Storyboards are used to define cinematic sequences in a game. Often games will develop story elements by using short cinematic sequences. These sequences are linear video clips and are often as sophisticated as any motion picture. They form a vital part of many games. Concept artists work with the game designer to visualize each cine-matic sequence. It is the responsibility of the concept artist to create storyboards that show how a cinematic sequence will work in the game. Sometimes the artist will work with a screen-writer to develop the sequences. In cinematic sequences, the storyboards are very similar to those used in motion pictures and television. A cinematic sequence is shown in Figure 6.4.

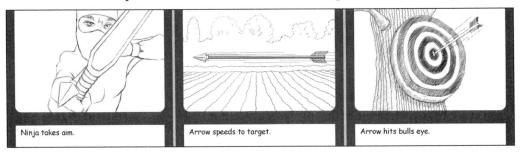

Ninja takes aim.   Arrow speeds to target.   Arrow hits bulls eye.

Figure 6.4
Storyboards are also used for cinematic sequences in games.

Creating the Storyboard

The first step in creating a storyboard panel is to draw a series of thumbnail pictures for each panel in the series. Because storyboards are used to describe an event, they usually will have two or more panels in a series. In this series there will be four panels to describe the heroine entering a room, discovering an enemy hidden in the room, defeating the enemy, and investigating the area where the enemy was hidden. Figure 6.5 shows the early thumbnail sketches for the series of panels.

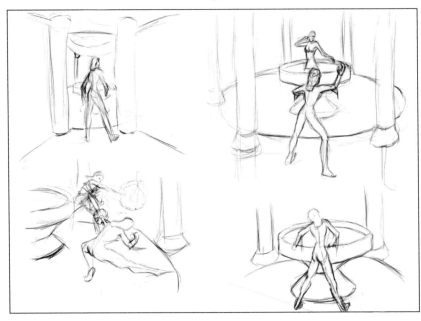

Figure 6.5
The first step is to create thumb-nails for each panel.

In the thumbnails, the artist works out the basic design of each panel. This is a third-person game, meaning that the main character is viewed from behind, and the player guides the character through the game. This limits the design in many ways, but it is still possible to come up with some interesting compositions.

Once you are satisfied with the composition of each thumbnail sketch, work on the actual panel can begin. Figure 6.6 shows the storyboard panel roughed in very lightly.

Figure 6.6
The initial panel is roughed in lightly.

It is important not to be too tight with the drawing in the initial stages. A looser, more fluid approach tends to help give the drawing a better feel. By not committing to any given line, you can feel the shapes as they are created. The loose initial drawing may change dramatically before the panel is finished, but drawing lightly helps get the artist past the blank sheet of paper that often stymies creativity.

Once the drawing is roughed in, you can start refining the shapes. Figure 6.7 shows the drawing starting to take shape.

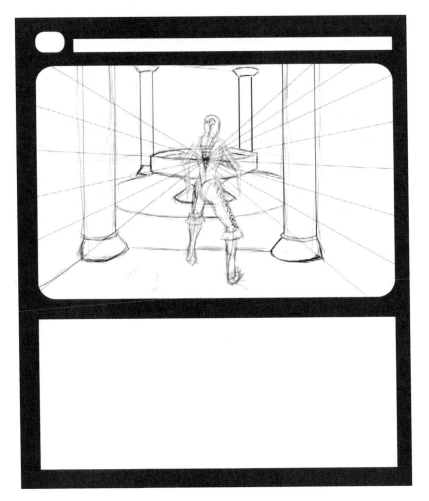

Figure 6.7
The shapes in the drawing are refined.

Notice that the lines are still relatively light. At this stage the artist should still be searching for the right proportions of the figure and other objects in the environment. In this example, the perspective lines converge on the center of the heroine's back. This design element helps to center the viewer's attention on the main character in the panel.

Once the major lines in the drawing are defined, the construction lines are then cleaned up as much as possible. Figure 6.8 shows the drawing in a more complete state, with most of the construction lines removed.

Figure 6.8
When the drawing is ready, the construction lines are removed.

tip

If the artist is using a digital drawing program, erasing and cleaning a drawing is not a problem. If the artist is using pencil and paper, then he needs to be very careful because erasing can cause damage to the surface, resulting in problems when the artist starts shading.

When all the major lines of the drawing are in place, you can start the shading process. It is usually a good idea at this point to do a quick thumbnail sketch like the one in Figure 6.9 to define the values that will be used in the drawing.

The final stage of the drawing is to add the shading. Shading a storyboard can be done with a pencil or with other tools such as markers, watercolor washes, or drawing pastels. You can experiment to see what works best for you. Figure 6.10 shows the sketch with shading.

Figure 6.9
Draw a quick thumbnail value sketch to help define the values.

Figure 6.10
The last step is to add shading to the drawing.

The storyboard drawing is now complete, but the storyboard is not finished yet. The written information still needs to be added before the storyboard is finished. Figure 6.11 shows the completed storyboard with the written information.

24-1 | Level 3/section2/room5

After fighting her way past the guards in the hall, the heroin approaches the challis pool room. The room is a two story circular room with a balcony supported by columns. In the center of the room is a challis pool emitting an eery blue light.

Figure 6.11
Finish the storyboard by adding the important written information.

In the top left corner of the storyboard panel, place the series number and panel number of the storyboard. The long narrow opening at the top of the panel is to write the game location where the event takes place. The opening at the bottom of the panel is for a written description of the event.

Now that the first panel is finished, the artist can go on to the next panel in the series. Try drawing some of the remaining panels yourself. You can use the thumbnails in Figure 6.5 as a starting point, or you can create your own.

Level Layouts

Games are often broken up into levels. The term *level* has its roots in the beginning of game development, when games were restricted by technology to a limited number of graphics loaded in the game at any one time. Each time the player moved from one area to another, the old graphics had to be eliminated and new graphics had to be loaded. Therefore, games were broken up into areas. Usually games progressed from simple areas to more complex as the player learned to play the game. These advancements in the play areas became known as levels, referring to the level of difficulty in each game area. Today the term has broadened to include any unique area in a game.

Level layouts are drawings created by the concept artist to show all the elements in a game level. These elements include a map of the terrain and all interactive characters or objects within the level. Often these layouts are drawn to scale on grid paper or with the use of a grid in a digital drawing program. Figure 6.12 shows a level layout for a safari game.

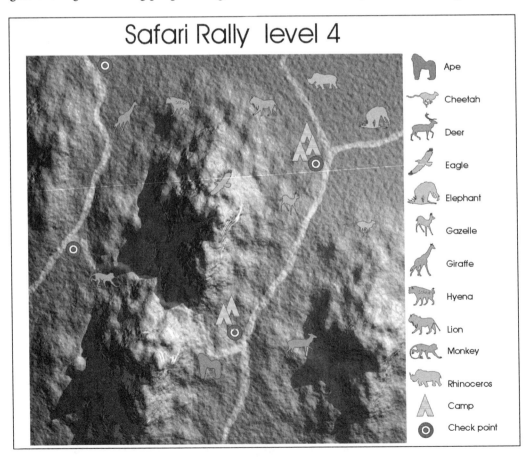

Figure 6.12
Level layouts show the terrain and interactive elements of a game area.

Level layouts often look like maps. In a way, they are maps of the game. They show where a player will start in the game area and how he can progress through the area. Sometimes the progression will take a specific path with a definite beginning and end position on the layout, while other games will use a more open system where there are multiple entry and exit points to the level.

Creating a Level Layout

The first step in creating a level layout is to define the area that the level will include. For this example, let's assume the game level will be the top floor of a hunting lodge. The lodge will have many guests that the player will need to meet and talk to during the course of the game. The top floor of the lodge needs to contain a secret room, a library, a lounge, a piano room, a bathroom, a kitchen, and some guest rooms.

Start by drawing a rectangle that will define the outer dimensions of the level, as shown in Figure 6.13.

Figure 6.13
Define the size of the level by drawing a rectangle.

The level layout for this level will look very similar to a simple floor plan. Not all level layouts will look like floor plans, but thinking of them as such can be very useful because, like floor plans for a home, the developers of the game will use them to construct the level.

Draw in the rooms as shown in Figure 6.14.

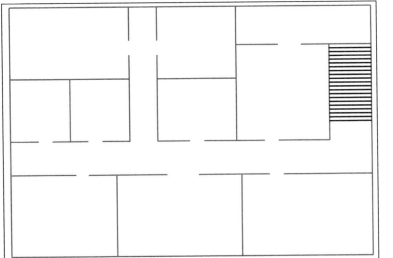

Figure 6.14
Draw in the walls of
the upper floor.

All good hunting lodges need doors. We need to put in doors for each room. When creating objects that are duplicates of each other, you don't need to draw each one individually. If you are using a drawing program such as Adobe Illustrator or CorelDRAW, you can create one door and then duplicate it to get all the other doors. If you are using paper and pen, create a door and then make some copies of the door. You can then cut and paste the doors in place. Figure 6.15 shows the doors for all the rooms, including the secret door to the secret room.

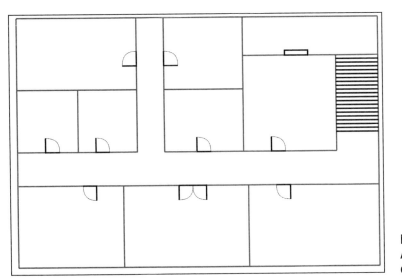

Figure 6.15
Add the doors to the
drawing.

Now we need to put the furniture into the room. Many drawing programs will have symbols in their font libraries for floor plans. You also can buy symbols from your local architectural supply store. Figure 6.16 shows the piano room with some couches, a chair, and a few other furnishings.

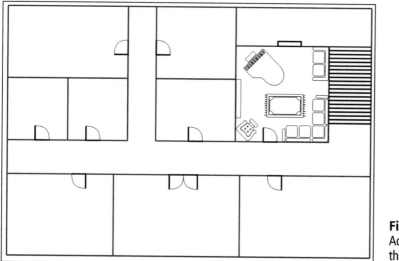

Figure 6.16
Add furniture to one of the rooms.

Continue to add furniture to the rooms. When you are done, the layout should look similar to Figure 6.17.

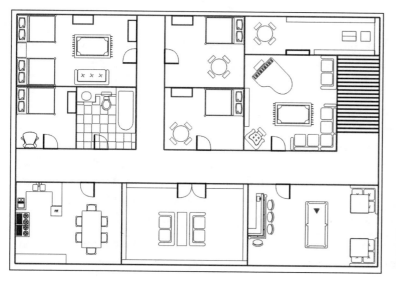

Figure 6.17
Furnish each room in the level.

This is an adventure game. The player must interview other people in the level to get information. The last step in the level layout will be to add the characters. Again a symbol is created to represent each character. The characters are numbered, and a list of the characters is added to the layout (see Figure 6.18).

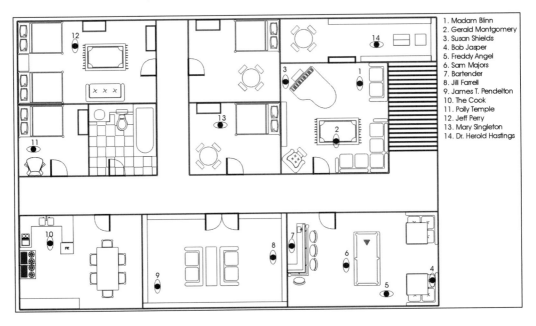

1. Madam Blinn
2. Gerald Montgomery
3. Susan Shields
4. Bob Jasper
5. Freddy Angel
6. Sam Majors
7. Bartender
8. Jill Farrell
9. James T. Pendelton
10. The Cook
11. Polly Temple
12. Jeff Perry
13. Mary Singleton
14. Dr. Herold Hastings

Figure 6.18
The characters are added.

Some games will have characters and objects that need to be listed in the layout legend. The legend is the numbered list by the picture. It can contain any important game information.

Environment Illustrations

An important part of the game design is *environment illustrations*. Environment illustrations are full-color illustrations of a game environment as it will be seen in the game. They are usually in the game design document with the level layouts to show the development team how the game should look. The concept artist will select important areas in a game and create illustrations that are then referenced on the level layout.

Environment illustrations help the concept artist communicate to the development team the feeling and mood of an area. They are used to show color schemes. They are also used to show greater detail in critical areas that is not possible in the level layout. A concept artist should use care in choosing what areas are illustrated so that each serves a vital purpose in the development of the game.

Creating an Environment Illustration

For this example we will create a drawing of a specific area in an action-adventure game. The main character is in a jungle. The location is near a vine-covered statue from an ancient building.

The first thing you need to do is rough in the drawing lightly to define the major elements of the drawing. Draw a few thumbnail sketches and then take the design you like and start your drawing. Figure 6.19 shows the drawing roughed in. The drawing at this stage is still very loose and free. All we need is to define the composition and content of the picture. Notice the composition lines that converge on the character.

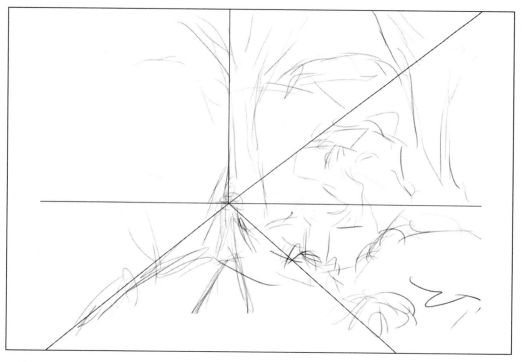

Figure 6.19
Rough in the composition of the drawing lightly.

Once you have the framework for the drawing, you can start to render in the different elements. Figure 6.20 shows the beginning of the rendering.

The two major points of interest in the drawing are the main character and the ancient statue. Define these two elements and then proceed with adding the other parts of the drawing. See Figure 6.21.

Continue to move to each section of the picture, defining the vegetation and other jungle elements as shown in Figure 6.22.

The drawing is of a path through the jungle. The jungle is a lush rain forest area, so the drawing needs to define that in the mind of the viewer. Add detail to the sides of the path so that the development team can see the types of plants that are needed in the game. See Figure 6.23.

Figure 6.20
Start to render the elements in the drawing.

Figure 6.21
Define the main character and the statue.

Figure 6.22
Continue to work on different sections of the picture.

We are almost done. Much of the foliage is now in the picture, and it is starting to feel like an enclosed, thickly wooded area. Figure 6.24 shows the picture as it nears completion.

Figure 6.25 shows the final picture. The development team should be able to get a good idea of how the game will look in this area from the drawing.

Figure 6.23
Add detail to the path.

Figure 6.24
Continue to add detail to the background of the picture.

Figure 6.25
The finished drawing

Character Designs

One of the most common items a concept artist will be called on to create is a *character design*. A character design is a sketch of a character that will appear in a game. *Characters* are people or creatures in a game that are controlled either by the player or through artificial intelligence. Some characters play major roles in the game, and some play minor roles, but every one needs to be designed. Figure 6.26 shows a character design.

The process of designing characters can sometimes be long, with the concept artist creating multiple sketches before coming up with just the right design for the game. Once a character design is chosen, the artist will usually create a detailed color rendering of the character. The rendering will become part of the design document and in some instances will be used to promote

Figure 6.26
Every character in a game needs to be designed.

the game. Figure 6.27 shows a character design that could be used for promotional purposes.

Characters in a game are valuable intellectual property, particularly if the game becomes popular. Several game characters, such as Lara Croft, Mario, and others, have gone on to become public icons. A character's name and image can be trademarked. The concept artist's design is usually submitted to the trademark office for the trademark.

Character designs sometimes can become quite detailed. Of all of the work a concept artist does, character designs tend to be the most widely used for other purposes.

Drawing a Character

As always, the best way to start drawing a character is to do a few thumbnail sketches of the character

Figure 6.27
Character designs are sometimes used to promote the game.

until you have something that looks good. Once you have a direction, you can then lightly rough in the character, as shown in Figure 6.28.

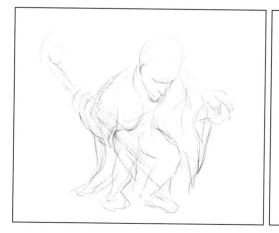

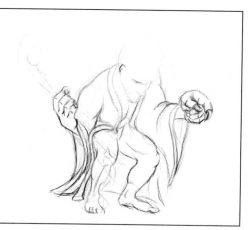

Figure 6.28
Lightly draw the construction lines for the character.

Figure 6.29
Add more definition to the drawing.

The early lines are called construction lines, and they are used to help define the character and placement of the character's features. This character is a shaman creature from some ancient underground race.

Keeping the drawing free and flowing continues to help define the creature. Figure 6.29 shows the progress.

The drawing is now beginning to take shape. Define the facial features and continue to work on the cloak and staff. The drawing should look like Figure 6.30.

Figure 6.30
Add facial features and detail to the staff.

Figure 6.31
Start refining the forms in the drawing by adding detail and shading.

Now that the character is more defined, you can start working on adding detail and shading to help define the character more. Figure 6.31 shows the character as he starts to come together in a more solid form.

Add a drop shadow and more detail to the character. The drawing is now finished. Notice that even though we didn't erase any of the construction lines, they are almost unnoticeable. If you always draw in the construction lines lightly, you shouldn't have too much clean up to do at the end of your drawing. See Figure 6.32.

Figure 6.32
Continue to add detail and shading until the sketch is finished.

Model Sheets

A *model sheet* is an orthographic detailed drawing of a character or object used by the development team to create the character or object. Model sheets are like drafting plans in that they show multiple views of the character. Most model sheets include front and back views of a character. Some model sheets include side and top views, particularly if the character is a four-footed creature. Figure 6.33 shows a model sheet for a human character.

A model sheet is often used in the creation of a 3D model of the character. The model sheets are

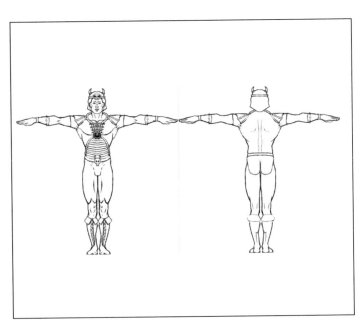

Figure 6.33
Most model sheets include front and back views of the character.

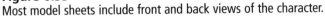

loaded as a template for the modeler to use as a guide for creating the geometry of the character as shown in Figure 6.34.

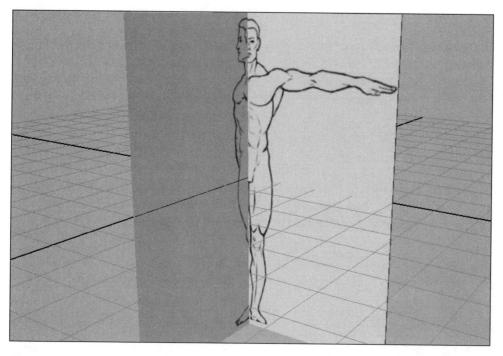

Figure 6.34
Model sheets are used in the creation of 3D models.

A game design may include multiple model sheets, one for each character in the game. Sometimes model sheets are created for important objects in a game. These objects are usually items that are critical to progress in the game or critical to the look of the game. A good rule in game design is to create a model sheet of any object that plays an important role in the game.

In some games the main character will change as the game progresses. For example, many role playing games allow the main character to change armor and weapons during the course of the game. In these games, multiple model sheets are needed for the main character.

Graphical User Interface (GUI) Designs

The *graphical user interface* (GUI) includes the onscreen game elements that are used to give the player information or navigate through the game. While user interface refers to everything involved in information and control between the player and the game, graphical user interface only relates to the onscreen elements of a user interface. Because these game elements often are present throughout the game, they need to be carefully designed. The GUI needs to perform a function, and at the same time it needs to be cohesive with the design of the game. Sometimes the GUI is as important to the mood and feel of the game as the rest of the game art itself. Figure 6.35 shows a design for a GUI.

Figure 6.35
The GUI plays an important role in the look and feel of the game.

Some games, such as role playing games, have very elaborate and complex GUIs. In these games the player has to manage multiple game elements. The more game elements a player has to manage, the more complex the GUI may become.

Good GUI design is critical to the game. A good GUI often can mean the difference between whether a game is a success or not. The concept artist needs to remember that while menus and buttons are part of the game, they are not the game. If the GUI is cumbersome or detracts from the core of the gameplay of the game, it needs to be redesigned.

An important part of GUI design is the *heads up display*, or HUD as it is sometimes called. The HUD includes all the onscreen interface elements present during normal gameplay. It is primarily for giving the player critical game information such as health status or current score. In many games it is on display constantly and is updated in real time. HUDs are tricky to design because they need to look nice while staying unobtrusive to the rest of the game. They usually occupy the edges of the screens to allow the main play action to take the center as shown in Figure 6.36.

Figure 6.36
The HUD occupies the areas near the edges of the screen.

Other Concept Art

Some game designs may require the concept artist to create other specialized concept art for the game. For example, a racing game may not have any characters but rather have vehicles. A flight simulator may have specialized encounter maps that deal with ground terrain on a very limited basis. A puzzle game may need to have solution charts.

There is no standard format for game designs because games vary so greatly. The purpose of the game design document is to communicate the nature and extent of the game. It gives the development team and other interested parties such as the marketing team and the management team a clear picture of the game. Each design needs to be customized to be as clear and easy to follow as possible. The concept artist plays a critical role in its creation. So much of a game is visual in nature that it would be difficult to have a game design without the concept artist.

Summary

This chapter was a quick overview of the types of art used in a game design. Concept art includes many elements, such as storyboards, level layouts, environment illustrations, character designs, model sheets, and GUI designs. Each type of art fills a vital role in the overall game design.

Sometimes specialized art is needed for specific games. Each game design is a unique document, so the design should be adapted to the needs of the game rather than follow a strict formula. This book will from time to time give examples of other specialized art to help with those games that have unique considerations.

Try creating some of your own art for your game design. If you are not a good artist, give this chapter to the member of your team who is and have him work on the projects. Remember that the better you can show your game in the artwork, the more likely it is that someone will want to look at your game design.

CHAPTER 7

DESIGNING AUDIO

Having great audio in your game can be attributed to the wise saying, "If you fail to plan, you plan to fail." Planning means not only preparing for everything from the beginning, but also adjusting the plan as the development progresses. There is one thing you can do at the start. For every project there is an initial meeting or series of meetings for design. These meetings turn out one or more documents related to technical design and game description. In the description, there's always a section about audio. Normally, an audio designer should write that section or at the very least have some input, so the first thing you can plan on is attending those meetings or having some collaboration with the audio person(s).

Audio is one of the most neglected aspects in the planning phase of a project. In relation to project development time, it is the smallest part for sure, but creating good audio is no small job, nor should a good book on game design imply that it's a mere twinkle to add on at the end of the project. I've never worked on a project whose game designer didn't have an audio "vision" as part of the overall plan.

Developers that have no in-house audio personnel are missing an important interaction in game planning/design. Hence it receives no attention till the very end, when contractors are brought in to fill the gap. And though they want to do the best job possible, they can never replace the benefits of being in the whole interactive process. (I've been in both positions—earlier is better. Sure, some stuff is good, but planning ahead makes it even better.

Yes, I would agree that freelancing is on the rise in the industry today, but small budgets and limited vision (a.k.a. no initial planning) have twisted audio production into more of a "widget factory" than a soundscape. Especially when they are brought in late, cram on the design, and spit out audio in a week's time. It is far better to have one in-house audio director to address all audio aspects.

As far as using the word *team*, I'm just referring to those doing the audio.

Remember that writing the audio portion of the document is not the important thing here. What's important is that you've made an assessment of the tasks at this point. A good self-check that you've done this is to read the audio portion of the design document. It should include all the audio assets and filenames for each phase, or milestone, of the project. It's also a favor to the team member who assembles the document, and it sets the tone from the beginning that you are in charge of the overall sound "vision" and not just a figurehead.

Whether you attend meetings or collaborate with the audio team, it's now your job to convince the team and management of the immensity of the work needed to get great audio. Artists concentrate on art, and certainly the programmers are not yet ready to jump into sound issues. To programmers, sound is icing on the cake when their current concern is to bake the cake. This is the point to introduce the mindset you need to have for success. We'll call it the two-way approach versus the three-way approach. Figure 7.1 shows an example of a two-way approach.

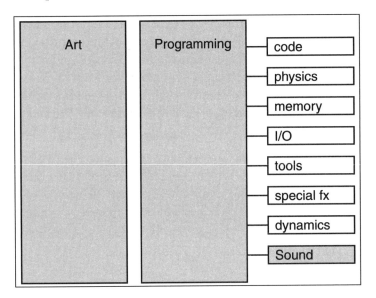

Figure 7.1
Example of a two-way approach

In the two-way approach, the game is conceived and designed according to what can be done with art and programming. Great amounts of time and effort are spent in attaining some new or cool thing in the handling and graphics. Some examples are the rudders and flaps on the P-51 Mustang of *Battlefield 1942*, or Max Payne's use of the "slo-mo" cam. The list goes on and on, of course, and it is a good thing. However, note where the audio is placed. It becomes a second- or third-rate task, usually handed off to a junior programmer. If left unchecked in a two-way approach, it leads to the overall soundscape being left to the junior programmer or a programming assistant (called a data-wrangler). The best mindset for approaching audio is the three-way approach. Figure 7.2 shows an example of a three-way approach.

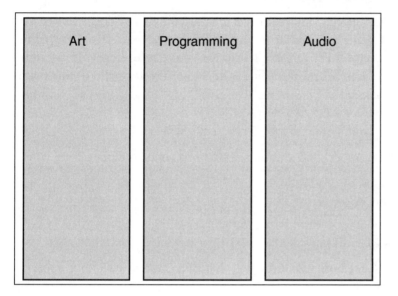

Figure 7.2
Example of a three-way approach

As is obvious in the three-way approach, we put sound, or audio, in equal balance with the other two facets of game development. This means that your audio requirements should be addressed as are those of art and programming. Your goals with a three-way approach should include three basic things:

- Educate your team on the audio requirements of the project. Now is the time to reiterate your needs and let them know what it's going to take to complete the project.
- Have specific audio-related tasks for each milestone. Break down your tasks and spread them over the milestones as needed. Be sure to allow the audio team the necessary time for creation, editing, and testing of assets.
- Acquire tools for testing and implementation. These tools are to be written by the programming staff with your audio team's needs in mind. You will need to stress that sound is to be in control of the audio director or sound designer. To keep control you will need tools, or at least a process for creating and testing a soundscape.

Your best bet for success is to collaborate in detail with the audio director, who will listen and usually be open minded about your overall design, including audio interaction. Then he can also bargain on your behalf for proper sound implementation.

Character Voices and Speech

In any project that involves speech, you will need to study the design document to get familiar with the type of game, environment, and number of characters, narrators, or other voices and arrange everything from script writing to voice recording. We'll separate this task into script, talent search, and recording. The audio director will be your main contact to oversee these tasks.

Script

First, let's look at straight numbers and amounts. Questions you should be asking yourself are these:

- How many characters do we want?
- How many are males?
- Would females add more to the game?
- Are there outside voices (those with no visual character) such as narrators, referees, or radio chatter?
- Does the environment call for additional voices?
- Are the voices normal humans or are there aliens, monsters, or other processed voices to create?

As an example, let's refer to the design document in Appendix A, "Design Document." We see that this is a racing game. In a racing game you might imagine the possibility of several unique characters, one for each vehicle raced. In motocross, most characters would be male, but there are female bike racers in the real world, so making some female would make sense and add depth to the game. Since it's a racing game, our environment will be a track or stadium, which calls for an announcer voice and crowd sounds. It also appears to be a realistic game, with no fantasy or non-human elements. This cuts out any need to create alien or monster voices.

Let's say you've come to a decision to design for nine total characters: six males, two females, and one announcer. You will be responsible for fleshing out the look and personality of each character in the game. Your next priority is to obtain a copy of this document as your director moves toward organizing a talent search. Below is an example of a character description used in Chapter 1, "What Is Game Design?"

Malden Stonebridge—Malden is a guard in the queen's palace. He is large for a dwarf and was chosen as a guard for his strength and skill with pole arms. He never leaves his post and is very dedicated to the queen. Malden wears a red uniform (similar to the English Beefeaters' uniform) with a white neck ruffle and gloves. Atop his head he wears a dragon-crested helmet. He carries an ornate spear as a weapon. A creature that looks like an overgrown rodent with large luminous eyes accompanies Malden on his rounds.

After fleshing out each character description, you can start to brainstorm on the type of voice he might have and the things he would say in the game. It is helpful to start a folder on each character where you can store notes. At this point you can either write the script yourself or hire someone to do it.

Writing Your Own Script

When writing your own script, it is best to plan for some research and rejection. With your design document in hand, try to immerse yourself in the character by using other reference materials such as TV, local events, videos, and so on. Look for people who fit the descriptions as best you can. Using TV, video, and local events will help broaden your script, especially if they are related to your game. Write down the things you hear people say. Take notes on their voice inflections, excitement level, and attitude. Use this to formulate scripts for your character.

Don't be surprised to find that some don't approve of your first draft of the script. Rather, expect it and consider it a blessing that the possibly unacceptable or mundane is being weeded out. This leaves you challenged to redo, but it can yield an even better script than you thought you could write. It would not be surprising to find that on your first draft, 50 percent of your characters need 50 percent of their speech altered in some way.

As an example, refer again to Appendix A. The best option would be to go to a motocross event. If that is not possible, try any outdoor event where there are crowds, announcers, and the stars of the event themselves. If that is also unavailable, rent some motocross videos or find a TV event to study. When you hear interesting comments and phrases, take notes with plans to modify them for your character. Then, of course, try to find variations for each character to make them as different from each other as possible. After researching, formulate an outline such as the following:

- Character 1—This character has a raspy voice that is mildly high pitched. He sounds like he has a cold or a sore throat. He's really excited in his speech.

    Phrases used: "Wow, I'm so hyped up!"

        "It's such a motivational factor."

        And so on.

- Character 2—Voice is deep and muffled, similar to putting a towel over his mouth. He's very careful in his speech, as if he's unsure of himself.

    Phrases used: "Well, it's been a tough competition…"

    "It's never quite…, well, fair…"

    And so on.

- Character 3—Voice is low for a female. Very sultry but not too slow. Has an insulting or challenging attitude. Reminds me of Ursula in *The Little Mermaid*.

    Phrases used: "Not too quick on the uptake, are we?"

    "Moto weeds out the weak from the strong."

    And so on.

From here you can construct more script, phrases, or sayings just by brainstorming or continued research. Other factors may include emotional states. Will they ever get angry or happy? The script will need to reflect this. Be sure to keep in contact with the other team members for review and suggestions. As your script progresses, stay organized and keep like items in groupings for each character. An example is as follows.

- Comments to:

    Character 2

    Character 3

    And so on.

- Positive comments
- Negative comments
- Narrations
- Exclamations

Hiring Out the Script

If time is short and you have sufficient budget, consider hiring someone to write for you. Options may include having the publisher take care of hiring, finding an author, or using local sources such as a college professor or even talented friends. You will be responsible for familiarizing your hired help with the scope of the game so that they understand character personalities and traits. Before ever using hired help in any area, you should have them sign a non-disclosure agreement (NDA).

You can usually find examples on the Internet. This allows you to talk about and pass around sensitive documents with their promise not to share information with anyone else. This may be desirable if you want to be sure your ideas are not stolen, but is not necessary except in more professional situations.

When you receive a script from a hired hand, you will then need to play the role of editor. Going through an entire script can be anywhere from short to formidable. Try to break up the characters and get as many people to proof it as you can. Some things may need to be changed or rewritten. As you review the text, look for the magic you want this character to have. If something falls short, make a note, and if you have a great idea, make a note. Be open minded, and don't be afraid to have your hired hand redo some phrases as needed. Again, you have responsibility to approve the final script and any changes.

It may be the case that you don't want to have voice in your game. Many games do away with the hassle of audible voice and just use text. This not only saves the cost of talent, but can save on expensive foreign voice talent when translations are needed to market the game in other countries.

tip
___
Have each person who reviews the script use a different color ink when making notes. This will help you identify each reviewing person's comments for later discussion.
___

Talent Search

Now that you have all or part of the script, you can begin organizing a talent search. Some of your most important consideration will be in obtaining good character voices.

Options

There are many options for getting the right voice, but we'll categorize them into three levels.

- Cheap. These are voices of friends, family, or anyone who will work for little or nothing just for the fun of being in a game.
- Midline. There are local people who may have done some voice work on the side. Maybe they've had experience such as giving lectures or being on radio talk shows. They usually charge a fee that ranges from $50 to $150 per hour or session.
- Expensive. Talent agencies are available in most cities and cost several hundred dollars per hour.

Talent agency voices are expensive and can add up quickly, so you have to find the balance between getting the best and exercising your options. This will mean starting at the bottom, or cheap level, and working your way up.

Having taken care of the script, you should be thoroughly familiar with each character in the game. Start with the first and begin to research, in the same way as the script, what this voice should sound like. Most other game designers are very opinionated about this and have a vision of what each voice should and shouldn't be. You will need to hold to your own vision as well. Together, you and the audio director need to produce a *read sheet*. This is a one-page-or-less selection of phrases from the script that best identify the character's personality.

Voice Appeal

Each option has some variances, but it all boils down to listening and evaluating the voice. In every instance it's important to see the character in your head while hearing the voice you are auditioning. It's best to have at least two sets of ears to do this: one to record and one just to listen. The ideal situation is to have three: one to record, one to evaluate script and inflection correctness, and one to evaluate overall voice type. You should be one of the people in attendance and attend all auditions.

Using the cheap method of talent search can be a bit more time consuming than the other two options. This comes from the fact that just because you hear a good voice doesn't mean the speaker is good in front of a microphone. You may have a friend who has a perfect voice in a natural setting, when he is calm and relaxed. But in a recording setup, he might be nervous and produce an unnatural sound or inflection. Thus, you sometimes need to try out many people to find the right one.

tip

When using portable equipment to record a voice outside a studio, make sure the microphone stays an even distance from the talent while recording. This is best accomplished with a microphone stand, but if none is available, have one of your associates hold the microphone or, if not him, the voice talent. Also, try to have the read sheet on a stand or table so that it doesn't rustle during the take.

Midline voice talent is the most sought after. They have experience in front of a microphone and are better able to deliver the voice you want at a reasonable price. If you find some midline talent and your script is shorter than one hour, expect to pay for a full hour as a courtesy. At this level, you have the option of recording in or out of a professional studio. Doing a session in the studio adds cost, but it reduces noise and errors. Most midline talent does not use their voice for a living, but as part of a living. Therefore, they may expect to be paid for the time it takes to do a read. If in doubt, simply ask.

Expensive voice talent is the easiest to record if you have the budget. There are many advantages to using a talent agency. In the first place, reads are free. You send a read sheet and the agency does all the auditioning according to your instructions and character descriptions. You may attend if you want.

A second advantage is the wide variety of voices available. Most agencies already have a demo CD of their talent that they'll send you free at your request. From the CD you can select whom you want to audition. Then, after all selections, they will come to the recording studio of your choice. Going to a recording studio is a must-do with this level of talent.

They will bring vouchers for you to sign at the studio, and the total bill will come later from the agency. Of course, the studio will charge separately.

Recording

So now it's time to hit the record button. Without getting too "techy," let's look at a couple of procedures you can use to help ensure a quick and successful session.

Microphone Placement

If you are recording voice talent yourself, as mentioned before, you need to ensure that the microphone and the talent stay an even distance from each other during the take. If your voice talent is of normal volume, start about eight inches apart. If the talent is louder, back off a couple of inches; if softer, creep up an inch. The key is to not have the volume of your talent cause distortion in the microphone. It's much easier to fix a lighter volume than to remove distortion. Also, if you have one, use a wind filter on the microphone. It's usually made of foam and slips over the top of the microphone. This will help remove popping "Ps" and other such "plosives" from speech.

Level

In conjunction with placement is level or, in other words, the sensitivity of the microphone. This is measured in decibels (dB). A simple tape recorder may or may not have a level adjustment and level monitor, but a digital audiotape (DAT) recorder will for certain. You simply turn it up for more sensitivity or down for less. As the person speaks, you can see the level jump up in the monitor. You can see a few examples of decibel levels in Table 7.1.

Table 7.1 Common Decibel Levels

Indoor Sounds	Decibels	Outdoor Sounds
Whisper (4 feet)	15	
	20	Leaves rustling
	22	Rainfall
Refrigerator	50	
Normal speech (3 feet)	65	
Classroom teacher	70	
Clock-radio alarm	80	
	90	Lawnmower
	100	Fire truck (no alarm)
Rock concert	110	
Threshold of pain	130	
	140	Rifle shot
	180	Space shuttle launch

As you can see, typical talking is around 65 dB at a distance of 3 feet. Recording at this distance is not recommended because other noises can creep in, such as room echo. Therefore, a good recording level is about 12 to 24 dB at the distances we've already covered.

Coaching

Since your talent is not as familiar with your character as you are, he will be a bit uptight about how he sounds. In all options you will need to help your voice talent achieve the personality and traits designed. This is called *coaching*. In simple terms, you will need to coach your talent, using some general guidelines.

- Fully prepare your voice talent by discussing the character in detail just before sitting down to record. In this discussion, indicate loud and soft passages, the character's attitude, and any varying emotional contexts you may need. If you're in a studio, conduct this discussion along with your studio engineer so that he can take appropriate notes as to volume and level.

- Start your session with the simplest script for the character. This will help break the ice and allow your talent to get into the appropriate frame of mind. If the initial sound or inflection is not right, give him hints and examples until it's corrected. Examples of known characters are extremely helpful. For example, tell him you want him to sound more like Darth Vader or to act sillier like the Animaniacs.

- Throughout the session, finish each phrase, line, or comment before going to the next. As an example, if the script line is "Captain Marvel reporting for duty," have the talent repeat as many takes as needed until you feel it is right. Only then should you move on to the next line. Constantly assess the overall sound of the voice for accuracy.

- Equally important to all the above is to give positive feedback. If he's doing a great job, tell him. If changes are needed, outline what's good first, then suggest the changes. Again, use examples and always work to keep the atmosphere positive. It's helpful to imagine yourself in the talent's shoes.

- Take enough breaks to relieve any frustration or fatigue. This is more appropriate with longer scripts, but it gives you a break, too.

You may have designed a game that requires a more "interactive" script. An example would be when one character talks to another. As they converse with each other, their responses may need to reflect different emotions while using the same dialogue. For example, the phrase "good luck" may need to be expressed in an angry state as well as a happy state. When coaching a voice talent in an interactive script, be sure to explain all the needed variances in a line of script.

When preparing an interactive script, prepare it in such a way that you can foresee all the possible directions a conversation would go. Conversation paths are often called dialogue trees, and can be quite extensive or purposely kept shallow for smaller budgets. It depends on how much interactivity you want between your characters. After you've made all your dialogue trees, run through them to make sure all the possible conversations flow well.

Coaching takes practice, but you'll get better as you go. There are professional coaching services available in bigger cities, but that will add to your cost. They are particularly useful in coaching a foreign accent if you have such a character. Generally, if you screen the talent, provide good examples, and coach well, you'll have a successful character voice.

tip

If you are recording in a studio, you have two coaching options. You can coach through a "talk-back" microphone inside the control room, or you can sit inside the recording room with the talent. The former can be more error free, but the latter can help you draw out a better sound from the talent.

For the Technically Curious

This section is intended to provide only a brief discussion of the physics of sound, the basic concepts you need. After all, you don't want to read a physics textbook, you want a basic rundown of the principles that will help you make better judgments about sound and music you want to design for a game. So let's jump in!

What We Hear

When you listen to your favorite song, what is it you hear? Most likely you can discern different musical instruments such as drums, guitar, and piano, but that is not what you are really hearing. The dictionary describes hearing as perception by the ear. What you are perceiving or hearing is sound waves traveling through the air (or other medium such as water or steel). Take the drumbeat in your favorite song, for example. When the drumhead is struck, the vibration bumps air molecules around it, which in turn bump other molecules, and so forth until the wave reaches your ear. Your brain then perceives that wave as a familiar sound—in this case, a drum. The manner in which this sound wave has traveled to your ear distinguishes it from other forms of waves and is called a *longitudinal wave*.

An easy way to think of longitudinal waves is to picture a crowded stadium. Have you ever seen "the wave"? It's started by a small group of people who stand up, lift their arms high, and then quickly sit down again. Others next to them see this and do the same, and thus it spreads around the stadium. Notice, though, that the people don't actually leave their place in the stadium, but instead, the action moves. This is very similar to how sound waves travel; the molecules stay, but the change moves through them.

That's the concept of a sound wave; now let's look at ways of measuring it. This will help you know what to modify in sounds you design and evaluate.

Wavelength

Why learn about wavelength? Because the number of wavelengths per second determines the pitch of the sound and is one of several terms you will need to be familiar with in the design process. Figure 7.3 shows what a sound wave looks like on a computer.

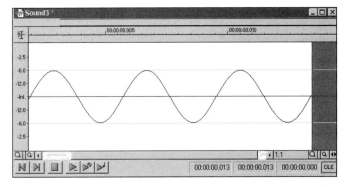

Figure 7.3
A sound wave

On this representation, there are peaks and troughs, but real longitudinal waves (such as sound waves) do not have these peaks and troughs. Instead, they have compression and rarefaction. You can create the compression and rarefaction of a longitudinal wave by using a Slinky™. If you stretch out a Slinky and shake the coils on one end horizontally, you can see the waves compress (compression) and stretch (rarefaction) as they travel across the Slinky. The wavelength is the distance of a complete cycle from one compression to another, or from one rarefaction to another. In Figure 7.4, the cycle from point A to point B is the wavelength for that particular wave.

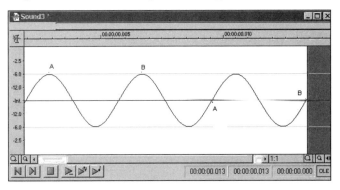

Figure 7.4
Wavelengths within a sound wave

Amplitude

Now notice the two waves in Figure 7.5. Would you believe they are making the same sound?

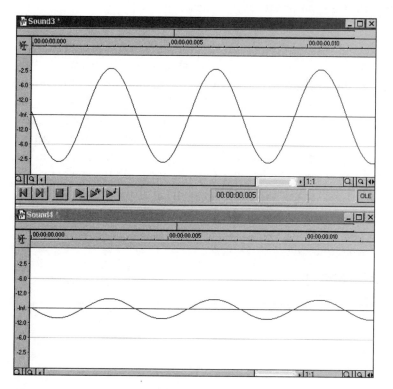

Figure 7.5
Wavelengths with different amplitude

In fact, they are making the same sound. Each has the same wavelength, but the top wavelengths are taller than the bottom ones. This demonstrates a difference in *amplitude*. There are complex relationships between amplitude and loudness that we won't worry about in this book. For the purposes of game audio, the higher the amplitude, the louder the sound is to the ear. The smaller the amplitude, the softer the sound is.

There is no shortage of decibels in the audio game world. A sustained level of 90 decibels on a regular basis can cause hearing loss and is a valid concern for the game designer, as well as the average music listener. Whether you use headphones or listen through speakers, a self-check you can perform is whether your ears are ringing after exposure to sound. If they are, then you're exceeding a safe level.

tip

Try not to use headphones if at all possible when evaluating sound and music. They can cheat you of the true frequencies, especially if they're cheaper headphones. Generally, if the audio sounds good on speakers, it will sound as good or better in headphones.

Frequency

As stated previously, wavelengths are measured in seconds, that is, the number of waves per second. The more waves in each one-second interval, the higher the pitch. The fewer per second, the lower the pitch. The scientific term for this is *frequency*, and the measurement for frequency is *hertz* (Hz). For example, you strike a key on the piano (in this case, an A), and it sends a sound wave to your ear. A musician would say, "The pitch is an A in the fourth octave," but a scientist may say, "The frequency is 440 hertz." As far as what you're hearing, they both mean the same. However, musicians and scientists don't always think alike, so Table 7.2 lists some terms you may come across that are similar in meaning.

Table 7.2 Common Term Similarities

Scientific	Musician/Game Audio
Period	Wavelength
Amplitude	Volume
Frequency	Pitch and octave
Hertz	Sample rate

No doubt you will want to include as many cool sound effects as you can in your game. The human ear generally can hear frequencies between 20Hz and 22,000Hz (22KHz). The speakers or headphones you use might not generate as wide a range of frequencies. This is known as the *frequency range* or *frequency response*. Frequency range is the span of frequencies that a monitoring device can reproduce, such as the human hearing range of 20Hz to 22KHz. Frequency response is similar but includes range *and* amplitude. In other words, if you see a frequency response graph on the back of a pair of speakers, it simply is a graph of what frequencies the speakers can reproduce at a certain number of decibels (amplitude). Figure 7.6 shows two examples.

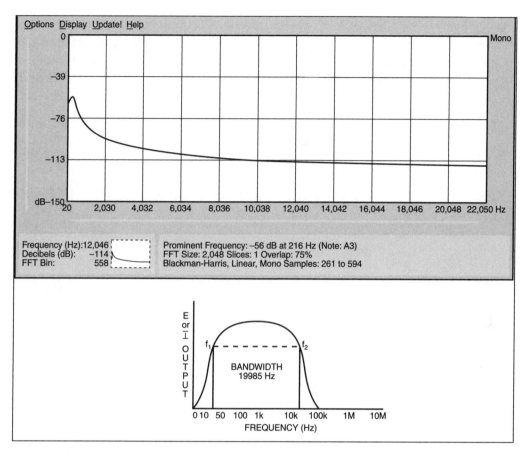

Figure 7.6
Frequency response graphs

It is important to note the type and quality of equipment you listen and evaluate sound on. Different equipment will produce audio sound differently, so be sure to make all evaluations on the same sound system. As an extra check, you could then try evaluating on a different system.

What the Computer Hears

Of course, your computer never really "hears" anything. But it can interpret sound using the same mathematical capability it has to function with any program. Sound is "heard" as a number, or sets of numbers, which you may be familiar with as *bits* and *bytes*. The computer converts sound into this numerical data by a process called *sampling*. Your computer is fast enough to sample sound many times per second, and a numerical value is then assigned to that sample.

Bit depth and sample rate are the ways of measuring the quality of your sound. Think of the sound that plays on a Game Boy machine compared to a CD. The quality of the sound is very different. Standard CD sound quality is a high 44KHz, 16-bit, stereo sound, as compared to a Game Boy, which is anywhere from 8KHz to11KHz, 4-bit, mono sound. Again, without getting too "techy," there are two basic rules for quality:

- Sample rate is the number of samples per second. The more samples, the better the sound quality. CD audio, for instance, is sampled at 44.1KHz. That means that the left and right channels are each sampled 44,100 times per second. Sampled into what? That's where bit depth comes in.

- Bit depth is how many bits are used to describe each of those samples. The more bits used to encode the file, the more accurate the sample. CD audio is sampled at 16 bits, so there is a 16-bit number to describe the amplitude of the sound wave for each of the 44,100 samples every second.

Figure 7.7 shows sample rate and bit depth in a graphical sense.

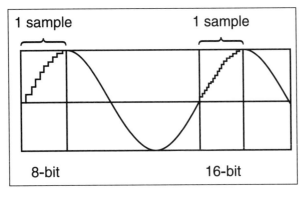

Figure 7.7
Sample rate and bit depth

These are the most basic specifications of all digital audio files, compressed or not. No wonder CD audio files are so big.

It may seem that going with the best quality is always the first choice, but increasing sample rate and bit depth also increases the size of the sound file. One minute of 44KHz, 16-bit, stereo sound is about 10 megabytes without any compression. To appreciate how large this is, consider that the Sony PlayStation machine allows only 2 megabytes of uncompressed sound (500K compressed). So how do they fit all that audio into a game? When working with sound, you need to find a balance between quality and size. Since human hearing usually ends at about 22KHz, many of today's game audio assets are set at that sample rate to achieve the highest quality at the smallest size. Bit depth is commonly left at 16-bit, but 8-bit is used occasionally. The memory limitations of game machines can be very small, as with a Game Boy, or very big, like the hard drive on your computer.

Sound Effects

A key contributor to the success of any game is the addition of sound effects. They can add an exciting depth to a positive gameplay experience, but can also take away from that experience if not carefully planned.

Realistic

As you have already reviewed your project in terms of character voices, you must do the same for assessing your sound effect needs. We will start by organizing sound effects (SFX) into two main categories, straight and Foley. Straight effects are already created and recorded; Foley effects are sounds you must design and create yourself.

Straight

Straight effects are those sound effects that already exist in the world and are readily available to you. Some examples would be rain and other weather sounds, automobiles, animal sounds, and so on. They are found mostly in CD libraries you can purchase over the Internet, or you can find a disc of sound effects at a local music or department store. It is important to note that there is a difference between a CD library and a sound effects CD. In most cases, if you buy a sound effects CD, there is a copyright connected to it. That means you cannot legally use any of those effects in your project without permission. Getting permission (known as a *license agreement*) may or may not be easy and involves contacting the company that produced the CD, explaining your intent, and getting a written document back. However, buying a CD library usually includes permission to use the effects in various ways. Figure 7.8 shows an example of a generic license agreement for a CD library.

The digitally recorded sounds included on this CD-ROM are licensed, not sold to you, as a single user license. All content on the CD-ROM is and remains the property of AB Company. It is licensed to you only for use as part of a live or recorded musical performance or for use in audio productions. This license expressly forbids resale or other distribution of these sounds, either as they exist on this CD-ROM, reformatted, or mixed, filtered, re-synthesized, or otherwise edited, for use as sounds, multi-sounds, samples, multi-samples, programs or patches in a computer, sampler, or sample playback unit. You may not sell them or give them away for use by others in their sampling or sample playback units. Any use for the sounds other than as provided herein must be under the terms of a separate license agreement with or by other written permission from AB Company.

Figure 7.8
Example of a license agreement

CD libraries are becoming more and more specific. In your initial design meetings, you may need to suggest CD libraries that contain sounds related to your project, such as one of the many automobile libraries if you have a racing project, or a set of "large impact" CDs if there are many collisions in your game. There are even Internet sites such as www.Sounddogs.com where you can purchase a single sound effect for a small fee. The sound is then downloadable to your hard drive and usable under a license agreement.

Straight effects (as well as Foley effects) are used to fill the realistic aspects of your overall soundscape. It is important not to spend more time and effort on a sound design than is required. For example, think of the movie *The Lord of the Rings*. It is said that every hair on the hobbits' feet came from the belly of a yak. Would you have enjoyed the show less if you knew the hair on their feet wasn't from a yak? Probably not, and it is a good lesson that can be applied to SFX design, as well. Sometimes the sound of rain is just the sound of rain. Don't waste valuable time overdoing a low-priority sound.

However, it is important to get the correct type of straight effect for your needs. If a rainy ambience is needed, there are many types of rain. In assessing realistic effects, you must pay attention to the environment. Rain falling on pavement will not sound the same as rain falling in the forest. Most CD libraries will have several options to choose from. Figure 7.9 shows a generic example from a CD library.

RAIN	LIGHT RAIN ON PORCH
RAIN	LIGHT RAIN ON PORCH
RAIN	ON METAL ROOF
RAIN	ON PORCH, WATER FROM EAVESTROUGHS, TRAFFIC IN b/g
RAIN	ON PAVEMENT, TRAFFIC PASSING BY
RAIN	ON PAVEMENT, TRAFFIC PASSING BY
RAIN	ON PAVEMENT, TRAFFIC PASSING BY
RAIN	ON PAVEMENT, TRAFFIC PASSING BY
RAIN	ON POND
RAIN	IN WOODS
RAIN	WALKING UNDER UMBRELLA
RAIN	LIGHT, ON PAVEMENT
RAIN	LIGHT, ON PAVEMENT WITH WATER SPLASH
RAIN	LIGHT, TRAFFIC IN b/g
RAIN	LIGHT, ON LAKE
RAIN	MEDIUM, ON PAVEMENT
RAIN	MEDIUM, ON LAKE, WATER DRIPPING ON DOCK
RAIN	HEAVY, ON PORCH
RAIN	HEAVY, TRAFFIC IN b/g

Figure 7.9
Example CD library index

The listed effects are ready to use, but they may need to be altered somewhat to fit your design. This task is usually handed to the audio professional, but as with any design issue, be sure to discuss the scope and nature of the sound effects with the audio team. The more involved you are, the better the fit of the sound effects. A general list of discussion points follows:

- Environment. Where is the effect occurring? Will the environment incur other sounds, such as echo, splashing, or debris?
- Composition and texture. What is the sound being made with? Metals, flesh, water, or assorted items? Is it weather related?
- Volume and intensity. Is it loud, soft, or both? Is there a lot or a little?
- Length. Long or short? Does it need to sync to some visual? Are the visuals accessible to the audio team? Does it need to loop?
- Variations. Will it repeat enough to be annoying? Are multiple variations needed?

Foley

Foley sound effects are those that aren't available on a CD library and must be created as they are needed. The method is named after Jack Foley, who invented many of the sound effect techniques in use today at major motion picture studios.

Foley effects include sounds such as footsteps, clothing movement, kitchen utensils clinking, paper rustling, doors opening and closing, all sorts of impact, glass breaking, and so on.

Since there are no real actors to record the sound-related events in your game, you and your audio team have complete control of the soundscape. You will want your audio team to have this control for timing, quality, and relative volume of the sounds.

Next time you are at a movie, listen to how the Foley is added, faded, and otherwise manipulated. For example, imagine a biker in a motocross game putting on a helmet. You could enhance it by adding sounds to match what you see. You would need to be sure your audio team adds Foley sound for donning a helmet.

Special artists who are trained to produce sounds usually perform Foley effects. Ideally, they stand in a Foley studio (a specialized sound studio) and have a variety of surfaces and props. The Foley artists watch a screen that displays the video footage they are to add sounds to and produce sound as the footage runs. This might include footsteps, jostling and wrestling, rubbing their clothing, handling props, and breaking objects, all while watching the screen to ensure their sound effects are appropriate to the visuals.

Renting a Foley studio and paying artists is expensive and may not be available in your area. Many simple Foley effects are created by other project members. The sounds are stored electronically and triggered by the audio team on a keyboard while watching digitized movies such as AVI files on the computer. There are great software programs available that use this process, such as Vegas Video and Adobe Premier.

tip

To add better depth and sound to your project, make sure you have several samples of the same effect. For example, the same footstep used over and over is immediately noticeable and quickly becomes annoying. Plan to have several versions of sound effects that are used repeatedly, so as not to have a dull and repetitive feel.

Without Foley effects, a game sounds empty and lifeless. The characters are dull, and the whole feel can be "blah." The audio team can set up the dialogue, but your game needs more than this to come alive. You need to hear the rustle of clothes, the clink of equipment, and so on, but you need to control those sounds so that they don't overpower the dialogue.

Another common use for Foley is for opening and transitional movies. Video footage is often without any noticeable sound, and movies created by your team are completely devoid of sound, so adding Foley becomes a necessity and helps bring those images to life. This can be quite intensive due to the number of specific sounds needed to create a realistic soundtrack.

Foley can also be used to enhance action scenes. In most movies you'll notice that many of the sounds are enhanced for effect. Most fistfights do not involve the actors really hitting each other, but even if they did you would not be able to record a satisfying punch sound. By punching, tearing, breaking, and outright destroying such objects as carrots, melons, and cabbages, you can record unique and much more realistic action sounds.

Keep this in mind the next time you watch an amateur movie or listen to a novice soundtrack. Does it sound thin or hollow? Even though the recording may be good (which it often isn't), the answer could be that the moviemakers did not add Foley to the soundtrack.

Non-Realistic

Many of the sound effects you will need are not present in the world you live in. You might call them fantasy effects. These are effects that require a unique sound, such as a wand casting a spell, an alien monster growling, or the whirl of a spaceship. Since there are no rules to follow in designing something that doesn't exist, you are limited only by your imagination.

Synthetic Sounds

Although a large CD library will have a section of sci-fi or other unusual sounds, there are those that are totally dedicated to fantasy-type sound. A synthesizer or other sound module that contains ready-to-use sounds is another option for fantasy sounds.

A synthesizer, or synth, is an electronic musical instrument that uses sound generating elements (such as an oscillator) to create audio samples. These samples are then combined and manipulated in specific ways to create a unique sound. Over the years, many different types of synthesis procedures have been developed and used, but only a few have become popular. Many modern synths provide digital control over audio parameters such as frequency, amplitude, filtering, and so on to create different variations.

A *sound module*, in simple terms, is a device that stores audio samples that can be accessed or controlled by various means, which your audio team will be familiar with. Often these devices can also accept or record other audio samples, along with the stored audio samples it came with.

However you obtain your sound samples, you will need to have your audio team alter, mix, or otherwise manipulate those samples until you get the sound that best fits your particular need.

Mixed Sounds

As a designer, you need not get into the nitty-gritty of mixing techniques. This is left to the audio team and rightly so, as they are trained to deal with those kinds of manipulations. However, you need to be aware of two general concerns in your project:

- Avoid canned sound. Remember that the same CD libraries, sound modules, and synthesizers are available to everyone. If you use a sound from one of those sources, it will be familiar to many who have heard it before, making your game less unique because it sounds like every other game.
- Be efficient. Use mixed and altered sound in every proper instance, but don't have your audio team overdo low-priority sound. Communicate to your team your desire to have unique sound effects in the game and specify what is high, middle, and low priority.

Music

Composing music is not an exact science. There are many rules and techniques you can apply that may help give a tune broader appeal. However, if you stick rigidly to rules, the result often can sound stiff, humdrum, and lifeless. If you ignore the rules altogether, the result is likely to be an untidy, self-indulgent piece with limited appeal.

Your goal is a balance between emotion and clarity. How do you find the balance that suits your project? That, unfortunately, is something only you as a designer can answer, but there is guidance available to help you through the process.

First Steps

Before you run to meet with your composer, take a moment to examine your musical needs for the project. What is the purpose of music in your project? What will the target audience enjoy? The answers to those questions can help you focus on your musical needs.

The purpose of music in your game is to enhance emotional awareness. You may be trying to accent the environment by the power of ambient music, you may be trying to create tension in the action scenes, you might be trying to create humor with funny character music, or you might be trying to cash in on a hot opening tune. Generally, for any of those scenarios to be successful, your chances are greatly improved by understanding the basic construction of a song, the emotions needed for the game, and where those emotions are needed in the game.

The Building Blocks

When you meet with your composer, you will need to have in mind the general parameters of each tune. General parameters are the length of a piece, the style of the piece, and usually a budget for creating the piece.

When discussing style, get specific as to the following building blocks in a musical piece.

- Instruments
- Rhythm
- Melody
- Harmony
- Effects
- Riffs
- Loops
- Lyrics (if needed)

To help yourself understand these features, you need to develop your listening and analyzing skills. A large step in understanding why some songs work better than others is simply to understand the building blocks of songs and how they fit together, and that involves "listening and analyzing."

To be on the cutting edge, you have to be able to assess the direction similar projects have taken. To do that you need to be aware of past developments and trends in that market. Try playing a couple of recently popular games from that market. This exercises your skills in decomposing a song into building blocks of sound. It will help if you can tune in only the music by lowering the SFX level or turning it off altogether. This will help to identify and clarify not only the features mentioned here but, more importantly, also the way in which they are used.

As you practice listening to and analyzing music, you will be able to strip a song to its building blocks just by listening to it once. You will spot trends in the types of blocks themselves and the way those blocks are arranged. These common factors will help you communicate to your composer each style of song that will fit into this project.

tip

As an example, when listening to a piece of music, try decomposing the percussion. Ask yourself these questions: What is the tempo? What is the time signature? What is the bass drum doing? What about the snare? Are there multiple snare sounds? What are the cymbals doing? Is there a lot of tom-tom work? How many bars does it take for the drums to loop? Are there other loops? What kinds of drum sounds are used? What beats are accented? Are there any special effects?

By decomposing each instrument in turn, you will increase in understanding of song architecture and song production. Discussing these aspects with your composer will help in assessing style, budget, and production time.

Generating Emotion

Determining the emotional awareness in each phase of the game lies largely with you as the designer. You will need to have the overall vision of the game and refer to it often, as direction is needed.

Fundamental emotional "game-states" are as follows:

- Ambient. This could include all calm states involved in the basic gameplay, such as searching, sneaking, or exploring.
- Alertness. Heightened status events such as finding a key, approaching danger, or losing too much time.
- Action. This speaks for itself and covers fighting, dueling, or any aggressive act or movement in the gameplay.
- Relief. This can include various comical attitudes and feelings, or a return to a calm level.
- Descriptive. You may need to describe specific characters or places with this type of music and can cover any emotion from pride to sadness.

Obviously there are many emotional states, but these can get you started thinking in terms of what emotional states you need for your project. As you discuss emotion in the game with the composer, try to have examples of existing music that can be used for reference. This will help point the direction for style and promote specific feature needs, such as instrumentation or melody.

tip

In the beginning stages of a game, you may be required to make a demo of the game that would have, for example, one level and one character interacting in the world. Since the music will not be complete at that phase of the project, you can purchase and download a song with the emotional representation you want over the Internet from companies such as www.sounddogs.com for a nominal fee. This can then be used as a temporary or placeholder tune.

Basic Organization

After you identify the emotional needs in your music, you will need to address the number of tunes you want the composer to create for each state. This is determined in part by your budget and in part by the overall needs in your game. For example, in any given state, a lower budget may have one or two long-playing songs rather than several short ones. And a higher budget may include many short pieces of music that transition well, providing more emotional variances.

As you determine the number of songs you need, you will want to organize them according to their positions in the game. The following is a typical list:

- Opening song
- Selection
- Gameplay
- Win/Loss
- Credits

Opener

This is what the player is going to hear first when he starts the game. What comes out first is paramount in how a player feels about the game. With that in mind, certain types of games gravitate toward certain types of music. A fast-paced racer, for example, will usually crank out a pumped up rock tune as its opening theme. The intent is to draw the player further into being a racecar driver, and rock music will do that.

As you stew over what your opening theme should be, consider what society-driven emotional aspects will draw in the player.

note

"Society-driven" is a term for what we as a society expect in any given situation. For example, music for a Halloween movie would include a creepy organ riff. There is no hard-and-fast rule that it must be so, but society has come to expect it.

Some existing game examples are Mario Brothers' happy-comic music, Halo's choir music opener, Starcraft's synth-orchestral music, and so on.

Selection

With most openers purposely trying to get your attention, the opposite is true with the selection music. After the opening sequence, a player usually needs to make choices as to character, equipment, colors, and so on. The musical goal here is to be subdued but anticipatory. A common option is to make a low-key version of the opener, with no melody, but just the underlying beat, or the beat and chords.

Some games will use only one selection tune throughout the selection screens. Other games will switch songs or increase the intensity of one song with each screen. It is purely a design decision, and you have to consider what is best for your project.

Gameplay

This is the most variable of all categories. Your gameplay tunes will cover all emotional states in your game and therefore could be quite numerous. There are many options as to how to execute the music, too. You and your programming and audio teams will need to collaborate on what process will be used. It usually falls into two areas: linear and interactive.

Linear

A linear system is one whose function is even or steady. Linear music is usually music that is streamed steadily from the CD-ROM, hard drive, or memory. To "stream" is simply to open a flow of data from one point to another. When done this way, the streaming of music is not related to events in the game. The only action that can be taken is to turn off one stream and start another. This lends itself to being mildly interactive in that an ambient stream of music can be turned off when danger is approached, with an action music stream being turned on. However, this manner of starting and stopping can be sloppy and ineffective.

If you choose a linear style, it is important to consider how the music will affect the gameplay events. You will not want the music to obscure the gameplay in any way. Instead, it must enhance the emotion you want to create. For linear gameplay music, underkill is better than overkill.

tip

A hard lesson to learn is that good gameplay music is not necessarily good to listen to on its own. Music for listening pleasure is made just for that purpose. Music for gameplay is made to enhance game events. Don't let the novice team member, critic, or client reject music just because it isn't good "listening" music. Try your best to evaluate music when it's in the game.

Interactive

Interactive music is music that interacts with game events. For example, suppose you are playing a game, and your character is walking around in a building. The music is calm and ambient. If you were to walk into a room with an enemy in it, the music would suddenly change to a higher-paced, action-oriented theme. Having the music adjust to the events of a game is interactive.

Most game consoles such as PlayStation 2, Xbox, and Gamecube can accommodate interactive music. This is normally achieved by executing the music tracks through Musical

Instrument Digital Interface (MIDI). MIDI has been an important step in the development of music in games in the past, and it has many intricacies that could fill an entire book. It is not necessary to know the details of MIDI in this chapter, except that it allows an instant change in the music as you progress from one point in the game to another. This has its advantages and disadvantages. The interactivity of music to the events of the game with MIDI is far superior to its linear counterpart. The disadvantage (usually) is the lack of sufficient memory to hold quality musical samples for multiple events.

Music development for games over the past few years has experimented and exploited different methods in combining MIDI sequencing with linear "chunks" of music. One common method is to split long tracks (bass, drums, synth, and such) into individual sample tracks and execute in the game as MIDI. This leads, for example, to using a synth track as the ambient music, and when danger is approached, a bass guitar track is overlaid and both are played together. Then the drum track is added to enhance an action scene, then when the danger is gone, it returns to the synth track only. This gives a greater sense of interaction than linear music without losing the higher fidelity and quality.

Another variation is to use high-quality samples and small linear chunks or riffs to be played or triggered by MIDI. This gives high-quality sound, like linear music, but limits the number of songs that sound sufficiently different from each other. Other possibilities include the use of both linear music streamed from the CD and the more interactive MIDI music that is played from memory.

Win/Loss

With every game, you play to win, achieve, or acquire something. You win a race, gain a level, pick up a rifle, hit a power-up, and so on. These can be accented by SFX, music, or a combination of both. You will most likely want to have several tunes that vary in intensity as you progress through the game. Normally, anything your character picks up, or acquires, is accented with SFX. Music normally is saved for level advancement or winning/achieving the main goal.

The style is fairly obvious as a celebratory theme, but make sure you regulate the intensity as you progress through the game, so that you have the least intense win theme first and the most intense last.

Credits

Most games have credit screens at the end that list the team members, developers, publishers, and so on. It's your decision, but it is typical to have an ending credit theme just as you would on a TV show. This is considered a low-priority tune that is often dictated by the remaining budget. The most common tune to hear during credits is a scaled-down version or variation of the opener. If your budget is tight, consider repeating the opening tune as it played at the beginning.

Summary

Designing good audio for your project requires you to remember the basic needs and functions of sound. First is successful overall planning and design, while maintaining a proper three-way mindset. Then initiate character voice scripting, talent search, and recording. Use the brief technical definitions in this chapter to further educate yourself in audio standards and to communicate well with your audio team. Address your sound effects needs effectively by utilizing real and/or non-real sounds. Lastly, specify music tracks that generate accurate emotion for your environments, and best enhance the sections of your overall project layout.

CHAPTER 8

GAME FLOW

In designing a game, it is very helpful to depict the flow of the game in some fashion. It not only helps the designers have a better mental picture of how the game and its parts fit together, it also gives the programmers something to follow as they implement the game. The game flow depiction is the main communication tool between the game design and the implementation of the game.

Note: With today's advancement in software development tools such as OOP (object oriented programming) and visual development tools (e.g. Java), flow design is becoming less of an issue with software development. However, not all games are or can be developed using visual development tools; therefore, I think it is important to cover game flow as part of a game design.

There are several different methods of depicting game flow. In this chapter, I will talk about the most common methods. I will also talk about different ways to break up the game flow depiction into smaller, more manageable pieces.

The Flowchart

The most common method is the flowchart. The flowchart is a graphical representation built with different shapes connected together by lines and arrows. Each shape contains text and represents different actions and decisions. The lines and arrows may have text associated with them, also. The text in a shape or associated with a line/arrow helps describe what is happening at that point in the flow of the game. The basic, most common shapes and their meanings are:

The Oval

Start/End – The oval denotes the place where the flowchart starts or ends. Usually the word Start or End is in the oval. Also, the name of the flowchart may be included. (e.g., Start Main Menu). The Start oval will have an arrow leading from it to the first step in the flowchart. The End oval will have one or more arrows leading to it. (See Figure 8.1)

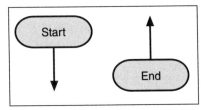

Figure 8.1
The oval depicts the start or the end.

The Diamond

Decision – The diamond is used to denote a decision. An arrow points to the top corner of the diamond showing how to get to this decision. The text of a question is inside the diamond. The two or more possible answers to the question are designated by text with arrows pointing from the other corners to the appropriate next step in the flow. (See Figure 8.2)

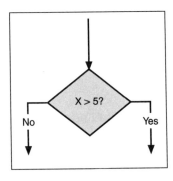

Figure 8.2
The diamond depicts a decision.

The Rectangle

The rectangle is used to denote an action or a reference to another flowchart. Usually an arrow points to the rectangle at its top edge and another arrow leads away from the rectangle from its bottom edge. The text inside the rectangle may be an assignment of a mathematical expression into a variable, a textual description of what happens, or the name of another flowchart. If it has the name of another flowchart, convention states that the vertical sides of the rectangle be doubled. (See Figure 8.3)

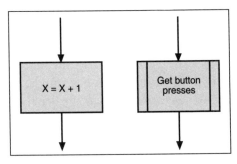

Figure 8.3
The rectangle represents a process.

The Circle

Connector – The circle is used to connect the flowchart together in areas where drawing the lines and arrows directly would make a big mess. Each set of connecting circles will be labeled the same. Most flowcharters use a single capital letter as the label. (See Figure 8.4.) Therefore, all the A's would be connected together, all the B's would be connected together, etc.

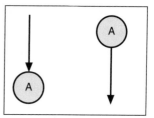

Figure 8.4
The circle connects things together.

You don't have to use these symbols as described and there are other less common symbols. However, whatever you do, make sure that the people who will be making the flowcharts and the people who will be using the flowcharts are all on the same page as to which symbols mean what.

A picture is worth a thousand words. The flowchart is like a picture of the game flow. The game designers are able to picture or visualize the game flow as they design the game. The programmers, hopefully, have that same picture as they implement the game.

A mathematical expression assignment is depicted as the variable name on the left followed by either a left arrow or an equals sign and then the mathematical expression. For example, $X = Y + 2$ says take the value in Y, add 2 to it, and put the result in X.

You can draw the flowcharts by hand or (if you can afford it) you can purchase a nice flowchart software package. If you draw by hand either with paper and pencil or by using drawing software and you need to make a change, then reconnecting the arrows can be a big pain in the "connector circle." A nice flowchart software package will keep the entire flowchart parts connected with possibly some minor adjustments.

Sample Flowchart

The flowchart in Figures 8.5 and 8.6 is an example of how someone might show the flow or steps for taking a shower. Since everyone has probably taken at least one shower in his or her lifetime, I thought that this example would be a good first exposure to flowcharting. Most likely, you could hand this flowchart to someone who hasn't had a shower before (but can read English) and they would be able to take a shower. Of course, if the person doesn't know how to do some of the steps, then those steps may need to be expanded into more detail. Some, like our mothers, may think that you should dry off before stepping out of the shower. In either case, the picture that the flowchart paints allows everyone involved to see the ins and outs of the game flow and to be able to make any necessary adjustments.

In Figure 8.5, the "Take a Shower" flowchart uses several decision techniques. The first one makes sure that the door is open. If not, then perform the step to open the door. The second decision technique is what is called a "loop." Certain steps are repeated until the desired condition is achieved. The danger with this kind of loop is that it can cause an infinite loop. In this case, the person feeling the water may never be satisfied that the water is neither too hot nor too cold. If the water is too cold, the adjustment to increase the hot water may make the water too hot and vice versa. To solve a problem like this, the programmer would need to make smaller adjustments and/or implement a wide enough range of acceptable temperatures that would allow the code to eventually get out of the loop. Now in Figure 8.6, the third decision technique is called an "iterative loop." Iterate means to repeat, so, in this example,

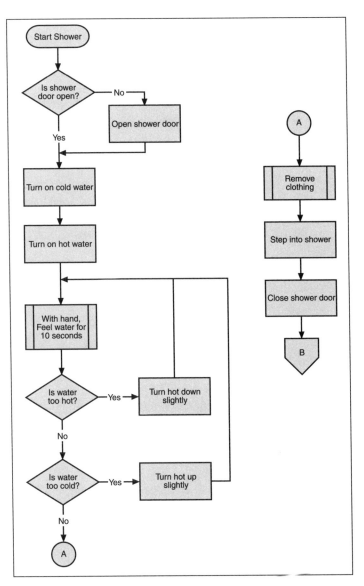

Figure 8.5
Everyone should know how to take a shower.

the shower flowchart wants the reader to shampoo, rinse, and repeat. To start an iterative loop a variable is initialized—in this case I is set to zero. At some point in the loop, the variable is incremented (or decremented), and then tested to see if it has reached the desired value, at which time, the flow exits the loop. The first time through the loop, I is equal to 0 and is incremented to 1. The second time through the loop, I is equal to 1 and is incremented to 2, at which point, the check for I < 2 is no longer true and the flow moves on.

Even though I didn't need to, I used a connecting circle to show how it might be used.

I also introduced a new flowchart symbol, the page connector. The page connector is shaped like a baseball home plate. Obviously the page connector is used to connect a large flowchart that doesn't fit on one page to its appropriate part or parts on other pages. Arrows going into a page connector indicate that the flow is going to another page. And arrows going out of a page connector indicate that the flow is coming from another page.

An Alternate to Flowcharting

If you don't have the means or you don't want to draw a flowchart, you can use what can be called a numerated text sequence. This can be less expensive than buying a flowchart software package and somewhat easier to modify than drawing, but it can be visually harder to follow.

Take a Shower Textual Sequence

Take a shower:

1. Is shower door open?

    Yes, go to step 2.

    No, open shower door.

2. Turn on cold water.

3. Turn on hot water.

4. With hand, feel water for 10 seconds.

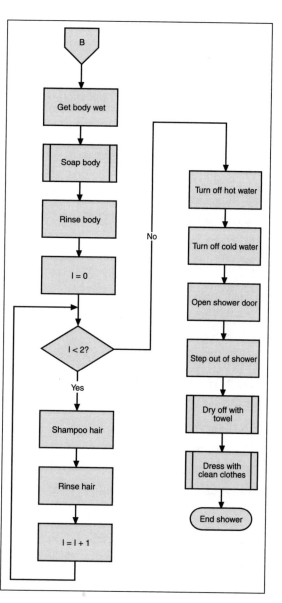

Figure 8.6
Don't forget to shampoo, rinse, and repeat.

5. Is water too hot?

> Yes, turn hot down slightly and go to step 4.
>
> No, go to step 6.

6. Is water too cold?

> Yes, turn hot up slightly and go to step 4.
>
> No, go to step 7.

7. Remove clothing.
8. Step into shower.
9. Close shower door.
10. Get body wet.
11. Soap body.
12. Rinse body.
13. Repeat 2 times:

> Shampoo hair.
>
> Rinse hair.

14. Turn off hot water.
15. Turn off cold water.
16. Open shower door.
17. Step out of shower.
18. Dry off with towel.
19. Dress with clean clothes.

Manageable Pieces

You will want to break the game flow into small, manageable pieces. I will talk about the methods to accomplish it and will give an example. The higher level game flow depictions would be included in the game design and the technical game design; whereas, the lower level (detailed) game flow depictions would only be included in the technical game design.

Game Flow Design Methods

Top-Down

This method of breaking the game flow into more manageable pieces is accomplished as its name implies: You start at the "top" by describing the major game flow (least detail) and then taking each part as its own flow and working "down" to more and more detailed game flows until you reach the "bottom" (as detailed as may be deemed necessary).

Bottom-Up

This is the opposite of top-down. Design the game flow details first and tie them together going up toward the top. This method works best if the details are known (hardware or engine capabilities lend to doing certain things better one way than another), but the designer may not know, at first, how those details may affect the upper level game flow.

Mixed

Many times it is best to use both top-down and bottom-up in combination with each other. Some details may need to be left until the upper levels have been designed, yet some details are already known and the upper levels will need to be based on those details.

Main Game Flowchart

As an example, I will use the top-down design method with flowcharts to demonstrate how you might depict the game flow of our sample *Motocross Professional Circuit* game. I will start from the top with the main game flow. Once the game has been initialized, the gameplay is shown as being repeated over and over again. There are two main parts to the gameplay. (1) The front-end is the part of the game which leads the player through a menu system and provides for the player to choose how he or she may want to play the game. (2) The race is the part of the game where the action is. Once the player has made his choices by navigating through the menu system, let the games begin. (See Figure 8.7.)

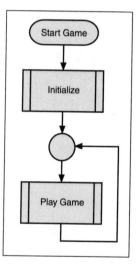

Figure 8.7
The main game flow starts out very simple.

Gameplay Flowchart

Figure 8.8 shows the main menu flow. For simplicity, I am doing something different with the menu flowchart. Normally you would show a decision as a diamond, but I am assuming that the programmer will implement a menu system that will show the choices on the screen and provide for the player to choose one. Depending on the choice, the menu system will set any appropriate data, save which menu it came from, and go to and display the next menu screen. I am also assuming that any of the menu screens will allow the player to go back to the previous menu. Again, for simplicity, at this level of the flowchart, I want to show the main front-end game flow from menu to menu, not the details of how the menu system works, yet. In the technical design document, I can design, in more detail, how the menu system works. So I use a rectangle (instead of a diamond) to represent the menu. The first line of text is the underlined menu name. The remaining lines of text indicate the possible menu choices. For each menu choice, an appropriately labeled arrow leads away from the rectangle to the next menu or action.

In my example, the Main menu is first. Main menu is underlined followed by four menu choices: 1 Player, 2 Player, Options, and Exit. If the player chooses 1 Player, then the game will move on to the 1 Player menu. If the player chooses Race or Practice, then the player will be presented with a pick track menu screen, a pick bike menu screen, and then moves on into the race. If the player chooses Career, then the flowchart goes to a separate flowchart, 1P Career. Exit will end the game.

2 Player is similar to 1 Player, except there will be a place for player 2 to select a bike.

The Options menu provides for the player to set or change options such as sound/music volume and saving and loading options. The game flow surrounding the Options menu could have been more detailed. But I wanted to show, for the game design, that there will be an options menu and I can make a more detailed description when I get into the technical design document.

In this flowchart, I used the connector circle to advantage. If I hadn't used the connector circle, then the five arrows that point back to the Main menu would have been messy.

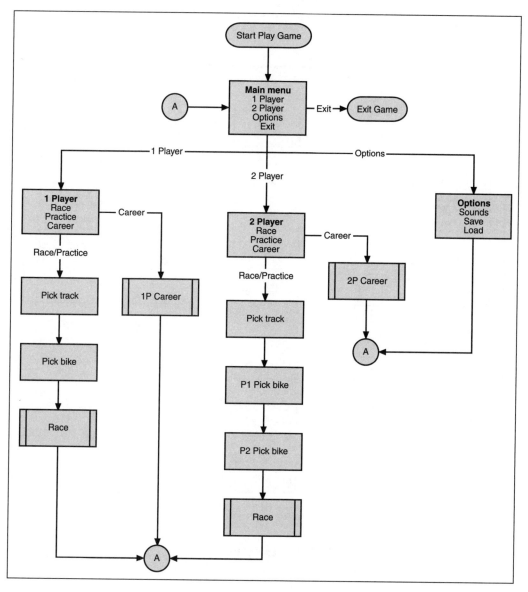

Figure 8.8
I used rectangles to depict menu choices.

A Sample of Not Using Connector Circles

The next figure, Figure 8.9, shows the same Gameplay flowchart without connector circles. I did this to show how messy and confusing a flowchart can get without the use of connector circles.

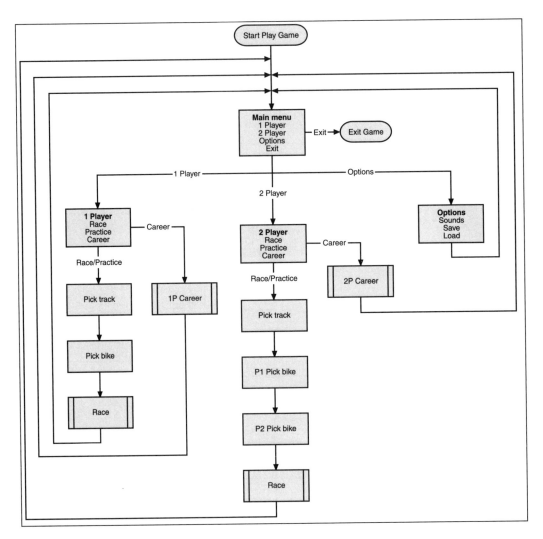

Figure 8.9
Fortunately all of those arrows are going to the same place.

One Player Career Flowchart

Figure 8.10 shows the flowchart for the One Player Career. As in the Gameplay flowchart, I use a rectangle to represent a menu screen instead of a decision diamond. This flowchart starts out by allowing the player to decide whether he wants to start a new career or continue an old one. If the player wants to continue with an old saved career, then he is presented with a screen to choose which career is to be restored. The career data is restored and the player is shown the Career menu screen. If the player wants to start a new career, he must choose which bike he wants to use, and the career data is then initialized before presenting the Career menu screen.

In this example, the Career menu allows the player to start the next race, see his statistics, save his career, or quit. Starting the next race, viewing statistics, and saving the career are pretty much self-explanatory. Quitting takes the game flow back to the Gameplay flowchart in Figure 8.8. The arrow takes you to the A connector circle, which leads you back up to the Main menu.

Here again the connector circle helped me to make a nice, neat looking flowchart, instead of having arrows all over the place.

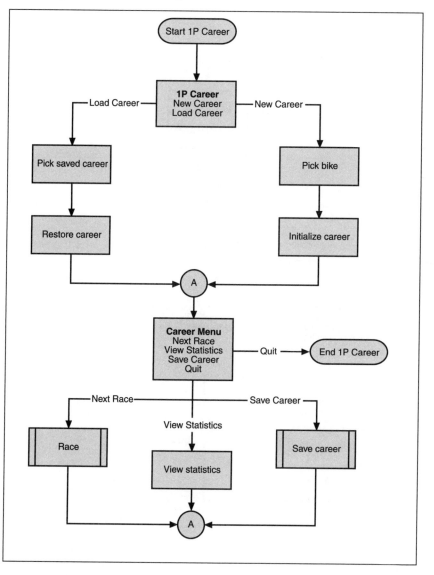

Figure 8.10
Don't forget to save your career!

Two Player Career Flowchart

The Two Player Career flowchart in Figure 8.11 is very similar to the One Player Career flowchart. In my example, the only difference is the fact that player 2 is allowed to pick his bike, too.

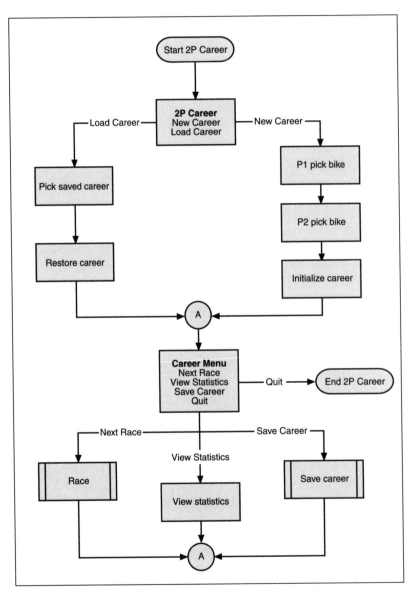

Figure 8.11
Two Player Career is similar to One Player.

Race Flowchart

The sample Race flowchart in Figure 8.12 is the beginning of a much more detailed description of the action part of the game. It starts out by initializing the race, which includes loading in the appropriate track and bike data, setting the Pause variable to false, setting the bikes to their starting positions, etc. Then it goes into the main loop of the race. Inside the main race loop, it gets the player's input (or players' inputs), which may include setting the Pause variable to true. If the Pause variable is true, display and handle the Pause menu. If not, then process the AI (artificial intelligence) for the computer-controlled bikes (if any) and process any motion/physics/collisions for all the bikes. The AI and the bike motion/physics/collisions will be the meat of the game. This could be (no, will be) where the programmers spend most of their time in developing the game. Even if the developer purchases a physics engine that is already written, the programmers will spend a lot of time on this part of the game.

Potentially, the next most time-consuming part of the game is the display of the game, depending on the complexity of displaying 3D objects. If the developer already has display code that was written for another game or has purchased a display package, then the job will be a lot easier and take less time.

In order for the game to be fun, it needs to look and feel good. That's another reason the programmers will spend much of their time on motion, physics, collisions, display, etc. With motocross, for example, you will want the bike actions to be as real as possible, but take my word for it, the game will be too hard to play and therefore not fun. Among other things, if you want the player's bike to be able to get lots of air and have plenty of time to perform tricks, the effect of gravity may need to be adjusted. So, with tweaking and fine-tuning, the final result will be somewhere between reality and make-believe. With that in mind, when you start planning your schedule as part of the technical design, you'll want to allow a good amount of time for "fine-tuning."

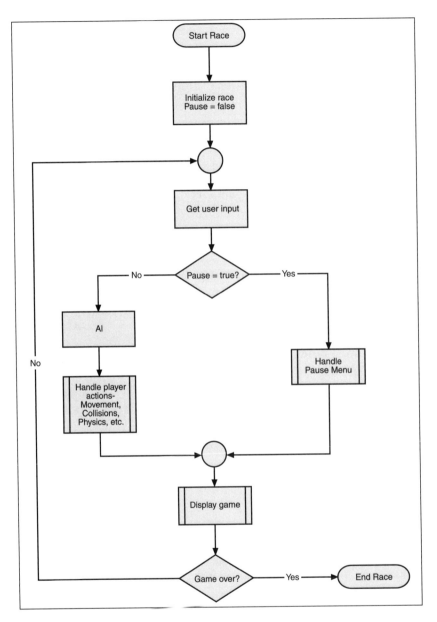

Figure 8.12
The race is the fun part of the game.

Summary

A picture is worth at least a thousand words. A flowchart is a picture of the game flow. Remember to keep each flowchart simple enough to stay as much as possible on one page and there will be less confusion between the designers and the programmers.

CHAPTER 9

USER INTERFACE DESIGN

A s you design your game, you are creating something that is interactive and therefore must have a way for the user to interact with it. The interface is the way a user can actually use your game, receive feedback, and control what is going on. For example, the player will have to roll the dice, see how far to go, move the pawn that many spaces, and then apply the result of landing on a particular space.

Whether textual, graphical, or spoken, the user needs to be able to perform the activities in order to play and then receive the necessary feedback to understand his status and progression in the game. There are several parts to the user interface that perform these functions; the main ones are as follows:

- Control for the player
- Feedback
- Visual elements

There are firms devoted just to creating the user interface for software products and games. This part of the design may seem like a big task, but breaking it down can help make it easier. By the time you finish this chapter, you should have a basic understanding of how to design a good user interface for just about any game.

What Is a User Interface?

The user interface is the representation of the information that allows the player to control the game and receive feedback. This creates interaction between your game and the player. The design is important enough to merit a chapter of its own. The topic covers quite a lot: from joystick control to dice rolling and from the credits to the heads up display. The following sections give the definitions you will need to pick out just the right parts for your game.

171

There are many parts to the user interface. You must figure out which ones you need in your game. Here is a short list of possible parts of the interface:

- Credits
- Intro scenes
- Cut scenes
- Menus
- Instructions
- Manuals
- Controls
- Presentation of the game world
- Player's state
- Heads up display

We will cover most of these points, and chances are you've already seen them in the games you play.

How Does the Player Receive Game Information?

There are many ways that the player can receive communication from the game, but the most common is a graphical representation. The player can see and understand what his current state is just by looking at the game. Another form is to present information as text through instructions and menus. Audio can sometimes communicate better than words, whether spoken or simple sound effects.

Can Interface Elements Be Incorporated into the Natural Play of the Game?

There are some games that start the player with no information at all other than what he has read in the instructions or heard from others. These games usually present a small video or short animation that sets up the start of the game so that the player has some direction. Information is then presented as the player progresses through the game. All of the choices the player makes by talking, walking, finding objects, or even picking a pocket are part of the user interface, but they are natural in that they are accomplished without a menu or written instructions. The player learns from watching other characters and talking to them. This is an extreme. *Pikmin*, *Pikmin II*, and many RPGs are good examples.

You can design your game with this form of interface, but be careful not to make it too difficult for new players. Be sure to use knowledge of the real world for interaction. Keep it simple by giving some clue as to how the interaction should take place. If the player walks up to a door, clicking with the mouse or pressing a button seems rather intuitive.

But if you map the controls so that you have to move left at the same time by pressing the up button and the left shoulder button, you have probably not kept it simple. If you blend the interface too far into the game, the player may not be able to understand what he needs to do.

> Be careful about breaking suspension of disbelief. To a degree, you have to do this; a person I met somewhere would be unlikely to say to me, "To open a door, press the A button," and if he did, I'd look at him kinda funny. But it is at least forgivable in the context of a character who has a reasonable desire to help the PC out. In some cases, it's better just to overlay a graphic on the screen or something of the kind—making the in-game help extraneous to gameplay—while avoiding making the characters in the game behave in inconsistent ways.

For example, I've played a particularly great game, a platform adventure, but I still don't know how to open a certain door. This has kept me from being able to finish and win, so I gave up on it. I could check online for clues or hints, but it just didn't seem worth it after spending so much time trying to find the correct sequence of events to get it open. I moved on to other games that interested me more. I may very well have opened the door, in which case the game should have provided more visual or audible clues.

How Can the Interface Affect the Game?

The user interface is about communication, which is a two-way street. The game provides the player with information needed to accomplish a goal, and the player provides the game with input on how he wants to act. If the lines of communication do not function, neither does the game. A good interface can make a game go from okay to great.

> When designing, you want to add lots of fun, cool-looking stuff, but it should also be functional. It should quickly and easily give the player the information he needs at crucial times during play. Someone built a level for *Warcraft III* in which a timer would activate waves of monsters. Without any warning, the monsters would descend upon the players to destroy everything, because the players had no idea of the oncoming hordes. Had they known, they would have better prepared their forces and constructions. This may have been what the designer had in mind, but it can be very frustrating for the player. A simple message or sound that something ominous was about to occur would have sufficed, but the designer may have wanted to keep from using somewhat unnatural methods for notification. Another point worth making is that, for skill-and-action games, the interface is often the game. That is, mastering the interface and being able to trigger exactly the right action at exactly the right moment is what lets you win the game. If this is the case, you not only want a clean interface, you also want the interface to cause people to do things that are entertaining and fun.

And another point: IA and user experience designers always insist that applications should be as transparent, simple, and easy to use as possible. For a shopping application, this is great advice. For a game, it is not always great advice. That is, you don't want to make it hard for the player to figure out what to do, but you *do* want it to be somewhat hard for him to actually do it. If the game is too easy to play, it won't be satisfying. So, you have to straddle a fine line between "too hard" and "too easy."

How Can the Player Control the Game?

What will the player do to control the game? This goes back to the genre and game style, but here are the controls. A player will need to move his game character or avatar about the playing field, even if it is a board game where the player is represented by a token or a set of tokens. This is part of the controls. Will the player use a joystick, use a keyboard, or do it manually?

Controlling Your Controls

"The keyboard and mouse give you neat instant response and near exact control. The controller is a far less precise, far more…well…leisurely input device."

—Warren Spector

When working on your design, you need to think about the requirements of the controls. There is a very large difference between a keyboard-mouse combo and a console controller. The information is broken up into the two major playing styles. The platform for which you are designing becomes a major issue when outlining controls.

Check out other games and see their controlling mechanisms. *Doom* and *Quake* are very similar in their controls. Both being first-person shooters, they use a similar camera design conforming to a standard for such titles, and their controls follow suit. *Starcraft* and *Age of Empires* both have similar isometric views for their cameras, and their controls are similar. Stick close to the standards of your genre.

There are some standards that transcend genres because they have been around so long. Pressing F1 asks for help or more information. Esc usually moves the game to the main menu and then exits the game. P means pause.

Consoles also have their own standards. During the development of a project, a development team came up with a color scheme that was important to members of the team. The problem was that the good guy—the player's character—was displayed on the map in red. Red is a vibrant color and easier to see than most other colors. This made it difficult for the player to understand the location of the unit he was controlling. This broke a standard, and the team was quickly reminded that they should stay with green for good guys and red for the bad.

Sometimes you will find or create something so new that there hasn't been a standard created or considered. In that case, design an action so that it compares with something in the real world or relate it to a similar action found in other games. That way, the player will not have as steep a learning curve because he will already have some kind of familiarity with the new action.

First Person

First-person games usually designate the mouse for looking, aiming, and firing, while the keyboard is laid out for movement and other actions. Adventure, shooters, racing, sports, and many other game styles can be played this way. On a console, the controls would be laid out differently because console players would not have or want to use a mouse. Newer consoles have two joysticks with which movement and looking can be performed. The camera in those games has to be a bit more intelligent in order to help the player with targeting and other movements. Buttons are then used for other actions such as jumping or strafing.

Sometimes the user is given a point of view and then clicks on the direction to move or look. The player is given an arrow indicator as feedback, for example, an arrow pointing left on the left side of the screen indicates turning in that direction. He can click a mouse on the objects in the view to interact with them. He can also manipulate them or take some other action. *Return to Zork, Myst,* and *Raven* are great examples of this form of gameplay. The graphics are pre-rendered to allow for more breathtaking views of their imaginary worlds.

Third Person

The third-person view is quite different, and the controls should be altered as well. The player is represented by a single avatar or token, a set of avatars or tokens, or maybe some combination of them. The movements of the tokens or characters are presented as if the player is watching from a distance. The controls need to reflect this.

The player can control a single avatar or token with the mouse by clicking in the view at the desired location. Right-clicking can be used for other actions, such as picking up items. These actions can also include bringing up a menu of options, displaying more information about an area, selecting cards on a playing board, or changing special features of the playing token. The use of the right mouse button can lead to problems if you are developing for a single-button mouse.

Multiplicity

When the player must control several tokens or characters, control can be similar to movement, but the player must be able to select the tokens he wants to control. Click and drag is intuitive to mouse users and makes sense for your design. It can be used to select small groups, which can then be assigned numbers on the keyboard for easy selection later. After making the selection, the player could Shift+click several locations, making points of interest for the movement of each group. In a combat game, these groups could walk or move to each point and then attack if there were enemies nearby.

Your game might use strategy, and a player would need to set up his tokens in a certain way in order to win. By selecting one or several tokens for movement, the player has a method for control. Suppose your game has a special character that the player must protect above all else; the game would need several other characters whose purpose it is to stand guard or attack incoming enemies. The player could use these methods of selection and movement for engaging in battle or rearranging the guard for better protection.

> Console note: Games with many controllable tokens almost *never* work well in a console environment, because of the difficulty of multiple selection and rapid movement from one side of the screen to another in the absence of a pointing device. (A mouse isn't necessarily required; you can do decent RTS games on a PDA, for instance, where a stylus replaces the mouse's functionality.) Those few console games that have the player control multiple tokens either (a) are turn based, with the player issuing orders to tokens one by one (*FF Tactics*, *Advance Wars*) or (b) have the player control one character at a time, with others following him around, controlled by AI (*Ico*).

Camera and Action

The joystick or controller pad on a console system can control the character so that the character's movement follows the direction in which the joystick or pad is pushed. If the camera swivels and turns in the direction the main character is facing, the controls make movement with reference to the character's left and forward. If the camera is more of an isometric view or one where the camera faces pretty much the same way all the time regardless of the movement of the main character, the controls work well if they move the character in reference to the camera view. For example, pressing up on the controls would make the character move up onscreen. This combined use of camera and controls works well for multiple players who share the same screen.

> Flight and Space Sims note: A convention with flight and space simulators uses a standard controller movement that is based on real-life aviation. Pulling back on the controller or joystick noses the craft up. It may seem counterintuitive to many beginners and to those not familiar with such titles but it is a standard not to be missed. Players of this genre are used to it and it only makes sense to follow this standard.

A game called *Baldur's Gate: Dark Alliance* uses an isometric view, though the camera can be swiveled by the player using the controller. As a cross-platform game, the actions need to work on several controllers. The developers mapped the actions appropriately for each of the controls. The camera is controlled from about the same location with the right hand, and player navigation is on the left. It implements movement with reference to the camera view. Independent of where the camera points or faces, pressing up still means up on the screen, but it could mean north, east, south, or west with relation to the world. What makes this interface a good one is that the player doesn't notice the change in camera position because it is seamless with the environment.

3D CAMERA

When doing a 3D game, you must *always* think carefully about how the camera will move or be moved, because if you do a bad job of this, players will often find themselves unable to see what they want or need to see at a particular time. A whole lot of different systems are used. In Halo, for example, one joystick controls character motion, while the other moves the camera about the character, giving you 360 degrees of vision without having to turn or move (this is similar to mouselook in PC-based FPS games). In most other console titles, the camera follows the character, either showing what the character would see (in first-person mode), or being above and behind the character (*Tomb Raider* is an example). In this style of game, you can't change the camera except by turning or moving. In still other games, the camera is under the game's control, following the character most of the time, but sometimes moving "on rails" as planned by the designer.

Configurable

When you are designing the control system, be sure that you allow for the end user to be able to change your configuration. Some publishers and manufacturers (Sony and Microsoft) require that the controls' layout not remain fixed. In addition, some gamers do not like the default configurations and like to change the settings to fit their playing style. If you map actions to every button on a console pad, you will probably need to make allowances for changes and may need more than one screen so that the player can better understand the controller setup.

In the development of one game, we had made a tight fit for all of the functions or actions to be mapped and displayed on a single screen. It worked and was visible but things became overly tight and somewhat difficult to understand when we had to localize the game for European markets. Words and descriptions no longer fit properly. Phrases and sentences were much longer in German and Italian than their English counterparts. Much care and time had to be spent rearranging the sequence and display of the controls. That was a powerful lesson, and I suggest you design with a couple of screens in mind for your controls.

Feedback

Feedback is what provides the player with the information about his state in the game. It's the communication between your game and the player. If there is no communication, then there really is no game. The player needs to know that he is being shot at, that he is going to fall if he does not move back from the edge of the cliff, or just simply that he needs to roll the dice to begin his turn. When the player makes a move, presses a button, or draws a card, he wants to know what the consequences are of his action. The player's token is in a new position, the player hears a sound, the player views the card—just a few examples of feedback.

One very important and simple rule should be adhered to: *acknowledge input immediately*. There should be no pause after an action is taken by the player. The actual method could be graphical or audible, and this should be added to the design. A statement such as "If the player selects a menu item, a ding is heard" would be appropriate and sufficient. Similar phrases can be added for other actions.

Another project included a few selectable units from a top-down isometric view. A problem that was not brought up by the testing department showed that players did not know if their unit was selected and was going to move to the location clicked on. There was no immediate feedback. The unit did move once the player clicked on the desired spot, but that wasn't enough. Those who had played it over and over during the development of the game never saw this because they knew what the unit would do.

With the advent of the Internet, new areas of gameplay have surfaced—the less visually stimulating and more textual gaming of wireless applications. In this realm, simple links by text and no client-side programming make it difficult to think of it as a gaming arena, though it is one of the fastest-growing markets for games. The interface is quite simple in this case, but feedback is critical. The information presented is mostly in text form, and there isn't much room for it, so you must be precise in its development. Every line counts. Short, concise statements should be used. Actions must be very apparent. Because response times vary, be sure the user understands the consequences of an action.

Further development has made mobile gaming move forward in leaps and bounds. BREW and J2ME are the base for application development and have allowed for more diverse gaming capabilities. More and more games are moving to the client side as more and more power is added to the mobile devices. 3D and animations are implemented with a thin client API. Developers have choices that make games quite easy to produce through this medium.

Information Presentation

It is imperative to present your feedback concisely. The more items you have, the more difficult it is to remember those options and take action. Short-term memory allows only five or six disjointed bits of information, so make the best of your player's brainpower. Get to the point.

For example, here is a main menu for a role playing game:

- Options
- Game Credits
- Game Information
- Play Game
- Choose Level
- The Creation of MyGame

This menu is too cluttered and does not help the player get to the game. The menu isn't even ordered correctly, as you probably have already noted. There is too much information that the player doesn't really need from the same menu. Here is another go at it:

- Play Game
- Options

That's it. There's no need for more than this in the main menu. The player will select Play Game to start and then Continue or Choose Level from the next menu—possibly Select a Character after that. If the player wants to adjust the game or see the credits and The Creation of MyGame, he will choose Options. That makes it simple and easy to use. It will keep the player happy because he can get right into playing.

As the player navigates through the menus, there should be some feedback that lets him know of the movement in a menu and the selection of items. Sound effects and other responses should be designed into the menus. Prompts for how navigation can be accomplished are also helpful—what buttons perform which functions. Let the player know what he needs to do. There usually are technical requirements for this sort of thing set up by publishers and manufacturers.

Personality

What will be unique about your design? What will draw the player into the interface? For both of those questions, I think about *Warcraft III* again. The menu screens are built to give you the flavor of being at the castle walls preparing for battle and start you down the path of warfare. The whole idea with the interface is to make the player feel as if preparations are being made for warfare. The sounds, the textures, and even some of the words play a part of this façade. Animation and movement in the background bring the menu to life.

Even with all the special effects and animations, the menus are simple and to the point. They are not overly long for a player who just wants to get into the action. The player has a quick route straight into the game. It is a style all its own that still incorporates simplicity.

Stop and Think

Think about your game and genre for a moment. What scenes play through your head as you think about the gameplay? Can these be used for openers, cut scenes, the main menu system, or printed instructions? See the following section, "The Visual," for more on this.

What will give your design its own personality? A special character from the game could help the player with the navigation by explaining how to play or what buttons do what. He could follow the selections made and repeat the player's choices either audibly or textually. Lip-syncing is getting pretty good nowadays. You will not want to overdo this character interaction, though; sometimes text is better. You will also need to make it possible to toggle on/off the character's speech and audio. So keep a secondary method of explanation handy.

A military game that we developed had a couple of special characters that stated the player's objectives and at the end of each level gave the player feedback and a report card to let him know how well the level was completed. When the player succeeded and accomplished most of the tasks, a reward would be given and an acknowledgment of high praise. Of course, if the player performed miserably he got chastised and possibly kicked out of the service.

The Visual

The biggest part of video and computer games takes place onscreen. The visual part becomes the largest part of the user interface. The interaction or communication starts with what is displayed to the player, giving the needed instructions. The onscreen elements used to control the game are called the *graphical user interface* (GUI).

What Is a Graphical User Interface?

A graphical user interface is any art used in a game for the purpose of player navigation or disseminating game information. That definition covers a lot, from onscreen display to menus to credit screens. In some games there is as much art in the GUI as there is in the rest of the game.

The amount of art required for the GUI in any particular game varies, depending on the type of game and the amount of information and navigation issues involved. A simple online puzzle game may have only a title screen and some onscreen game controls. On the other hand, a flight simulator may have extensive navigation and information systems.

Information Screens

An information screen is a screen that gives the player specific game information. A title screen is an information screen. Almost all games have a legal screen, which lets the player know who owns what copyrights and trademarks in a game. Many games have high score screens or other specialized information screens.

The very first thing a player sees in a game is a GUI element. It may be simply a loading screen, or it may be an elaborate full-motion video. It is important to make a favorable first impression on the player, so an interesting and visually impressive opening to a game goes without saying. The concept artist is the person who is responsible for creating a great opening for the game.

The most important aspect of an information screen is to give the player information. In a legal screen, the information is spelled out in very specific legal text that needs to be clear. In a title screen, the information may not be so much in the text but more in the emotion of the art. Each screen will have its own purpose. The concept artist needs to be aware of the purpose of each screen and design the screen with that purpose in mind.

Some of the more common types of information screens are as follows:

- Title
- Loading
- Legal
- Level
- High score
- Win
- Lose
- Credit

Title Screens

The title screen may be the most important of the information screens. At least as far as budgets for screens, it is the one that typically has the largest. The title screen is the opening screen for a game and includes the game's title. It is the one that introduces the game to the player. First impressions are very important.

A common practice in games is to have the title page be the same art as that on the game box, if the game is sold retail (in stores). Online games don't have a box. If the game will be sold at retail, then the concept artist may want to wait to design the title page until the box art is designed. The main issue with using box art is that the box layout is different from a screen layout. Figure 9.1 shows the layout for retail boxes and game screens.

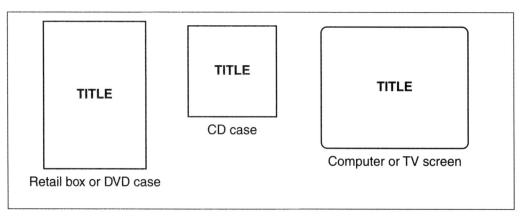

Figure 9.1
The layouts of boxes are different from those for a screen in the game.

Notice that the box is either a vertical rectangle or a square. The screen is a horizontal rectangle. Sometimes the box art will not look good when adapted for the title screen.

In addition to the title screen, the game many times will have an opening movie. The movie, like the title screen, is an information element in the game. If the game includes a movie, the concept artist will need to create a storyboard to explain the movie.

Loading Screens

Loading screens are also important initial screens in games. Games that are on either a CD or a DVD take time to load the game graphics into system memory. During the loading time, a loading screen is displayed onscreen. This screen can be as simple as a loading bar that grows as the game loads, or it can be a lot more. It is up to the designer and concept artist to determine what they want to put on the loading screen.

Some games get very creative with their loading screens. A racing game may have a car move across the screen instead of a loading bar. Some games even have simple little games that the player can play while waiting to load. Figure 9.2 shows a sketch for a racecar game loading bar.

Figure 9.2
A racecar is used in the loading bar for this concept drawing.

Legal Screens

Legal screens have very specific legal requirements that make them less creative than other screens. A legal screen tells the player who owns what part of the game. The ownership is usually determined by a trademark or copyright. There are specific requirements for displaying notices for both. Some games may contain patented software, although that is less common.

Before designing a legal screen, it is a good idea to check with the attorney responsible for the game to get the legal text. The same attorney should make sure the text is accurate and check the concept design when it is completed.

In a legal screen, the text should be clear and legible. The logos should be large enough to be recognizable. The composition should be simple and in most cases formal.

Level Screens

In many games there is an introduction screen for each level. Often the level introduction screen is also a loading screen. Level screens are similar to title screens, with the exception that the level screen introduces the level and not the game. Level screens are often used in racing games to show the layout of the upcoming course. Figure 9.3 shows a design for a level screen from a racing game.

Unlike the title screen, one game may have many level screens. The number of level screens is dependent on the number of levels in the game.

Some high-budget games will have movies between levels. This doesn't happen too often because of the expense in creating Full Motion Video (FMV) sequences, but the industry is moving more and more in that direction.

Figure 9.3
Racing games often have level screens to introduce a course.

High Score Screen

A high score screen is a statistical screen that shows how the player's score compares to other players. High score screens are similar to legal screens in that there is specific information that needs to be communicated. They are different from legal screens in that there is a lot more creativity that can go into a high score screen.

Win Screen

A win screen is the reward for the player when the game is won. Win screens need to be something special because the player has just spent a lot of time with the game. If the reward is not very much for winning, the player will be disappointed. It is common to use FMVs as the reward.

Lose Screen

A lose screen is like a win screen except that the player sees the screen when he has lost the game. A lose screen is often seen several times during the course of playing the game, but a win screen is seen only when the player successfully completes the game. A lose screen should encourage the player to return to the game and try again.

Credit Screen

Like movies, games also have a number of people who contribute to the development of the game. Everyone who has a part in creating the game should be included in the credits for the game.

A credit screen lists the names and maybe pictures of the people who contributed to the development of the game. Credit is very important to members of the development team, and the information included is very specific, like the legal and high score screens. It is closer to the legal screen in that the credit information needs to be clear and easy to understand. Many people in the industry rely on credits to help them get work or to upgrade their jobs. Some even become celebrities in gaming circles if they have worked on a popular title.

Menus

Menus are the most common GUI element for front-end navigation. Menus are onscreen selection elements with selectable graphics, usually in the form of buttons, but they can use other types of graphics as well. Each button on a menu has a function. The player navigates the game by selecting buttons with the game control device, which in the case of a PC game is usually the mouse. Figure 9.4 shows a design for a game options menu screen.

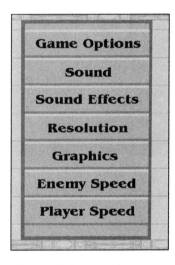

This example uses buttons to make selections. Buttons are virtual devices, and there is very little functional difference between a button and any other onscreen selectable item. The only real difference is in the animation of the button. There are several types of selectable elements that can be used in designing games. A few of them are as follows:

- Menu lists
- Buttons
- Icons
- Objects
- Characters

Figure 9.4
Most menu screens use buttons.

Menu Lists

The simplest type of menu is a list. Most people are familiar with menu lists in computer applications. The most common form of menu list is the pull-down menus usually found at the top-left area of the screen. There are other types, including marking menus and static lists. Marking menus float over the screen and are accessed either by a mouse click or a button press on a game controller. Figure 9.5 shows a design using a marking menu.

Figure 9.5
Marking menus are floating menus.

A static list is a menu that is part of the static artwork in a screen. Static lists are very common in Internet Web pages. Menu lists are widely used in Internet and computer applications, but they are not as common in games, where a more graphically interesting approach is desired.

Buttons

A button is a graphic device that has the appearance of a physical button. Many buttons are animated so that when the player activates it, it appears to be pushed. Figure 9.6 shows a button in its two stages of animation.

Buttons are common in games because visually they are more interesting than menu lists.

Figure 9.6
Many buttons are animated to show when they are pressed.

Icons

Icons are very similar to buttons, with the exception that an icon is a small symbol or picture. It may be pressed like a button, or it may just change colors when selected. Figure 9.7 shows an icon in the selected and non-selected states, with a simple color shift to indicate the difference.

Figure 9.7
Icons often use a color shift to indicate the selected and non-selected states.

Most people are familiar with icons from their use in computer software. The desktop of most operating systems contains multiple icons. Icons are used often in games because of their use as symbols. Often the need for text is eliminated because of the symbol on an icon. The example in Figure 9.7 shows a child reading. The player doesn't need text to indicate that reading is what the icon represents.

Objects

A very common practice in games is to use objects as interface devices. Unlike other interface devices, an object can exist as part of the game world. It doesn't have to be a separate interface device. It can be part of the setting. Doors leading from a room to other play levels are an example of interface object art.

Many games have pick-ups. A pick-up is an in-game element that the player can acquire during gameplay. They are not traditionally thought of as interface art because they are part of the actual play of the game. However, in many ways they act as interface devices because they are selectable items in a game.

As games become more advanced, the line between the interface and the game is becoming less defined. Game designers are starting to include many systems that were once interface elements in the game itself. This is really stretching the definition of a menu, but it is basically the same thing. For example, if a player selects the play level by the door selected in a room, it is the same thing as selecting the level from a menu list. Menus do not have to be 2D word lists.

Characters

Using a character for a selection item in many ways is similar to using an object, except that the character may be able to talk to the player to explain the selection. A character in a room is an obvious way to create a character selection menu, but characters can go beyond just the selection of characters. Characters are great for information. Using characters for interface elements is a lot more interesting than a menu list. For example, a player can interactively change the character's clothes, hair color and style, skin color, and body type.

Onscreen Displays

Many games have graphics that remain onscreen during gameplay. These graphics often give the player information about the game. They may indicate the health of a character or show the speed of a vehicle. They might display the score or the number of items a player has collected. Their purpose is to give the player vital real-time information.

An onscreen display is often called a *heads up display* (HUD) in the industry. The name comes from the displays used in military aircraft to give the pilot vital flight or enemy information while flying. Figure 9.8 shows a HUD for a racing game.

Figure 9.8
Racing games often have several HUD elements.

In Figure 9.8 there are three HUD elements. In the upper-left corner is the track display, with the relative position of each racer. This is also known as a radar map. In the lower-left corner of the screen is the position of the player. It indicates that the player is in first place. To the right on the lower part of the screen is the speedometer. Each element has a purpose to help the player during the game. From inventories to radar maps, from item menu displays to spell casting, each has its role in helping the player interact with his game world.

It is very important to design the HUD carefully because the HUD is onscreen while the game is played. It is arguably the art that is seen most often by the player.

The concept artist needs to be aware of the video safe area. The video safe area is that part of the screen that will not be hidden by the game system. Some game systems do not display the full screen during the game. This is especially true for video game systems that display their signal on a standard TV. Computer games typically do not have this problem because they use a digital rather than an analog signal. As more display systems become digital, this concern will disappear. Figure 9.9 shows the video safe area of a TV video game.

Figure 9.9
Some video game systems do not display the full game screen.

When designing the HUD, the concept artist needs to place the onscreen elements in such a way that they do not interfere with the game action. The area where most of the game action takes place is called the focal area. Figure 9.10 shows the area typically used for the focal area of a game.

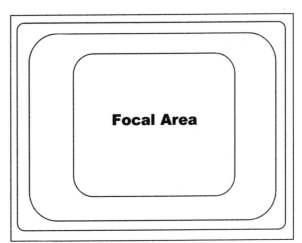

Figure 9.10
The center of the screen is usually the focal area.

The area between the focal area and the edge of the video safe area is the best location for placing HUD elements. This will make them less likely to intrude on the action of the game and still keep them from being cut off. Figure 9.11 shows where the HUD elements should go.

Creating Game Navigation Design

This first example is of a game options menu in a science fiction adventure game. The design will use simple shapes. The first step is to define the screen area and lay in the background. In this case the background is a dark gradation, as shown in Figure 9.12.

hint

A vector drawing program is a very useful tool in creating interface art designs. These art programs are very good at creating clean geometric shapes. They are also very useful in laying down gradations or flat colors. More intricate drawings can be created in painting programs and then imported into the vector program.

The next step is to create the basic menu areas. These shapes are drawn in, as shown in Figure 9.13.

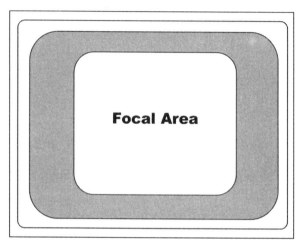

Figure 9.11
The area between the focal area and the video safe area is the best location to place HUD elements.

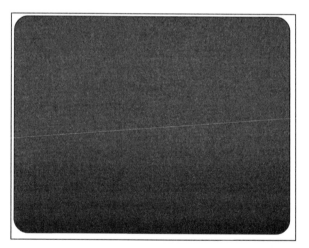

Figure 9.12
Start by defining the area of the screen.

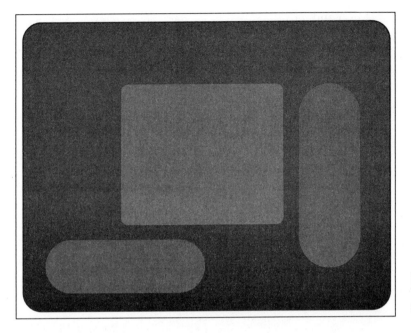

Figure 9.13
The menu areas are
drawn in.

The center shape will be a monitor. It is now drawn in, as shown in Figure 9.14.

Figure 9.14
The center shape is a
monitor.

A character will speak to the player from the monitor. A character sketch is added to the monitor, as shown in Figure 9.15.

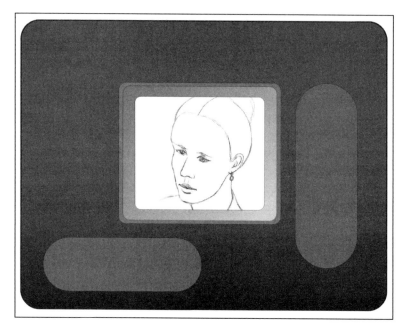

Figure 9.15
A character sketch is added to the picture.

To give the design a more technical feel, some tubes are added as support devices to the onscreen shapes. Figure 9.16 shows these tubes.

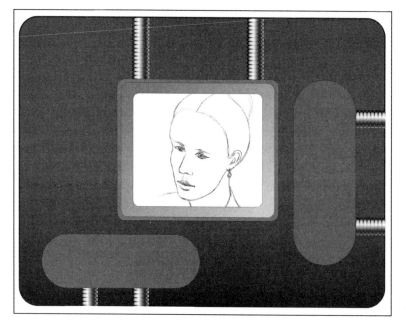

Figure 9.16
Support devices are added to the drawing.

Now the buttons can be added to the picture, as shown in Figure 9.17.

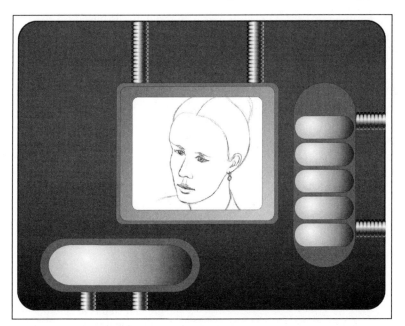

Figure 9.17
The buttons are added to the shapes to create menu panels.

The last step to complete the concept sketch is adding the text on the buttons. Figure 9.18 shows the finished concept sketch of the game options screen.

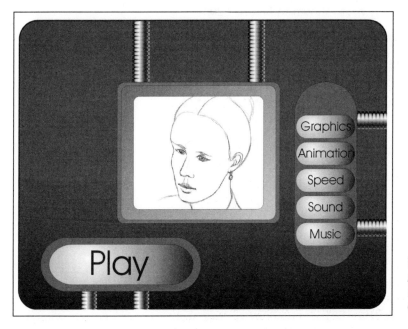

Figure 9.18
Adding the text finishes the game options screen.

Creating Onscreen Elements

This example is for a PC racing game HUD design. Because the game is based on the PC, there is no need to deal with the video safe issue. The first step is to define the screen area, as shown in Figure 9.19.

Figure 9.19
The first step is to define the dimensions of the screen.

HUDs are art that overlay the game. A sketch of a racing game is added to indicate what the game action will likely be, as shown in Figure 9.20.

Figure 9.20
Add a sketch of the game.

Now the HUD elements can be added. The game design calls for an onscreen track layout that shows the progress of each car in the race. The first element added to the design is a miniature map of the track, as shown in Figure 9.21.

Figure 9.21
A miniature map of the track is added.

Small circles are then added to the track to represent each car, as shown in Figure 9.22.

Figure 9.22
Circles are added to the track to represent the cars.

The next HUD element is the position of the player. Figure 9.23 shows this element added to the design.

Figure 9.23
The position in the race is added to the design.

The last element to add to the picture is the speedometer. This will be placed in the lower-right corner of the screen. The speedometer will be circular, so the first step in building it is to create the shape, as shown in Figure 9.24.

Figure 9.24
Create the shape of the speedometer.

Text indicating the speed is added to the speedometer. The test wraps around the inside of the circle much like a real speedometer, as shown in Figure 9.25.

Figure 9.25
The speed is added to the speedometer.

The last element is to add an indicator of how fast the racecar is traveling. This is done by adding a needle, as shown in Figure 9.26.

Figure 9.26
Show how fast the car is going.

Summary

The use of simplicity, feedback, similarity, and familiarity will help you design a good user interface. In your design, be sure to investigate the platform(s) you expect to use, and then find out the technical certification requirements.

- Simplicity: Keep it simple. Be sure not to overload the user with non-essential information, especially in menus. When they are simple, multiple menus are fine and can help keep the player in the correct flow, which moves him right into gameplay. The player wants to play, not spend time in menus.

- Feedback: The key to feedback is visibility. Visibility means providing good and helpful information to the player, giving audible clues according to action, as well as using simple coloring to show selections and other functionality. Highlighting menu options with a background color change alongside the foreground color change helps the player stay on target.

- Similarity: As selectable options change, don't change the method of selection. Moving from menu to menu, it's a good idea to keep the same method for selecting items and changing the selected item. Any in-game menus should correspond to those in the front-end of the game, for example.

- Familiarity: Remember to check out not only games that are similar in content, but all kinds of games, in order to better understand how good user interfaces are designed. Compare them to your needs and borrow elements. Players have played these games, and you need to conform to the norms that players will understand and with which they are familiar. When you find elements that you like and that are suited for your content, be consistent throughout your design.

From the information in this chapter, you should have a handle on what it will take to make a good user interface that is not only functional but also user friendly. It's not hard to do, but there are definitely some things that need to be remembered and implemented.

CHAPTER 10

TECHNICAL DESIGN

The technical design document (TDD) picks up where the design document left off. The TDD describes the nitty-gritty of how you are going to accomplish the development of your game. It takes the design document and adds more detail, such as more detailed flowcharts and information on memory use, what software tools will be used, and your time schedule. It especially should include descriptions of any special things that are unique to your game. For example, in the *Motocross* game, the user might be able to build tracks and race them. If that is the case, the TDD should describe how you expect to accomplish putting together the pieces of track and so on. The TDD should also include a section describing any concerns or problems and how you expect to solve those problems.

As a general rule, the more time spent on the TDD, the less time will be spent in development. At some point, though, you need to stop designing and start developing. You can usually tell when that time has come, when there are only questions that can't yet be answered. Simply put those questions in the Concerns and Potential Problems section and describe the processes that will be used to answer them. Of course, it may not be that simple, but do the best you can.

Parts of a few sections of the design document may be included in the technical design document. Some of these sections could be the basic game description, flowcharts, target audience, target hardware system(s), and milestone table. Including those sections helps to have continuity between the two documents. As you describe some of these sections in more detail, it also helps to have the original paragraph or two followed by the more detailed description.

The Sections of a TDD

I will talk about the purpose of each section that should or may be in a technical design document. Some sections should always be included in a TDD, while including other sections will depend on the genre of game and the target hardware system. I will also include an example or partial example to give you an idea of what can be in each section.

Target Hardware System(s)

You will always include this section. After all, the readers will want to know the system or systems the game will be played on. Knowing this will help you to direct the writing of the rest of the TDD. If the game will be developed for a console, simply mentioning the console will most likely suffice. However, if the game will be developed for, say, the PC, then you will want to list the minimum or suggested system requirements.

For example:

- Target system
- Windows PC with the following minimum system requirements:
  - Pentium III or equivalent
  - Windows 98 or higher
  - 128 MB RAM
  - 32 MB video card
  - 8x CD-ROM drive
  - DirectX 8.0
  - Sound card
  - 650 MB of available hard drive space
- For network play, the system will also need a network card

Target Audience

You will probably want to just copy this section from the design document. Most likely, there won't be any additions to it. It's good to have it in the TDD because then the reader won't have to refer back to the design document to retrieve the information.

Processor Use

This section would be included only if your target system is a console system or has multiple processors with different purposes. The PlayStation 2 has several processors that have different purposes. It has a main processor, an input/output processor, two graphics processors, and a sound processor. Even though each processor has its own specific purpose, sometimes you can have a processor that may not be busy all the time do certain tasks such as performing calculations for the artificial intelligence (AI).

Memory Use

This section will be a "best guess" on your part. You will need to determine, as closely as possible, how much memory will be used and for what purpose. The reasons you want to go through this exercise are because it's a sanity check to make sure your estimated memory use fits within the minimum system requirements and because it will be used as a target as you develop the game. As the game develops and you find that your memory use is going outside the limits you had originally set, you have to either bring your memory use down or determine if the minimum system requirements can be raised. If you were developing this game for a game publisher, most likely, the second option wouldn't even be considered, because they've already determined their market size by how many potential customers have that much memory on their computers.

For example:

- 1 MB—Code
- 2 MB—Sounds
- 2 MB—Front-end art
- 16 MB—Bike 3D art (2 MB per bike)
- 32 MB—Track
- 53 MB Total

Saving and Loading

Almost all games have something to save. Even if the game doesn't have a career or some other type of progress to save, it will most likely have options. In this section, you will want to describe what data will be saved and how it will be saved. Will all career data be saved in one file or will each career be saved in its own file? How large will the files be?

If you are designing and developing a game for a console that uses a memory card, you will also need to describe how much of the memory card will be used.

For example:

The career data will be saved in one file for all careers. Up to 10 careers can be saved. Each career will be saved with the following information: Player's name, current bike being used, any bike upgrades, rank information, current level, which race in the level, and track order for the current level. Each career data should be no larger than 256 bytes, so the career file will be no more than 2,560 bytes.

Supported Input Devices

In this section, you'll describe which input devices will be used and how they will be used. For a PC game, your choices would include the ever-present keyboard and mouse and a vast variety of joysticks. If the keyboard will be used, which keys will be used for what? Will your game support some of the extra features that some mice have, such as a third button or a scroll wheel? Will your game support just a standard joystick or other varieties?

For example:

> Supported input devices will be the keyboard, the mouse, and any standard analog joystick. The mouse will be used only in the menu system. The keyboard can be used for gameplay input. One player will use the arrow keys as follows: left arrow—turn left, right arrow—turn right, up arrow—accelerate; down arrow—brake. A second player will use the A, S, W, and Z keys as follows: A—turn left; S—turn right; W—accelerate; Z—brake. The standard analog joystick can be used for one or two players, and the controls will be analog stick left to turn left, analog stick right to turn right, button 1 to accelerate, and button 2 to brake.

Supported Output Devices

Besides the TV or monitor, some games use other output devices. If your game needs to print anything, such as a certificate, you'll need to explain in this section how printing will be handled. Will it use the standard Windows printing interface? If not, what printers will be compatible with your game?

AI

Not all games need artificial intelligence (AI). If your game has non-player characters (NPCs), then your game will need AI to control these NPCs. NPCs can be anything from other bikers with whom you are racing to the big boss you have to defeat in order to complete the level. In any case, you'll need to explain as much as possible how each NPC's AI will be calculated.

For example:

> We will use the blind data capability in Maya to attach a value to certain polygons in a track. The NPC bikes will use this data to follow the track. Certain values will be used to indicate how to traverse the track. Such values would include:
>
> Straight—Full throttle
>
> Right turn coming up—Slow down in anticipation of the turn
>
> Left turn coming up—Slow down in anticipation of the turn
>
> Right turn—Turn right

Left turn—Turn left

Extra boost—Jump coming up, use the extra boost to jump

Trick—Perform a trick here

Multiplayer

Will your game allow more than one player? If so, you need to explain the ins and outs of whether you'll be able to play on a network or over the Internet. Will your game handle more than one player on one screen? If so, explain how the screen will be split—horizontally, vertically, or both.

For example:

> This game will allow two players to play on the same machine and up to eight players over a network. Because of the potential for large latency on the Internet, there won't be Internet multiplayer capability.
>
> Two players on one machine will be able to use the keyboard or joysticks. The players will be able to choose a horizontal or vertical screen split, and the default will be horizontal.
>
> In network play, it is anticipated that one computer will act like a host and keep track of all racers and AI bikes. Each computer will control its own bike and transmit that information to the host. The host will take all the bikes' data and transmit that data back to the other computers. The host computer will resolve any conflicts between computers.

Concerns and Potential Problems

This is where you put unanswered questions and any other problems you are concerned about. You anticipate that these questions will be answered in the process of developing the game. Either you will plan to have some research time to try to answer a question or, as the game progresses, you will be better able to address the problem. In either case, explain as much as you can.

For example:

> The host computer being able to handle conflicts between other computers on a network is unknown at this time. As soon as possible, we intend to get the physics working with placeholder bikes and tracks and begin testing and working out what conflicts may occur and the best way to handle those types of conflicts. One of the more obvious conflicts that may occur is in colliding with other bikes. One computer may erroneously calculate that a collision has occurred based on not having received information from the host that the other bike had just turned enough that the collision didn't occur.

Software Tools

This section should contain a list of the software tools that you anticipate you will use to develop your game. This includes the tools that will be used to build the 2D and 3D art, the sounds, and the game code.

You will pick these tools based mainly on two criteria: Does the tool do everything you need it to do? Can you afford it? If you have the time and skills, you can go with a cheaper tool and make up the difference by writing some of your own tools. If you will be writing your own tools, you can describe them briefly in this section.

For example:

Art Software tool list:

Maya for creating and editing 3D art and motion.

Photoshop for creating and editing 2D art.

Data Wrangling

I've named this section "Data Wrangling" because the person (usually a junior programmer) who deals with getting the art and sound data into the game is often referred to as the *data wrangler*. This section is where you need to describe this process. This process is also referred to as the art or sound path or pipeline. This process may take some thought and organization, but if done correctly, it will pay off in the long run, especially if there is going to be a large amount of data.

In the following example, the So-And-So Graphics Engine is fictitious.

For example:

3D art pipeline—We will use the Maya plug-in for the So-And-So Graphics Engine to output the 3D art into the format used by the So-And-So Engine. A filename standard will be used to keep track of each art file. For the bike files, we will use the following naming standard:

The first four characters will be "bike."

The fifth character will be bike size (0–125cc, 1–250cc, 2–500cc).

The sixth character will be which of the bikes can be chosen (0 through 7).

Therefore, a filename for the fourth 250cc bike might be bike13.sas.

Database Handling

Not all games will have a database. If yours does, then you will need to describe what data is in the database and how it will be used in the game. A database is a set of data organized into records. Each record contains fields. Each field contains the same type of data as in the other records. For example, a "person" database would have "person" records. Each person record in the database would have fields, which could include the person's first name, last name, address, and phone number. A monster database might be used to define what monsters are located where in the game. The fields for such a database might include which 3D art file to use and its level, starting location, initial hit points, and regeneration time.

Some databases are simple enough that you can build a table by hand in your game code. If the database is large, you may want to keep track of your data in a spreadsheet and then "wrangle" it into your game.

Scheduling

This is where you estimate when certain tasks and milestones will be completed. You'll want to coordinate the tasks so that a task that is dependent on another task is not scheduled to start before the other task has been completed. You will probably spend a good amount of time figuring out and coordinating the schedule. Nevertheless, it will give a plan to follow. If a given task is falling behind, you can see how it might affect the rest of your schedule, and you might be able to plan around it and make appropriate adjustments.

Even if you don't care about when the game is finished, at least it can give you a picture of where the project is and how close it is to being done.

I like to use a project software package. Figure 10.1 illustrates how a schedule might look.

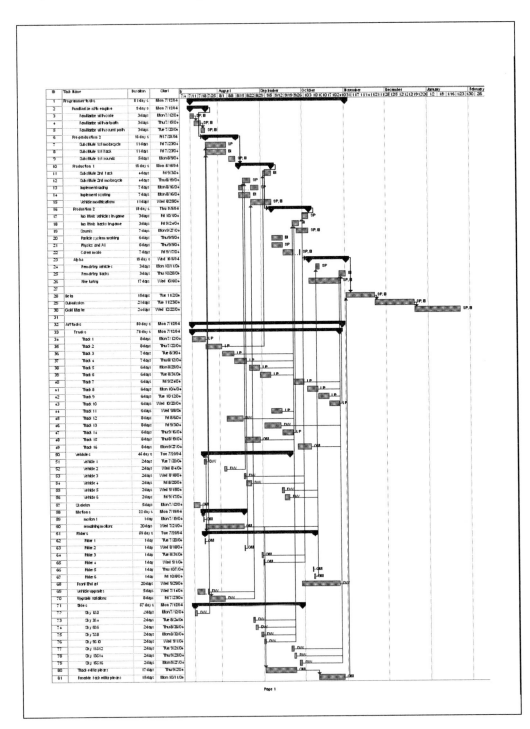

Figure 10.1
This sample schedule shows dependencies.

Game Flow

Again, you can start with what was in the design document and make more detailed flow-charts. See Chapter 8, "Game Flow." You'll want to be as detailed as possible without going overboard. Deciding how detailed to get is dependent on those doing the programming.

Figures 10.2, 10.3, and 10.4 show part of the expansion of Handle player actions from the flowchart shown in Figure 8.12 from Chapter 8, "Game Flow."

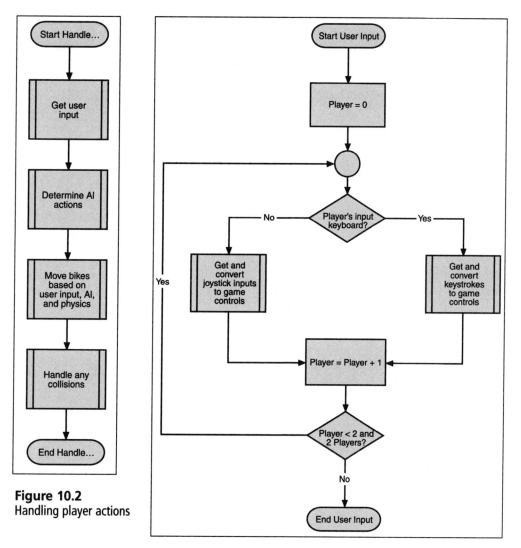

Figure 10.2
Handling player actions

Figure 10.3
Handling user input

Figure 10.2 expands the Handle players actions function shown in Figure 8.12. It expands into a simple sequence of events: Getting the user input, determining any AI actions, moving the bikes, and handling any collisions.

Figure 10.3 expands the Get user input function from Figure 10.2. It loops through each player (assuming one or two players) and gets that player's input from the keyboard or the joystick.

Figure 10.4 expands the Get and convert keystrokes to game controls function from Figure 10.3. It checks for certain keys being pressed and converts them to the appropriate internal game controls such as turning left.

Game Engine

What will drive your game? Will you be using an existing engine or will you be writing your own? A brief but thorough explanation of what you plan to do goes in this section.

For example:

> We will be using So-And-So's 3D Graphics Engine to develop the display aspects of the game. So-And-So's 3D Engine version 6.3 is a client-based, multimedia technology platform with unique compression technology. The So-And-So 3D Engine takes advantage of modern processor and graphics card hardware acceleration, scaling content

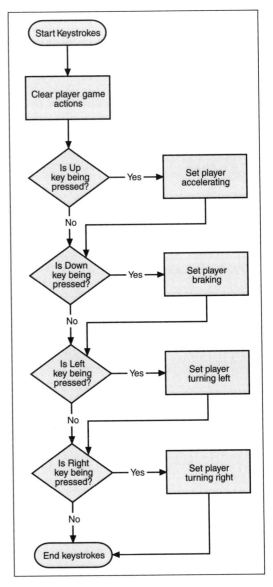

Figure 10.4
Handling keyboard input

to the optimal level of the computer's power. The engine SDK immerses developers in an interactive browser- or standalone-based 3D world, supporting flexible and seamless creation of leading-edge, innovative content.

Needed Assets

This section will involve a good amount of time and effort. You will list, by category, every single bit of 2D and 3D art, motion, and sound that you anticipate will be used in the game. Not only does this give you an idea of where the "end of the tunnel" is, this information aids greatly in your scheduling. If you know that you will need 25 similar type pieces of 2D art and you estimate that each piece will take one day to complete, you can estimate that it will take 25 days on your schedule.

For example:

> 2D art needed for the front end and gameplay:
>> Legal screens (the screens that contain the copyright and other legal information)
>>
>> Main screen
>>
>> New Game screen
>>
>> Load Game screen
>>
>> Training screen
>>
>> Options screen
>>
>> Exit screen
>>
>> Race Briefing screen
>>
>> Save Game
>>
>> Gameplay interface or heads up display (HUD)
>>
>> Score screen
>>
>> Career Progress screen

Languages

If your game will handle different languages, this section is where you explain how you plan to accomplish it.

For example:

> The game will handle American English, British English, Spanish, French, and German. We will make and use a language database tool that will build a phrase dictionary file for each language. When the user chooses a language, the appropriate language file will be loaded. Internally, a unique number will refer to each phrase. Any time text is to be displayed, the desired phrase number will be used to "fetch" the correct phrase from the dictionary.

Audio Handling

This is where you explain how the sounds will be played. Most likely, sound effects will be preloaded and played instantly. Other sounds, such as music and speech, may need to be streamed. Because of the way streaming works, there will be a delay between the time a sound is queued to play and the actual playing of the sound. If the delay may cause problems, you will need to describe what techniques you will use to reduce the effect of the delay.

For example:

> The So-And-So Engine handles sound files. The engine can handle preloaded sounds as well as streaming sounds. All of the sound effects will be preloaded and played as needed. The background music and the announcer speech files will be streamed. We don't anticipate that the slight delay for playing the announcer speech will be a problem.

Physics

If your game has physics—and a motocross game definitely has physics—then you describe in this section how your physics will work. Will you use an existing physics engine or will you write your own? If you will use a prewritten physics engine, tell which one. If you will be writing your own, explain what techniques you will be using. How realistic will the physics be? Remember that, in most cases, totally real physics makes the game too hard to play. If you don't know the answer to this question, say so and write a blurb about how you plan to start and then adjust the physics. If the person doing the programming knows the plan, he can write the code in such a way as to make adjustments relatively easy to make.

For example:

> The So-And-So Engine has collision detection, so we will use the engine for handling collisions. We will need to develop our own physics handling. We will use the basic physics equations for calculating acceleration, deceleration, velocity, momentum, and friction. Each bike type will have a certain mass. We will try to be as real as possible by initially using the equivalent to the earth's gravity. In order to allow for a little more hang time in the air to pull off tricks, we will probably need to adjust gravity to be less than the earth's. We may also need to fine-tune the friction coefficients.

Sample Art

Definitely have some sample art of how the game might look in different aspects. Include samples of what some of the menu screens might look like and what some of the actual gameplay might look like.

User-Defined Worlds

Will the user be able to build or define his own worlds? If so, describe in this section how the user interface will look and work, how the pieces will be pieced together, and how the AI will work. In the example of the *Motocross* game, the user can make his own tracks and race them. This could be one of the more difficult parts of the game to accomplish. Not only do you need to put the different track parts together seamlessly so that the bikes don't fall through seams, but you may have problems getting the AI to work.

For example:

> We plan on using Maya's hidden data to flag the vertices that will be tied together when assembling a user-defined world. The same method will be used to tie together the AI track.

Summary

Writing a TDD can be a lot of work, but will definitely be worth it in the long run. Use this chapter as a jumping off point. You may not need all the sections mentioned in this chapter and there may be other sections that you will need to add. It depends on what your game is and for what platform. Additional sections may include discussing your final product format (CD, floppy disk, DVD), copy protection, your game's handling of force feedback devices, and (if you're really shooting for the moon) your game's handling of virtual reality devices.

CHAPTER 11

SCHEDULES AND BUDGETS

What is it going to take to make the game?

Well, you're getting close to having the game design complete at this point! Now it's time to determine how long it will take to develop the game. Then you will be able to figure out how much it will cost to build it. Let there be no doubt in your mind that this can be a difficult part of the design process. If you are doing all the work by yourself and you have no time constraints, then it is less difficult. If you are working with your buddies and no one is being paid, then you won't be concerned about a budget.

Since that isn't likely to always be the case, let's assume that you are working with some of your buddies and that you want to complete the game in as short a period of time as possible. As a result, you will have to "accurately" decide how long it will take the artists to do the artwork, the technicians to put the artwork in the game, the programmers to code the game, the audio director to squeeze in the audio that he has put together, the testers to test, to fine-tune for gameplay, and so on.

So that you will understand the process more fully, let's also see how a budget for the development project can be created. If you continue to develop games, schedules and budgets will become increasingly important, so now is a good time to be introduced to both of them.

Your proposed budget will be based on your development schedule. If you are wrong on how quickly your team can develop, it will likely come out of your pocket, not the publisher's. So now is the time to develop a feel for budgeting—when it isn't really costing you anything, not later when it really will hurt to make a mistake!

In this chapter, we will discuss some important elements of the schedule and budget that you should consider as you prepare yours.

What Comes First, the Chicken or the Egg?

While this is generally considered to be a rhetorical question, it is appropriate in this situation for you to answer. Are you in the situation where you have designed the game just the way you want it and will be developing the budget to support the schedule? Or are you in the situation of having to pare down the development schedule to fit the publisher's budget? Both situations occur. Obviously, as a developer you hope for the former. But, with many publishers, the latter occurs more frequently.

At this stage, you are developing a game with no outside pressure from anyone. You are making all the decisions. If you finish the game next month, great! If you finish it next year, that's okay, too. There is no pressure on you except what you and the other people working on the game self impose. However, that will not always be the case.

With that in mind, it is very important that you, as a game designer, understand the development cycle of a game. There are a few overriding elements that tend to hurt developers and put their long-term viability at risk.

The first element is created by the developer. Many teams think they can do X in Z amount of time, when in reality they can do Y in Z amount of time. Now, if X is less than Y, then the developer is in great shape. However, for most development teams, Y is generally close to 2X. Obviously, this doesn't work economically. Consequently, there are lots of developers who are here today and gone tomorrow.

The second contributing element is caused by the publisher. Obviously, the publisher wants the most bang for his buck. Okay, that is not entirely true—the publisher wants *more than* the most bang for his buck! This is compounded by the fact that you are assigned a producer from the publisher to work with. He wishes you were given more money for the development process as well. But regardless, his job is often based on how great a game is produced. He will be pushing you to put more and more into the game to make it better and better. At some point, you have to know when to say "no more."

The third element that sometimes arises is when you have designed a $1M game, but the publisher that picks it up decides that the budget is only $500K. Obviously, the publisher, and you to a lesser degree, would love to have all the bells and whistles in the $500K game that you designed in the $1M game! Unfortunately, you decide that if you work a little harder and put in a few more hours each day then you can cram more into the smaller game. This, combined with the time element, often leads to financial disaster for the developer. Occasionally, it also leads to a strained relationship with the publisher.

tip

Now is the time to start learning how to understand the elements you will have control over. As you start working with others to complete projects, you must learn how long it takes each of them to complete their tasks. You should be comparing how long it takes you or them to complete the task with how long you or they said it would take! Are you one of those who take twice as long to complete a project as you said it would take? Or are you the type that completes it in two-thirds of the time you said it would because you always build in a buffer? It really doesn't matter what type you or the others are, as long as the person building the schedule and budget knows what types you all are.

These are a few things that you need to be aware of as you create your development schedule and budget. Sometimes the egg will come first, and other times the chicken will come first. You must be able to deal with both situations and do it in a way that keeps you and your team viable throughout the process and beyond.

In our situation, let us decide that the egg comes first. In other words, we're going to develop the programming schedule based on our design document and then create the budget to fit that schedule. For learning purposes, we are also going to assume that you are working with some buddies. The group is going to handle all the programming, art, and audio work.

Now, even though you're not working with a publisher right now, scheduling and budgeting are important issues. Master this area now while the games that you are developing are small. It will make it so much easier when you move to larger, more complex development projects.

In presenting the scheduling and budgeting materials, we will make it as simple as possible. You should be aware that work breakdown structures, Gantt charts, critical path analysis, and the program evaluation and review technique are all important aspects of scheduling that you should become familiar with as your development projects increase in complexity. For the purposes of this book, we are going to assume that you know little, if anything, about scheduling and budgeting. With that in mind, let's get started.

Breaking Down the Tasks

Now is the time to break down each element that will lead you to the completion of the developed game. The overall list should include each major element that is needed in developing the game. The following is a simple list of broad areas that generally are contained in a development schedule.

- Design
  - Refinement of game design
  - Technical design document
- Programming
  - Graphics engine
  - Sound engine
  - Music engine
  - Input engine
  - Physics
- Art
  - 2D artwork
  - 3D artwork
- Audio
  - Music recording
  - Voice recording
  - Sound effects
- Video
- Testing and game-tuning

Your schedule may include some of the items listed and others that are not. With the list of activities that are needed to complete your game, you now have a framework that you can flesh out into a full game development schedule.

From this list, you then will break each element down into manageable tasks or activities. Each task or activity should be able to be accomplished in a week or less, with one day as the smallest unit of measurement. Rarely should the activity take more than two weeks. If the activity takes more than a week or two, then it should be broken down further into tasks that can be measured and accomplished in a smaller amount of time. For example, if the activity is to create eight motorcycles for the *Motocross* game in four weeks, then this activity should be broken down into smaller tasks. For example, it can be broken down into two motorcycles per week or one motorcycle every two and one-half days. By doing this, you are creating a schedule that can be monitored and managed more effectively. In your weekly progress meetings, you can review actual progress and see more clearly where the development cycle actually is. If you have eight weeks to complete an activity, it is more difficult to track the progress than when you have to have two motorcycles completed each week.

Staying on track with the schedule is itself a difficult task. Everything you can do to help monitor the process is a bonus to you and, someday, will be to the publisher as well. It is difficult to be honest with yourself and the team when having to acknowledge that you are slipping behind. But it is much better for everyone involved if such honesty occurs when you are early in the development process than when you arrive at the point when the game should have been complete, only to have to tell the publisher that the completion date has slipped three months. Learn to handle this situation now when you are working by yourself or your buddies so that when you encounter it with a publisher you will know how to handle it.

At the same time you are breaking down each element into a manageable task, you should also be identifying dependencies. A dependency exists when a task cannot be started or completed without another task being completed first. For example, programming cannot put the sound into the game until the audio engineer has completed it. The art technician cannot put a piece of art into the game until the artist has completed it. It is crucial to recognize and understand these dependencies start here.

Creating the Framework of Dependencies

With the elements of the development cycle broken down into small manageable tasks, you can now lay them out in a manner that shows their dependencies.

For example, let's take the following broad list and work with it. To keep things a bit more simple, assign a letter to each task and include the estimated time that you determined you will need to complete that task. The times you estimate are certainly going to be different from those that are listed:

A—Refinement of game design, 5 days

B—Technical design document, 10 days

C—Graphics engine, 10 days

D—Music engine, 5 days

E—Sound engine, 5 days

F—User interface engine, 10 days

G—General programming and gameplay, 15 days

H—Physics, 10 days

I—2D artwork, 15 days

J—3D artwork, 20 days

K—Music recording, 5 days

L—Voice recording, 5 days

M—Sound effects, 5 days

N—Video, 10 days

O—Level design, 10 days

Now with the tasks laid out, let's identify any dependencies that exist. In other words, let's identify what task or tasks must be completed before you can complete each task. For example, this is how I would indicate the dependencies for the list:

A—depends on (none)

B—depends on A

C—depends on B

D—depends on K

E—depends on L, M

F—depends on C

G—depends on C, D, E

H—depends on G

I—depends on A

J—depends on I

K—depends on A

L—depends on A

M—depends on A

N—depends on A

O—depends on H

With the dependencies identified, you can begin to see what has to occur for the project to be completed. Notice that each one hinges upon the design document being completed.

Next let's put this information into a form that will be more useful. We will use a Gantt chart, which is discussed in the following section.

Gantt Charts

A Gantt chart is a visual tool that will help you in planning your game development. The Gantt chart was developed by Henry L. Gantt, an American engineer and social scientist. The Gantt chart is a graphical illustration of the schedule that is very helpful in planning and tracking the specific tasks in the project.

You can create a simple chart using graph paper, or you can use a variety of software products to create a Gantt chart. Initially, it will probably be easier if you just use a spreadsheet or the Table feature of your word processor. You can add rows and columns as necessary, and it's easy to manipulate the data. As your projects become more sophisticated and complex, you will probably want to start using Microsoft Project or a similar project management program.

Let's start by building the chart in the following manner. Across the top, we will put the weeks needed to develop the game. At first, we aren't going to actually know how many are needed, but start at the left and begin numbering toward the right. We will assume that each week contains five workdays. Down the left side of the chart we will list the listed tasks (A–O).

Starting with task A, mark off how long it will take to complete the task. It is estimated that task A, refining the design document, will take 5 days, or one workweek. So week 1 is blocked off to show when task A begins and when it will be completed. For task B, we noted that it could not be started until task A was complete. As a result, we can't start it until week 2. Since it will take two weeks, or 10 workdays, to complete it, both weeks 2 and 3 are blocked off. Continue to block off the time to complete each task, making sure that you don't start a task until the task upon which it is dependent has been completed. When the chart has been completed, it will look similar to Figure 11.1.

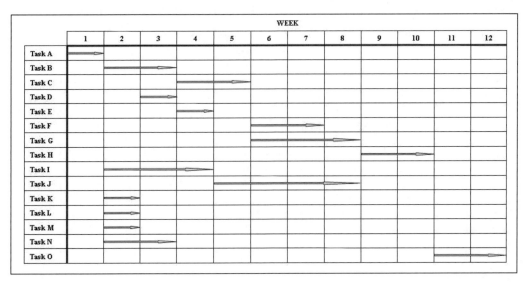

Figure 11.1
A sample Gantt chart

There are at least two important things to pick up from looking at the chart. The first is what is called the *critical path*, the shortest path to completion of the game. The second is how to place the tasks in such a manner as to allow the work to be completed in the shortest amount of time using the smallest number of assets.

Critical Path

Again, for our purposes we will define the critical path as the shortest path of tasks to complete the game. As you know from the list of dependencies, some tasks of the game's development are dependent on other tasks being completed first. You can see those dependencies as you look at the Gantt chart. Understanding these dependencies will allow you to develop the game in the shortest amount of time. This means that not only does the game get finished more quickly, but it also means that it will likely cost less to develop.

Here is what is meant by the shortest path. Notice that several of the tasks on the Gantt chart are overlapping. For example, while the programmers are working on the user interface engine, other programmers are working on general programming and gameplay. Another way of completing the work would be to complete the user interface engine first and then complete the general programming and gameplay. Obviously, the latter method is not very efficient and would increase the time needed to complete the game. It is also obvious that you cannot go to the opposite extreme and complete all tasks simultaneously because some tasks are dependent on others. We want to find the shortest path and then follow it during the development process. By adding up the periods of time associated with each task in the critical path, we will also know how long it will take to complete the game.

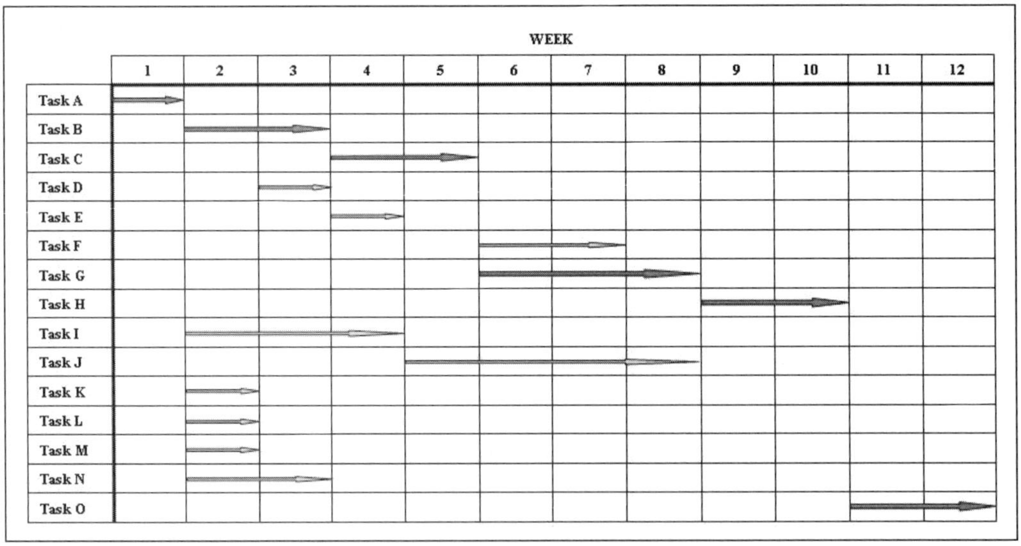

Figure 11.2
Critical path highlighted by red arrows

Figure 11.2 shows the critical path for this project indicated by the red arrows. Regardless of how the game tasks are scheduled, the game cannot be completed in less than 12 weeks.

You must understand that if any task in the critical path takes longer than what has been allotted, it pushes the game's completion off by an equal amount. For example, if task G, general programming and gameplay, ends up taking 20 days instead of 15 days to complete, then the completion date of the game has been automatically extended an additional 5 days. This is because task H, physics, cannot be started until task G is complete. Task O, level design, cannot begin until the physics has been finished.

Scheduling

Now let's build a development schedule for the project. With the tasks identified, dependencies identified, and each task assigned an estimated development time, we can now complete the schedule. The critical path becomes the foundation of the game's development schedule. Remember that the tasks along the critical path are dependent upon each other and must be developed consecutively. As a result, the fastest way to complete the game is to complete each task in the critical path in the shortest amount of time.

When the critical path is laid out in sequential order, you end up with something similar to what is seen in Figure 11.3.

WEEK											
1	2	3	4	5	6	7	8	9	10	11	12
Task A	Task B		Task C		Task G				Task H		Task O

Figure 11.3
Scheduling the critical path

At a glance, you can see during which week a task should be started and finished. This is a valuable tool during the scheduling process. Now the job at hand is to lay out the remaining tasks. However, you can quickly see at least one of the issues involved with this task by looking at the bolded tasks in Figure 11.4.

Task	1	2	3	4	5	6	7	8	9	10	11	12
Task A	■→											
Task B		→→→										
Task C				→→→								
Task D			→→									
Task E				→→								
Task F						→→→						
Task G						→→→						
Task H									→→→			
Task I		→→→→→										
Task J					→→→→							
Task K		■→										
Task L		■→										
Task M		■→										
Task N		→→→										
Task O											→→	

Figure 11.4
Overlapping tasks

Notice that tasks K, L, and M are all overlapping. This means that the projects can be worked on and completed simultaneously. The problem with this is that all three are audio related, and if you have only one audio engineer, it's not going to happen simultaneously! If possible, we want to complete K, L, M, and N consecutively. The same applies to all the different areas. We know that we can't complete the project in less than 12 weeks, so the key is to schedule all the remaining tasks in such a manner that you do not increase the project's development time but in such a way as to keep the assets required to develop the project to the fewest possible. With that in mind, let's look at Figure 11.5 to see how we have filled in the remaining schedule.

1	2	3	4	5	6	7	8	9	10	11	12
Task A	Task B		Task C		Task G			Task H		Task O	
	Task L	Task M	Task K	Task D	Task E	Task F		Task N			
	Task I				Task J						

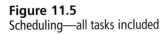

Figure 11.5
Scheduling—all tasks included

Let's look first at the audio/video related tasks. Remember, it was earlier noted that we don't want to complete K, L, M, and N simultaneously; rather we hope to do them consecutively. Notice, however, that the tasks are being completed with K first, L second, M third, and N as the last task. Why? This sequence of completion shows you how important it is to understand dependencies.

If you refer to the dependencies listed above, you see that K, L, and M are dependent only on A. That means that any or all of the three can be started as soon as the design document is complete. However, it you look further, D is dependent on K, and E is dependent on L and M. This means, of course, that D cannot be started until K is complete, and E cannot be started until both L and M are completed. Note that neither D nor E is part of the critical path. However, it is very important to note that G, which is part of the critical path, is dependent on both D and E! Notice that N, the video for the game, is dependent on A, but nothing is dependent on it.

Can you begin to see what can happen when you start putting the schedule together? Remember that when we determined the critical path using the Gantt chart, we simply laid out the tasks to be completed *as early as the tasks could be.* Having done that, we could then determine the critical path or those tasks that had to be scheduled consecutively to complete the game in the shortest amount of time. With that accomplished, we went about laying out the tasks on the schedule to develop the game using the fewest resources or people possible. You must be extremely careful at this point to make sure that you don't accidentally extend the development time of the game.

For example, look at Figure 11.6 to see what would have happened if we had decided to complete N before finishing any of the other three audio/video tasks.

WEEK											
1	2	3	4	5	6	7	8	9	10	11	12
Task A	Task B		Task C		Task G			Task H		Task O	
	Task K		Task N		Task D	Task F	Task L	Task M	Task E		
	Task I			Task J							

Figure 11.6
Scheduling errors

If we had inadvertently put together a schedule like this, at the beginning of week 7 we would have wanted to go jump in the lake! One important dependency has been overlooked in the above schedule. Task G cannot begin until E is complete. Consequently, Figure 11.6 is not a valid schedule. Rather, it should look like Figure 11.7.

WEEK															
1	2	3	4	5	6	7	8	9	10	11	12	13	14	15	16
Task A	Task B		Task C								Task G		Task H		Task O
	Task K		Task N		Task D	Task F	Task L	Task M	Task E						
	Task I				Task J										

Figure 11.7
Scheduling a development extension

Since E is not scheduled to be completed until the end of week 9, G cannot begin until week 10, and the game's earliest completion date has been pushed off until the end of week 16 instead of week 12. Obviously, such an error in scheduling would probably have a catastrophic effect on the financial viability of the company and could easily result in the game not being completed.

It is very important that, after you have determined the critical path of the game, you don't mess it up when you start filling in the blanks of the development schedule! With that in mind, let's take a look at Figure 11.8 to see the schedule with a little color added to it.

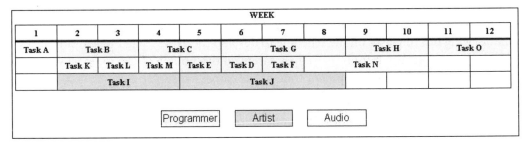

Figure 11.8
Scheduling tasks by workgroup

In Figure 11.8 we have added color to the tasks to indicate which workgroup will be responsible for completing each task. If each task were to be completed by one person, we could easily determine the manpower requirements for the project. Since I and J will be completed consecutively, it will take one artist seven weeks to complete the required work. According to the schedule, only one audio engineer will be needed for the development project. However, with the schedule laid out in color, we can see that there is a three-week gap between the audio engineer's third and fourth tasks. Unless there is a special reason for this, it would be better to schedule N to begin during the fifth week rather than the eighth week. We'll correct that. Finally, when looking at the programming tasks, we see that we will not be able to complete the game with only one programmer unless we're willing to push the development time of the game out an additional three weeks. If we are to complete the game in the shortest amount of time, then we will need two programmers during weeks 5–8. With that in mind, Figure 11.9 will be the project schedule used to complete the game.

WEEK											
1	2	3	4	5	6	7	8	9	10	11	12
Task A	Task B		Task C		Task G			Task H		Task O	
	Task K	Task L	Task M	Task E	Task D	Task F					
	Task I			Task J							
				Task N							
			Programmer	Artist		Audio					

Figure 11.9
The final schedule

You may be asking yourself if you really need to go through all this for the game you are designing. The answer is "Yes, you should!" While you might easily get around it for the size of the project you are developing, this is the time to learn how to do it right. You can easily see how complex it can be and will become as your development projects become more and more sophisticated.

Budgeting

Now that we have the development schedule, let's figure out the budget for the game. Again, for the purposes of this project, we're going to keep this pretty simple. But with what you learn here, you will understand how to handle the budget as your projects grow in complexity.

Direct Labor Costs

The first step we're going to tackle is determining the direct labor costs involved in creating the game. We'll define direct labor costs simply as the amount of money you're going to have to pay to the people who are developing the game. For our purposes here, we will continue to use the project that we used in scheduling.

All this can be done by hand, but you will find it significantly easier if you develop and use a spreadsheet. Additionally, you can make quick changes and see how it affects the entire budget.

Figure 11.10 is a sample spreadsheet created for our project. Let's walk through the spreadsheet so that you understand how and why it has been laid out this way. Of course, there are countless ways to do this, so feel free to change it in any way that you desire.

Again, this is a very simple spreadsheet, and you can make it as sophisticated and complex as you want. On the other hand, a simple spreadsheet like this is very useful and is generally sufficient for even large development projects. Also, please realize that all the figures in this spreadsheet are fictitious.

Sample Game Project Spreadsheet

	Days	Hours	Direct Labor	Equip-ment	Fixed Costs	Total Costs	With Profit
Programming	70	560	$ 5,600.00	$ 1,875.00	$ 5,600.00	$ 13,075.00	$ 16,343.75
Art	35	280	2,240.00	-	2,240.00	4,480.00	5,600.00
Audio/Video	30	240	2,160.00	-	2,160.00	4,320.00	5,400.00
Design	5	40	480.00	-	480.00	960.00	1,200.00
Testing	10	80	600.00	1,500.00	600.00	2,700.00	3,375.00
Totals	**150**	**1,200**	**$ 11,080.00**	**$ 3,375.00**	**$ 11,080.00**	**$ 25,535.00**	**$ 31,918.75**

	Hourly Wage	# Needing Equipment	Average Cost of Equipment w/ Software	
Programmers	$ 10.00	1	$ 1,875.00	
Artists	8.00		3,000.00	
Audio/Video	9.00		2,000.00	
Designer	12.00		1,000.00	
Testers	7.50	1	1,500.00	
Fixed Cost %	100%			
Desired Profit %	25%			

Figure 11.10
A sample spreadsheet

Let's concentrate for a few minutes on the top half of the spreadsheet, as shown in Figure 11.11.

Sample Game Project Spreadsheet

	Days	Hours	Direct Labor	Equip-ment	Fixed Costs	Total Costs	With Profit
Programming	70	560	$ 5,600.00	$ 1,875.00	$ 5,600.00	$ 13,075.00	$ 16,343.75
Art	35	280	2,240.00	-	2,240.00	4,480.00	5,600.00
Audio/Video	30	240	2,160.00	-	2,160.00	4,320.00	5,400.00
Design	5	40	480.00	-	480.00	960.00	1,200.00
Testing	10	80	600.00	1,500.00	600.00	2,700.00	3,375.00
Totals	**150**	**1,200**	**$ 11,080.00**	**$ 3,375.00**	**$ 11,080.00**	**$ 25,535.00**	**$ 31,918.75**

Figure 11.11
Cost centers

In the first column of the spreadsheet, each of the cost centers has been listed. These are the groups that are going to cost money to develop the game. Note that testing has been added to the group. It was left out of the schedule for simplicity's sake, but it definitely costs money to test the game, and we'll include it in these figures.

Along the top of the spreadsheet are several different areas. The first area is Days, meaning the number of days for this cost center to complete the work scheduled. This will be discussed in more detail later.

The next column is Hours. This is a simple computation changing the number of days to the number of hours. For example, design is suppose to take 5 days to complete. This means that if you work 5 days with 8 hours in each workday, you will have worked 40 hours.

The next column is Direct Labor. Again, this is a computation in which the number of hours worked is multiplied by the hourly amount you are paying this group. For example, if you are paying the programmers $10.00 per hour (I wish!), then the computation is 560 hours $\times$ $10 = $5,600.00 Additionally, if you're covered by your parents' health insurance now, you don't have to include it in the Direct Labor, also known as payroll related expenses, but the time will come when you'll need to include it and several other items in this area. For our example, we have limited Direct Labor to hourly wages.

In the next column, the one-time equipment costs that you might have are computed. This will be explained in greater detail later, so don't worry about it now. Just understand that with many projects, there will be additional equipment—hardware, software, audio and video equipment—that must be purchased to complete the project. You need to account for that in your budget. This is where that occurs.

Fixed Costs, the next column, is where you account for the overhead involved. If you're developing the game in the basement of your parents' home, then your overhead will probably be minimal, but over time it will increase. Included in the overhead are rent or lease, utilities, office supplies, maintenance and repairs, telephone, postage and mailing costs, and so forth that are necessary for you to run the business.

The Total Costs column simply adds all the preceding sums together.

The final column is With Profit. This is only necessary if you are a "for profit" type of person. This is where you build in your desired profit margin. You will see how to make adjustments in the column a little later in this chapter.

However, this is probably a good time to discuss profit. In the spreadsheet, you can subtract Total Costs from With Profit and determine that there is $6,383.75 built in for profit. You must understand that this doesn't mean that you *will* have that much in profit at the end of the project. It only means that if you complete the game exactly the way you have scheduled and budgeted for it, you will end up with that much profit. On the other hand, if it takes longer to develop than what you have budgeted, the profit will evaporate.

Now, the opposite is also true. If you are fortunate enough to complete the project ahead of schedule and budget, the profit for the project will be more than you anticipated. Keep in mind that the former situation is more often the case than the latter!

Do you begin to see now how important it is to be as accurate as you can be in building the schedule? You must be as brutally honest with each other as you can. Now is not the time to think you can do something in 15 days when you know deep down that it will take you 25 days.

Obviously, when building a schedule and budget it is better to err on the conservative side. Don't cut yourself short.

I want to say one last thing on this subject. As you can see, if you are off a little on your schedule and it ends up taking a little more time to develop the game than you budgeted, you can take that out of the profit and still make all your payments. That is nice. But, as a company, you can't afford to do that for very long or on too many projects or you will still end up out of business. Companies need to profit to grow and develop. If you keep spending the profit to complete the game, then you need to adjust your schedule and budget to make sure it doesn't happen in the future.

Easy Adjustments

Now let's look at the bottom half of the spreadsheet as shown in Figure 11.12. This is technique and is provided simply to show how you can make easy adjustments to your spreadsheet.

	Hourly Wage	# Needing Equipment	Average Cost of Equipment w/ Software	
Programmers	$ 10.00	1	$ 1,875.00	
Artists	8.00		3,000.00	
Audio/Video	9.00		2,000.00	
Designer	12.00		1,000.00	
Testers	7.50	1	1,500.00	
Fixed Cost %	100%			
Desired Profit %	25%			

Figure 11.12
Spreadsheet techniques

In Figure 11.12, the spreadsheet cells highlighted in yellow are those that are most easily used to make adjustments to the budget. Because of the manner in which the spreadsheet is created, it is easy to do "what if" checks and make changes as conditions change.

Under the Hourly Wage column, you indicate what you are paying each category. If you have only one person in a category, it's easy. If you have more than one, you need to average the pay. For example, if you have only one programmer, then the $10.00 indicates that is what you are paying the programmer as an hourly wage. On the other hand, if you have two programmers, and you are paying one $12.00 and the other only $8.00, you would average the two wages together and arrive at $10.00. Obviously, this would assume that both programmers work about the same number of hours a day. If you have programmers making different hourly amounts and one or more are part-time, then you will need to weight the average to accurately indicate the average hourly wage. Of course, you would build these calculations into your spreadsheet as your needs increase.

The # Needing Equipment column is where you indicate how many persons need equipment, such as a new computer with associated software. Then you indicate how much such a system costs in the next column, Average Cost of Equipment with Software. Of course, when you put in these figures, remember to add all the incidentals, such as a mouse, a specialized keyboard, monitors, software, and so on.

Finally, the last two cells in which you can make changes are the Fixed Cost % and Desired Profit %. As described previously, you will have to determine the fixed costs of your business. In this example, it was determined that the fixed costs equal the direct labor costs. With the desired profit margin, you have to decide what you want and how much the market will bear. In this example, a 25% profit margin is used.

Putting the Budget Together

With all this in mind, let's look at Figure 11.13 to see how to use the spreadsheet in developing the budget. Once you have determined your schedule and know what resources will be needed, including people and equipment, it's time to put that information into the spreadsheet.

Sample Game Project Spreadsheet

	Days	Hours	Direct Labor	Equip-ment	Fixed Costs	Total Costs	With Profit
Programming	70	560	$ 5,600.00	$ 1,875.00	$ 5,600.00	$ 13,075.00	$ 16,343.75
Art	35	280	2,240.00	-	2,240.00	4,480.00	5,600.00
Audio/Video	30	240	2,160.00	-	2,160.00	4,320.00	5,400.00
Design	5	40	480.00	-	480.00	960.00	1,200.00
Testing	10	80	600.00	1,500.00	600.00	2,700.00	3,375.00
Totals	150	1,200	$ 11,080.00	$ 3,375.00	$ 11,080.00	$ 25,535.00	$ 31,918.75
	Hourly Wage	# Needing Equipment		Average Cost of Equipment w/ Software			
Programmers	$ 10.00	1		$ 1,875.00			
Artists	8.00			3,000.00			
Audio/Video	9.00			2,000.00			
Designer	12.00			1,000.00			
Testers	7.50	1		1,500.00			
Fixed Cost %	100%						
Desired Profit %	25%						

Figure 11.13
The final spreadsheet

The yellow cells indicate the areas in which you should put in data. The other cells with numbers are where the information is displayed that will be useful to you. The first thing to do after creating the spreadsheet is to determine what goes in the bottom half of the spreadsheet that generally won't change too much from project to project, such as hourly wages, average cost of equipment with software, fixed cost percentage, and desired profit %. Then determine what equipment will be required for this project and add it to the corresponding cells in the Equipment column.

With that done, it's time to add the final numbers to the top half of the spreadsheet and see what it will cost to develop the game. Let's take the schedule used earlier in the chapter which is laid out by the cost center that will accomplish each task (see Figure 11.14).

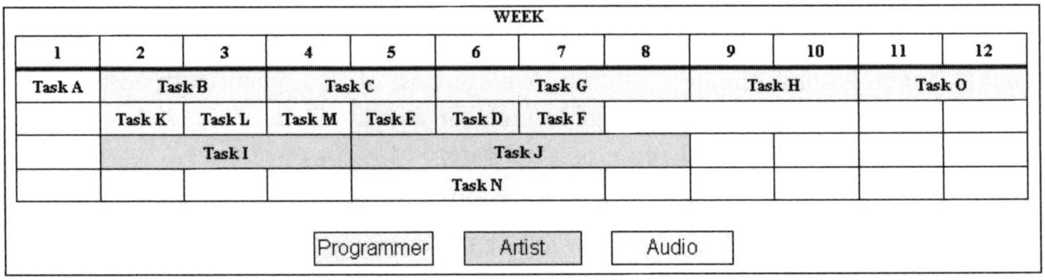

						WEEK						
1	2	3	4	5	6	7	8	9	10	11	12	
Task A	Task B		Task C		Task G			Task H		Task O		
	Task K	Task L	Task M	Task E	Task D	Task F						
	Task I				Task J							
				Task N								

Programmer   Artist   Audio

Figure 11.14
Scheduling by cost center

Start by adding up the weeks needed by each group to complete all the tasks for that group and put that number in the corresponding cell of the spreadsheet. For example, it will take the artist seven weeks to complete tasks I and J. With five workdays to the week, it will take 35 days for the artist to complete the artwork ($7 \times 5 = 35$). Then you put 35 into the correct cell.

If you have correctly put the formulas in the spreadsheet, the answers in the other columns will be automatically computed. For example, look at Figure 11.15, the Programming line of the spreadsheet.

	Days	Hours	Direct Labor	Equip-ment	Fixed Costs	Total Costs	With Profit
Programming	70	560	$ 5,600.00	$ 1,875.00	$ 5,600.00	$ 13,075.00	$ 16,343.75

Figure 11.15
Programming figures

It was determined in the schedule that the programmers would need 70 days to complete their tasks. Seventy days equates to 560 hours, and at an hourly wage of $10 per hour, the direct labor costs will be $5,600.00. As indicated in the lower half of the spreadsheet, one programmer needs equipment at a cost of $1,875.00, and the fixed costs will be $5,600.00 for the programmers. When the labor, equipment, and fixed costs for the programmers are added together, we arrive at a total cost of $13,075.00. When the 25 percent profit margin is added, we now know that our budget for programming is $16,343.75.

Figure 11.16 shows the Totals row and the final summations of these numbers when this is done for each cost center that we have designated.

	Days	Hours	Direct Labor	Equip-ment	Fixed Costs	Total Costs	With Profit
Totals	150	1,200	$ 11,080.00	$ 3,375.00	$ 11,080.00	$ 25,535.00	$ 31,918.75

Figure 11.16
Budget totals

You can see that the cost of labor will be $11,080.00 for this project. Additionally, $3,375.00 will be spent on equipment, and $11,080.00 will be needed for fixed costs. With a 25 percent profit margin added, you will need $31,918.75 to develop this game, based on the schedule that has been put together. If you're a teenager reading this chapter, the figures that were used may have scared you! Hopefully, you won't let them bother you. While it is important that you understand scheduling and budgeting, there are things, in the beginning, you won't be concerned about and ways to work around other things. For example, if you and your buddies are building the game together, you probably are not paying yourselves or thinking about profit. Additionally, as a student you may be able to purchase software and hardware at a student's discount which will reduce your costs significantly.

Summary

Following the critical path will result in completing the game in the shortest amount of time. Carefully scheduling the remaining tasks will help you complete the game with the fewest resources. Of course, extreme care must be taken to allot sufficient time to each task.

The actual budgeting is greatly simplified by using a spreadsheet. The positive correlation between scheduling and budgeting requires that you be as accurate as possible when scheduling, or you will not know how much it will cost to develop the game.

Most people would agree that the scheduling and budgeting part of game development is the least exciting aspect—especially when you're working by yourself or with some of your friends. On the other hand, you can see how important both items are and how complex they can become as a project's sophistication grows. As your game designing develops into a business, scheduling and budgeting will take on a whole new meaning of importance. Learning and mastering these two tasks is part of being a good designer.

CHAPTER 12

SPECIAL CONSIDERATIONS

Game designs differ widely, depending on the type of game. This chapter will take a look at several different types of games and the important design elements needed for each one.

By now you should have a good understanding of game design documents and many of the elements that go into making a great game design. Now it is time to take a closer look at different types of games and how the type affects the design document. We can't cover every genre because there are just too many, and new ones are being conceived every day. Your game might not fit into any genre, but by looking at a variety of different types here, you should gain an understanding of how to adapt your document. We will cover the following game types in this chapter :

- Puzzle
- Platform
- Adventure
- Racing
- Fighting
- Sports
- Real-time strategy
- Turn-based strategy
- Shooters
- Simulations
- Role playing
- Massive multiplayer online

Each genre has elements that are unique and important for that genre. For example, a fighting game will focus very heavily on character animation, while a racing game may have little or no character animation. A good game designer will recognize the unique and important elements for the genre and move those to the front of the document so that the reader will see the critical information right away.

Puzzle

A puzzle is an activity designed to test the player's ingenuity. You are probably familiar with physical puzzles such as jigsaw puzzles or Rubik's cubes. You may have played word puzzle games such as word search or crossword puzzles. In computer games, a puzzle game is one that focuses on problem solving. You might say that all games have problem solving, and that is true. Puzzle games are more focused on pure problem solving and are not as likely to have stories, characters, or plots.

When you are designing a puzzle game, the puzzle is the important aspect of the game. The first question a reader will ask when looking at a puzzle game design, as seen in Figure 12.1, is "What is the puzzle and why is it fun to solve the puzzle?" The design document should have a clear and compelling example early in the document of what the puzzle is and how it is played.

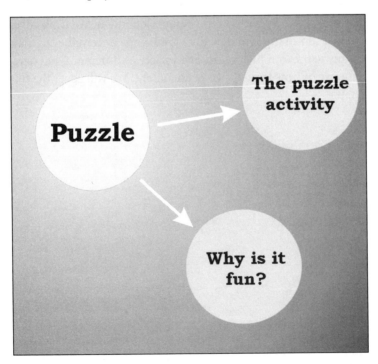

Figure 12.1
The most important issues in puzzle games are the puzzle activity and why it is fun.

As with any design document, the sooner the designer can get the reader to imagine playing the game, the better the document will be received. Pictures are a great way to present a puzzle game to the reader in a game design document. Showing pictures of the game early in the document will help to communicate the idea of the game to the reader. Figure 12.2 shows a screen shot from a picture puzzle game. The object of the game is to remove blocks to identify the picture beneath.

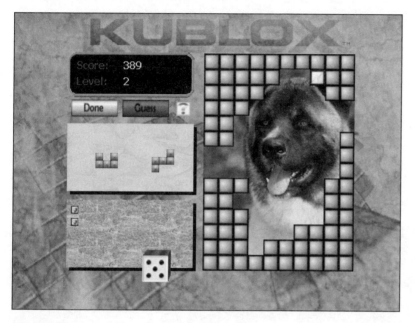

Figure 12.2
Use picture examples to show how a game is played.

The picture shows clearly what the game looks like. The picture can then be used to explain the gameplay. In this case the player rolls the dice to get potential game pieces that can be removed from the puzzle board to the right. Without the picture the concept would be more difficult to explain. With the picture it becomes much easier.

Not all puzzles are visual in nature. The puzzle may be in the sound rather than the pictures. For example, maybe the puzzle is in a song or a series of musical notes. Maybe the puzzle is in an audio question or riddle posed to the player. In these cases, a picture may not be very effective in communicating the concept of the puzzle to the reader. A written description may work better. If the document is electronic, sound files can be attached to the document to show how the puzzle will work.

Some games have multiple puzzles instead of just one. When dealing with multiple puzzles, the design document should show clearly a list of the puzzles in the front of the document and later define each puzzle for the reader. If the game is tied together so that each puzzle is part of a specific sequence of events or all have a specific theme, those ideas should be brought out early so that the reader understands them prior to reading about the individual puzzles.

Sometimes puzzle games are subsets of other games. The game may be an adventure game where access to certain areas is dependent on solving a puzzle of some kind. In these games, the puzzle aspect of the game takes a back seat to the overall game. The puzzle elements should be well defined and in separate sections so that the reader has easy access to them. A good example of using puzzles in an action game is the *Zelda* games.

The key to communication in a design document for a puzzle game is to give the reader a good understanding of what the puzzle is and how it is fun.

Platform

Platform games are one of the oldest genres in the industry. A platform game is a character-based game in which the player controls a character through what is basically an obstacle course. They derive their name from the old practice of placing characters on platforms within a world, as shown in Figure 12.3.

Figure 12.3
Platform games get their name from the old practice of placing characters on platforms.

A platform game is a skill-based navigation game. The navigation of the world is central to the platform game; therefore, level design is a critical factor. The other aspect of the game that is very important is the attributes of the character, as shown in Figure 12.4.

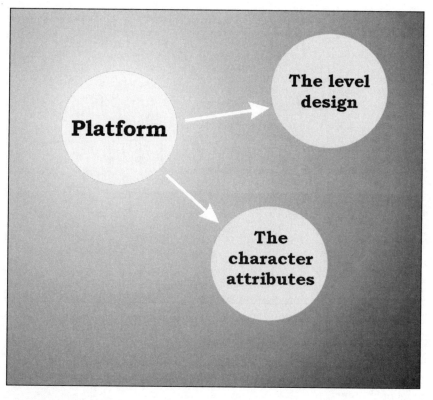

Figure 12.4
Level design and character attributes are the two most important issues in
platform games.

There are, of course, many other issues that you will have to deal with in creating a platform game design, but these two issues are central to the game and should be given a position of prominence in the design document. The best way to handle each is to combine
good descriptive text with some level layouts and attribute charts. Figure 12.5 shows a
sample level layout of a platform game. The dotted line indicates the path of the character to navigate this part of the level.

Figure 12.5
The level layout is a good way to communicate the level design.

Not all platform games are pure platformers. Some have elements of puzzle games, and some have elements of shooters.

In the early days of games, platform games were all side-view games. Now the platform game has gone to 3D, like many other games. Regardless of whether the game is 2D or 3D, the principle of controlling a character through an environment still applies.

Adventure

An adventure game is a story-based game. The player plays the part of a character as a story unfolds. The way the story unfolds is partly up to the player and partly up to the events of the game. Of all game types, adventure games have more to do with storytelling than any other type does. The story is at the heart of the adventure game. Other important aspects of an adventure game are the characters and the game progression, as shown in Figure 12.6.

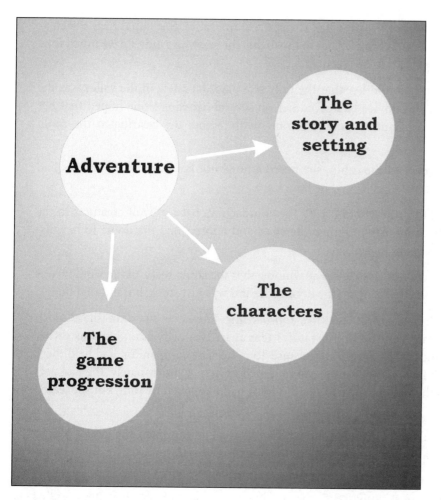

Figure 12.6
Story and setting, characters, and game progression are important to adventure games.

In an adventure game, the player lives a story. A good adventure game will immerse the player in the plot of the story to the point that the player becomes emotionally involved in the outcome. When designing an adventure game, you should include enough of the story to get the reader's attention early in the document. The full story of the game will most likely be lengthy, so place only a synopsis at the beginning of the document.

A good way to get the reader involved in an adventure game is to describe a particularly interesting sequence in the game as a game walkthrough. A game walkthrough is a one- or two-page description of events as if someone were actually playing the game. The following is an example of a game walkthrough.

Jennifer was out of breath when she reached the cabin. She could hear the creatures out there searching for her in the night. She knew she didn't have much time before they picked up her scent.

The old man had told her that the only safe place he knew in the valley was the cabin. So far his advice had saved her on several occasions. She hoped that her luck would continue to hold. She ran swiftly across the clearing to the cabin porch.

As she approached the cabin, she heard a howl not far away. The creatures had found her scent. They would be here soon.

Not willing to make a sound with the approaching pack of wolf creatures in the woods, she cautiously mounted the steps and approached the door. To her dismay, the door was locked.

There was only one door and one window that she could see, and the window was barred. She tried pulling on the door to see if it was just stuck, but it didn't budge.

She could hear the wolf creatures approaching. She knew she didn't have much time. She had seen the wolf creatures tear apart two of her companions earlier that day. She had escaped only because Tom, her last companion, had held them at bay with his knife while she ran in search of help. Unfortunately, she had gotten lost in the woods. She had no idea what had happened to Tom, but she feared the worst.

She heard a faint noise. It sounded like it was coming from the cabin. Maybe someone was inside and had locked the door. Should she knock? She didn't know.

She heard a rustling at the edge of the clearing. The wolf creatures had ringed the cabin and were starting to approach. They moved cautiously, their hatred-filled eyes darting from side to side as if afraid of the place.

She had no choice now. It was either get in the cabin or die, the victim of these demons in wolf form. Panic-stricken, she pounded on the door and called to whomever was inside for help.

She didn't hear anything from inside the cabin. The wolf creatures were becoming bolder; they were just a few yards away. She screamed at the door and pulled at it with all her strength.

Then she heard footsteps from within. A latch clicked, and the door opened. She fell inside and the door closed. It was dark inside. She couldn't see anything except dark silhouettes of shapes that could be anything.

The footsteps retreated and she heard a match strike and saw someone light a lamp. It was the old man she had talked to at the service station. He had been the one who had warned her about the valley and told her about the cabin. Relief and confusion flooded her mind as she climbed back to her feet. He was smiling?

"The beasts shan't have you tonight," he said as he set the lamp on the table, giving light to the small interior of the cabin. "They fear the cabin."

The old man walked across the room to the table. "We are so pleased that you could join us," he said.

She noticed that there were three other figures sitting motionless at the table. Ice filled her veins as she realized who they were. There sat Tom, Susan, and Paul— or rather, what was left of them after the wolf creatures had torn and ripped them. They were obviously dead, yet they sat there as if animated by some evil power.

"I warned you about this valley," the old man said as he sat at the table. He looked different now somehow. Instead of the kind, benevolent old man, there was a look of triumphant evil on his face.

"Won't you have a seat?" he said, pointing to an empty chair by the table. "It has been a long time since we had a living guest."

This tells only a small part of the game story, but it gives the reader enough information to get a feel for the type of adventure the game will hold. The game obviously is a horror adventure game. Placing text like this at the beginning of the design document will help the reader understand the game and get involved in the story.

The other major aspects that are important to adventure games are characters and game progression. The design document should emphasize good character design with well-written descriptions and illustrations of each of the main characters in the game. In addition, the design should contain a chart that shows how the character progresses through the game. All of these items should be placed prominently in the document so that the reader can find them easily.

Racing

Racing games are performance games that have as their main theme competitive course navigation against opponents. They are fast paced, and the difference between winning and losing is sometimes a fraction of a second. The key ingredients of a racing game are the vehicles, the courses, and the control, as shown in Figure 12.7.

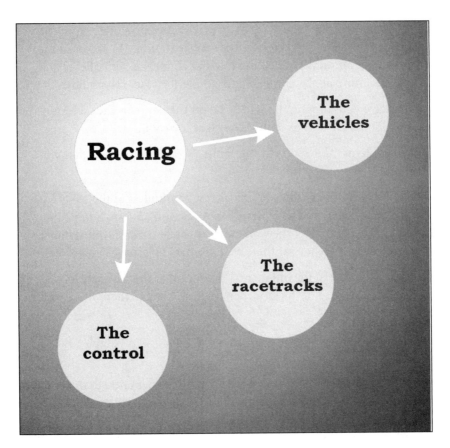

Figure 12.7
The key ingredients of a racing game are the vehicles, the course, and the control.

A big issue to a lot of racing game fans is the vehicles in the game. They want to know what they can expect to drive or use in the game and what unique features each vehicle will have. You can treat vehicle design in a racing game in much the same way that you treat character design in other games. Each vehicle should have an illustration with the vehicle's features labeled and a concise description.

Another key factor in the design of a racing game is the courses. Each course should have both a layout and a description of any unique factors relating to the course. Figure 12.8 shows a couple of example racecourse design illustrations.

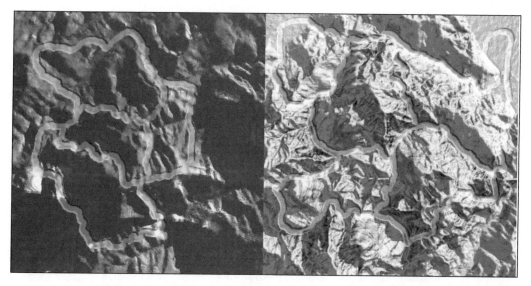

Figure 12.8
Racecourse design is a central element in racing game design.

The vehicle control is perhaps the most important aspect of racing games, but it is the hardest to show. Control is a matter of both the interface system and the physics simulator in the game. Both are hard to describe in a game design document. You can say that the game will have the greatest physics anywhere, and you will be just like every other racing game designer. That is why most publishers will not look at racing game designs unless they are accompanied by a game demo.

In the game demo, the designer can work with the programmers to show how the game performs. If you want to design a racing game, you will need to consider building a demo that shows how your game will perform. You may need some help here. A game demo is not an easy thing to build.

Fighting

A fighting game is generally defined as a game that focuses on the individual fighting skills of characters in the game as they combat other individual opponents. Like racing games, they are performance games in which control is a vital issue. The three most important issues for fighting game design are the fighters, the arenas, and the game control, as shown in Figure 12.9.

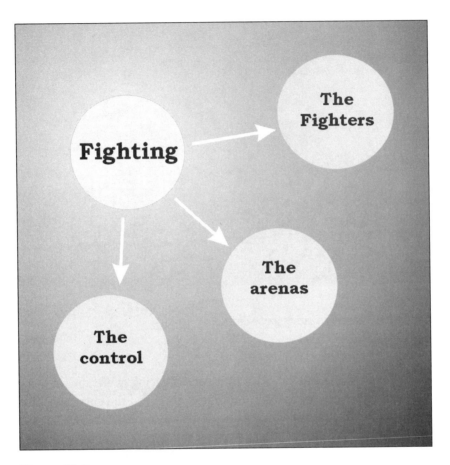

Figure 12.9
The fighters, the arenas, and the game control are important ingredients in fighting games.

Fighting games are about close personal combat, so the characters in a fighting game are central to its success. Character design in fighting games needs to be a lot more detailed than in other types of games. The character design is not just about how the character looks but about how the character fights, as well. In addition to character illustrations, the design should contain sketches of the characters' special moves and fighting styles. Figure 12.10 shows a sample animation design for a jumping spin move.

Figure 12.10
Animation design sketches are good to have in a fighting game design.

The arenas are also important in fighting game design. Many games have interactive arenas, which are becoming the standard for fighting games. An interactive arena is an environment where the player can pick up objects and use them in the game or where elements in the environment present hazards to the players. An example of this is an arena where the two combatants are fighting on a catwalk high above molten steel in a manufacturing plant.

As in racing games, game control is very important in fighting games. The control of the characters is vital to a good fighting game. Unlike a racing game, there are elements of fighting game control that can be part of the game design document.

Most fighting games have special button press sequences called *combos* that control the character's actions. These combos are a vital part of the game. When creating a design for a fighting game, you should create a chart that has all the combos for the game. This chart should be a prominent part of the game design document.

Sports

Sports titles cover a vast array of games, from traditional sports such as football, basketball, and tennis to less-traditional sports such as skateboarding and sky surfing. Because the rules for most sports games are well defined and understood by the players, sports games rely on other game elements to compete with each other. Some of the most prominent of these are the game graphics, the game features, and the player control, as shown in Figure 12.11.

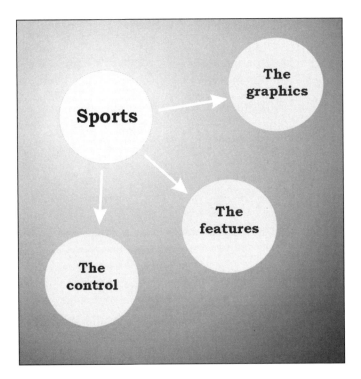

Figure 12.11
Sports games rely heavily on graphics, features, and player control.

Game graphics have become a very dominant factor in sports games. Many sports games are pushing the limits of the game systems to create some of the most amazing game graphics in the industry. At first glance, some games look like a video of a real game. With this kind of competition, any design document for a sports title needs to have some great graphics.

Game features are a key area of interest in sports games. Feature sets include items such as the number of statistics the game tracks, the number of teams, play editors, character editors, and many others. A feature might also be a license to use a famous sports brand. When you create a sports game design, you should include a game feature list. This is a list of game features in bold type and a short description of the feature in normal type. Feature lists make it easy for the reader to see what the game will contain without having to wade through a mountain of text.

Player control is also an important part of sports games. In games such as skateboarding or tennis, there is only one person to control, so those games are similar to many others. Other sports games, such as football or soccer, have large teams of players. The game has to have a way to control individual team members while at the same time controlling the rest of the team. Most of the time team control is in what is called a *playbook*. A playbook contains plans for how a team will work together.

The most obvious use of a playbook is in football games. In a football game, there is a break in the action so that the teams can set up plays. In a video game, the player sets up plays using a playbook. If the game you are designing has plays to control the team's actions, then the playbook should take a prominent role in the game design document.

Even if the game is not a team-based game, player control is still important to the success of a sports game. Just as in real sports, timing in sports games can mean the difference between winning the game or being a loser. If the game is difficult to control, players will become frustrated. Player control should be explained in the design document, but you may need to build a demo to show how it will work in the game.

Real-Time Strategy

Real-time strategy games are those in which the player controls multiple units to beat his opponents strategically. *Real-time* means that everything in the game is happening independently, similar to how things happen in life. When it is a multiplayer game, you are working on your base while I am working on mine. If we attack each other, someone else may come in and attack us both. The important elements of real-time strategy games are the command system, the units, and artificial intelligence, as shown in Figure 12.12.

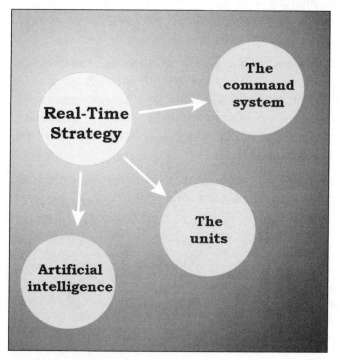

Figure 12.12
Real-time strategy games focus on the command system, the units, and artificial intelligence.

The command system is the way the player controls a large number of units. Some real-time strategy games may have hundreds of individual units. The player needs to be able to control what each unit is doing in the game. Designing a good control system is a real art form. If the player has to control every unit individually, the whole game can become tedious. The best real-time strategy games have a way of giving group commands to large numbers of units. This system for giving commands should be an integral part of the design document.

Units are very important to the real-time strategy player. Each unit in the game will have a specific ability. Some very powerful units will take a long time to build and have a high value in the game because of some special ability. Each unit needs to be balanced against other units controlled by the other players. This brings up a very complex system that needs to be explained in the design document. The best way to explain the system is to create a chart that shows each unit and what the unit does. The chart should also show how each unit counters an ability of an opposing unit. In this way, the reader can tell at a glance that each unit in the design has a clear reason for being in the game.

Real-time strategy games require that the player control many individual units. Some games have hundreds of units. It would be impossible to control every move of that many units. The solution for control of multiple units is to give individual units intelligent actions. In other words, if an enemy approaches a unit, it will react to the approach in a predictable manner.

Creating intelligence in a game unit is part of the game's overall artificial intelligence. Artificial intelligence is an important aspect of real-time strategy games. It needs to be explained in the design document so that the reader will know how each unit's actions will be determined. Will a unit always fight when attacked even when facing overwhelming odds? Will there be some determination of moral or strategic advantage? Can the player have some control over the orders for each unit?

The best way to show unit intelligence is to create a chart in the design document that shows unit by unit how each reacts to a given threat or encounter.

Turn-Based Strategy

A turn-based strategy game is one in which the players take turns in their moves. Chess is a prime example of a turn-based strategy game, as shown in Figure 12.13. There are two players who take turns moving play pieces on a board. The time it takes to make a move usually is not limited. Some games of chess may take hours to make a single move because the player is carefully weighing every option and even planning several moves in advance.

Figure 12.13
Chess is a turn-based strategy game. Copyright 2004 Corel Corp.

Turn-based strategy games are much more deliberate than real-time strategy games, but there are many similarities. The important aspects to consider when creating a game design for a turn-based strategy game are the terrain or play board, the unit abilities, and the opponent, as shown in Figure 12.14

In chess the game board is a flat surface with a grid of squares. The board makes up the play area of the game and controls the movement options of the players. The same thing is true for other turn-based games, but rather than a flat board with a grid of squares, there may be actual terrain with obstacles such as water or buildings. The navigation of the terrain is a key factor in the game. The game design should show detailed layouts of the terrain and explain the challenging features in each layout.

In chess the unit's abilities are primarily in how they each can move on the game board. Other strategy games may have other abilities such as combat abilities or defense abilities. The abilities of each unit have a great effect on the strategy of the game. The game design should contain a chart showing each unit and any abilities of the unit.

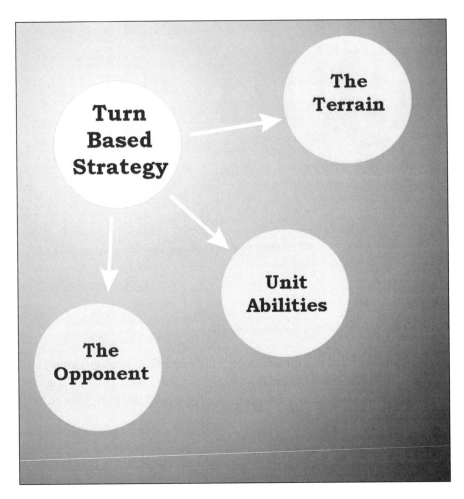

Figure 12.14
Important aspects of turn-based strategy games are the terrain or
game board, the unit abilities, and the opponent.

In turn-based strategy games, the player has time to control multiple units. Because the player controls each unit, it becomes very important that the intelligence of the player's opponent be challenging. This is true only when the player is in a single-player game against an artificial opponent. (The selection of real player opponents is up to the player, and the game designer has little say in whom the player chooses to play against.) The design document needs to state clearly how artificial players will be implemented and how they will challenge the player throughout the game. As the player's skill level in the game improves, the level of challenge needs to improve as well.

Shooters

Shooters are games in which the player controls one character or vehicle and tries to eliminate other players or characters by use of projectile weapons. One of the first shooters was a game called *Asteroids*, in which the player had a spaceship in an asteroid field. The object of the game was to destroy asteroids by blasting them apart. The player had to blast asteroids while trying not to get hit by any flying pieces from the asteroids.

Asteroids was a flat 2D game. Now almost all shooters are 3D games. Some of the best-known shooters are from a first-person perspective, where the player is looking out of the eyes of his player character. These games are aptly called *first-person shooters*. Other shooters put the player in a third-person perspective, so that the player sees the character or vehicle onscreen. These games are often called *third-person shooters*. In either case, the important issues are the weapons, the terrain, and the enemies, as shown in Figure 12.15.

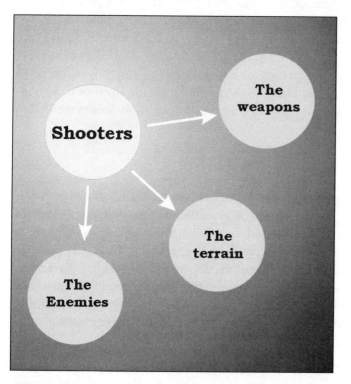

Figure 12.15
The critical factors in a shooter are the weapons, the terrain, and the enemies.

Weapons in shooters are important because they are usually the way the player advances in the game. Most shooters start out with simple weapons that have very limited fire-power. As the player progresses in the game, more powerful weapons are obtained, giving the player the ability to go up against more powerful opponents. The game designer should pay close attention to the weapons in the game. Not only are the weapon's capa-bilities important, but where the weapon is placed in the level is also important. Each weapon should have an illustration with a description similar to a character design. The location of each weapon should be part of the level layouts.

The terrain is also an important aspect of shooters. Some games make great use of cover where the player can find protection from enemies. In addition, levels may have areas that are difficult to reach because they contain well-guarded stashes of weapons or ammuni-tion. The layout of the terrain can have a huge impact on the game. The designer should create detailed level layouts with explanations for why the level is in the game. Each level should have a purpose, even if it is just to test the player's skills.

Enemies are important to shooters because they represent the challenge in the game. There may be some navigation issues in shooters, but the primary focus of the game is on finding and destroying opponents. Some games are totally geared toward players playing against each other. It is almost always more fun to play against a real opponent, because a real oppo-nent can be more creative than computer game intelligence. That said, almost all games are based on some level of individual play where the player squares off against computer-controlled opponents. If the game design calls for any single-player play, it needs to detail how the enemies will be controlled and placed in the game. An enemy attribute and place-ment chart is usually the best way to communicate this information in a game design document.

Simulations

A simulation is a game that tries to approximate the feel of actual life as closely as possi-ble. Simulators were some of the first computer games, although they were not thought of as games at the time. Simulators were first used in training. Some of the first simulators were flight simulators. It was much less dangerous and expensive to train new pilots in simulators than it was to have them crash in real life. The simulator also had the advan-tage of control over events, so new pilots could experience extreme conditions that they might not encounter in normal day-to-day flying. Even though they were not thought of as games, it didn't take long before people realized that simulators had many of the same elements as games, and they made the jump to entertainment.

From that early time of flight simulators, this type of game has grown to include almost every activity in life—from hunting to racing and from sports to raising a family. Almost every genre of game mentioned in this chapter and more have games that are very much oriented toward simulation. This makes it harder to define simulators, but it is important that the game designer understand the unique aspects of simulators as opposed to other games. These aspects are realism and controls, as shown in Figure 12.16.

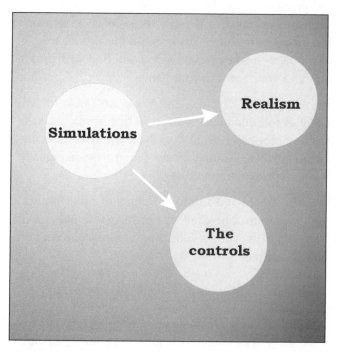

Figure 12.16
Realism and controls are of great significance in simulations.

The whole idea of a simulator is to make the experience of playing the game as close to reality as possible. The simulator is successful when the player feels like he is actually flying the jet or swinging the golf club. The magic of a simulator is that there is a real sense of accomplishment, even though the player is only playing a game, because the game is closely mimicking a real-world event. Unlike other games, simulators can have a strong impact on a player performing a task well in real life. To be effective in mimicking a real-world event, a simulator must be as true to the actual event as possible.

When designing a simulator, you have to communicate how you will be making the game as close to real life as possible. The realism has to extend to more than just technical accuracy. It also must be in the presentation as well. This includes the graphics and sound of the game. The more realistic the graphics look, the more likely the player will be to feel like he is actually doing what the simulator is simulating. If any part of the game looks or feels fake, the whole game can be put in jeopardy.

While making a game feel real is not easy to put in a design document, you have to indicate how you intend to make the game feel real. A game demo may be your best option, but if you don't have the resources to create a demo, the next best thing is to explain how you intend to create the feeling of realism. For example, if you want to create a flight simulator, you can include in the document extensive information about the aircraft and, for example, that you will be using a pilot as a consultant. Often you will find that professional friends are happy to help you build accuracy into your games.

When designing a simulation game, it is vital to have the controls as similar to the real thing as possible. Some games go so far as to build physical controls that mimic the actual controls used in the vehicle or aircraft. Some games even have hydraulic systems to simulate the movement of the craft. Most of these simulators are found in video arcades because they are very expensive for a game player to purchase.

In a PC game, the standard control is a keyboard and a mouse. Neither of these tools is a good choice when creating a racing simulation. The challenge to the game designer in designing a simulation is to find a way to get the game's control system to feel right even though it is very dissimilar to the actual controls.

Role Playing

Role playing games are those in which the player takes on the role of a character and develops the character throughout the game. The character becomes the central element of the game for the player. Unlike adventure games where the player also takes on the role of a character in the game, role playing games are focused on the character first and the story second. In fact, the character may continue from one game to the next. For example, the character may advance from the first game to the second game in a series of games.

Role playing games are best known in the area of fantasy to the point that most people equate role playing games with fantasy games. They are often referred to as *FRPs*, which stands for *fantasy role playing*. Role playing, however, extends beyond fantasy into many other types of games, including science fiction, war, sports, and racing. In fact, many games have role playing elements even if they are not pure role playing games.

Obviously, when dealing with a design for a role playing game, character progression is of primary importance. In addition to the character, the other elements that need to be addressed are the world or game environment and the game graphics, as shown in Figure 12.17.

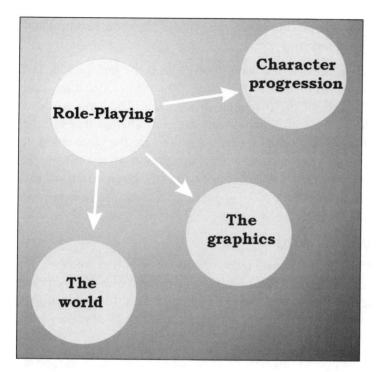

Figure 12.17
The world, the graphics, and character progression are very important in role playing games.

Character progression is the system by which a character advances in skills and attributes during the course of a game. Character advancement is usually defined by levels, and in most role playing games a character will have a set number of levels of advancement. With each level of advancement, the character improves. Depending on the game, that improvement might be in any number of areas, including strength, health, weapon skill, spell casting, dexterity, and so on.

It is important in the design document to spell out clearly how characters advance. If the game includes more than one type of character class, then the advancement of each class needs to be charted. The chart should include each character class and the number of levels of advancement. It should also include the effect of each level advancement on the character in every area that changes with the advancement.

The reason graphics are included on the list of important items for role playing games is the amount of competition in that area. Role playing games are among the most popular games to develop within the development community. Because they are so popular, the level of competition is quite high. One way to make a game stand out from other games is to have better graphics. Thus, role playing games are some of the most beautiful and graphically intense games on the market.

The third area that needs to be addressed in a design document is the game world. The game world includes much more than the terrain. It includes the creatures, characters, and everything else that affects the lives of the characters in the game. The game world is important because many players base their purchase of a game on whether they like the world. The design document needs to give the reader a good feel for the game world. It needs to illustrate the environments and include written descriptions of the places and characters in the world. In a lot of ways, it is a geography book of the game world, just like the geography books you study in school.

Massive Multiplayer Online

Massive multiplayer online games are played over a large area network such as the Internet. They get their name from the fact that hundreds if not thousands of players are playing the game at the same time. Some games may have hundreds of thousands of registered users. These games are like simulators in that they can be any type of game where hundreds of people can play together.

The games that lend themselves best to this type of game are those in which individual worlds or universes are created and the players represent the people who live in those worlds. Fantasy games are a natural, as are military games. Both of these types of games scale well to hundreds of players. Other games—racing games and platform games, for example—don't work as well because they are more individual in nature.

Massive multiplayer online games are very similar to role playing games in that the play is heavily focused on the game character. Figure 12.18 shows the three areas that should have prominence when doing a game design for a massive multiplayer online game.

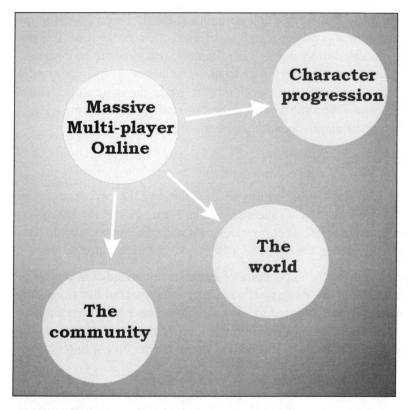

Figure 12.18
Character progression, game world, and game community are very important
to massive multiplayer online games.

Character progression in massive multiplayer online games is as important as if not more
so than it is in standard role playing games. Some characters in massive multiplayer online
games gain real value and are auctioned off on the Internet. Designing characters that
progress in skills and traits encourages players to invest a lot of time and effort into building their characters. This translates into hours of playing the game online, which generally means more revenue for the game. Character progression charts in the design can be
similar to those used in standard role playing game designs.

The importance of the game world in massive multiplayer online games is similar to that
of role playing games. The world is one of the major draws to players. The world for a
massive multiplayer online game is different in that it must be usable by a lot of players at
once. This means that whereas a role playing game might be able to have a more linear
design based on a specific story like an adventure game, the massive multiplayer online
game needs to be more open, with many stories happening simultaneously.

A game factor that is unique to massive multiplayer online games is the game community. The game community is the way players interact with each other in the game. It is not something that can be strictly controlled, but it is something that needs to be designed. You have to design the interaction of players in a way that encourages new players to enter the game while still giving long-time players a chance to live in the same world. Older players beating up on the new players ruins many games. You have to design game systems that help both older and newer players to work together.

Summary

This chapter has been a quick look at different types of games and the important design considerations for each. This is admittedly a subjective topic. The magic of your design may not be in the areas mentioned in this chapter. Your design is still valid, but you should consider each of the areas mentioned in the chapter for the game you are working to create.

Some argument may be made for the importance of elements not included in this chapter. These arguments are valid because everyone will look for the parts of the design that are most important to them. What you need to do as a game designer is take a good hard look at the game you are designing and determine the most important aspects of the game. Once you know what is important, it is easy to set up the document to reflect the important areas.

Designing a video game takes a lot of work and effort, but it is a rewarding and fulfilling job. The game designer plays a pivotal role in the development of new and better games. If you have enjoyed reading this book and developing game designs, you should continue your studies and work on some game designs of your own. The industry needs great game designers.

APPENDIX A

DESIGN DOCUMENT

Motocross Professional Circuit

Design Document

by

Alpine Studios

Copyright © 2004 by Alpine Studios, Inc.

Version 1.0

August 23, 2004

Table of Contents

Introduction

Motocross Professional Circuit is the sequel to the original *Motocross PC*. It is not simply an upgrade of the original game but is an entirely new game with a new engine and added features such as a course editor. The game is primarily a racing game but also has a fun arcade mode. Players will be able to upgrade their bikes and save them to the hard drive. Skillful play will unlock new courses with more challenging course features. Players will be able to move from amateur to semi-pro to pro status, encountering more highly skilled opponents as they advance.

Game Overview

Motocross Professional Circuit is a fast-action, high-energy motorcycle arcade-simulation game, offering exciting progressive racing action, competitions, and a unique career path seamlessly tying these elements together into a compelling experience. The game will follow the same format as motocross racing, with amateur, semi-pro, and professional circuits. Players will be able to advance from one bracket to the next based on their performance. With each progression, the opponents become better and the speeds increase.

The game starts out with the player choosing a bike and entering the amateur motocross competition at a local track. When the player wins at the local track, an invitation is extended to race in the amateur circuit. Completing the amateur circuit with enough wins will give the player an invitation to race in the semi-pro circuit. After completing the semi-pro circuit with enough wins, the player can move on to the pro circuit.

Rather than focusing on characters, the game will focus on bikes. The player's bike will be central to the game. Winning a race will give the player a choice of possible bike upgrades. To stay competitive with the other racers, the player will have to build a hot bike. Players will be able to save bikes to the hard drive and then use those bikes in races with their friends.

All unlocked tracks will be available for arcade mode. In arcade mode, the player will be able to receive bonuses for tricks. The track will also have a variety of pick-ups that the player will be able to grab and use in the race.

Platform

Personal computer with the following requirements:

- Pentium III or equivalent
- Windows 98 or higher
- 256 MB RAM
- 32 MB video card
- 16x CD-ROM drive
- DirectX 8.0
- Sound card
- 650 MB available hard disk space

Genre

The game fits into the sport racing genre.

Target Audience

Primary demographic: Seven- to fourteen-year-olds of both sexes.

Languages

English, French, German, and Spanish.

Street Date

Q-2 2005

Key Features

- **Three levels of expertise.** The game will follow the same format as motocross racing, with amateur, semi-pro, and professional circuits. Players will be able to advance from one bracket to the next based on their performance. With each progression, the opponents become better, the tracks become longer and more difficult, and the speeds increase.
- **Progressive racing action.** Each course will have three levels of difficulty. Players will start with the amateur course. If they win at the amateur level, they will be able to unlock the semi-pro course. Winning at the semi-pro level will unlock the professional course.
- **Bike upgrades.** In order for players to compete in the higher racing brackets, they will need to improve the performance of their bikes. With each win, a player will be able to choose from a group of possible upgrades.

- **Single and multiplayer.** The game will support two-player, split-screen racing.
- **Track editor.** Players will be able to design their own courses to race against their friends.
- **Two classes of bikes.** The player competes in the amateur and semi-pro classes with a 125cc bike. Once the player has completed the semi-pro level, he will be able to compete in the 250cc class.
- **Arcade mode.** All unlocked tracks as well as the 125cc and 250cc bikes will be available for the arcade mode, and nothing will be unlockable. This will be strictly exhibition-type racing. In arcade mode, the player will be able to receive bonuses for tricks.
- **Player selection.** The player will be allowed to select either a male or female rider and choose from approximately four different outfits.
- **Bike selection.** The player will have the ability to select either two- or four-stroke selections for each circuit.

Unique Selling Points

- **Sequel to the popular *Motocross PC*.** The game will take advantage of the popularity of its predecessor.
- **Realistic career mode.** Advancing from amateur to semi-pro to pro is in keeping with motocross.
- **Track editor.** Players can create their own tracks for both racing and arcade modes.

Career Path

The player will take the role of the amateur motorcycle racer. The player will then be able to advance from amateur to semi-pro to pro sequentially by placing in the top five in each circuit. As the player progresses through a sequence of events, he will be able to upgrade his bike with better equipment, thus making the player more and more competitive. Achieving given rankings in given circuits will unlock levels and hidden areas. Advancing to the professional circuit will allow the player to choose from the best equipment available. The 250cc bikes will be available only in the professional circuit. The final goal is to advance to #1 in the professional circuit.

Game Structure

Camera Viewpoint

The default camera will follow behind and slightly above the bike and will be aimed at the bike. Additionally, the player will be able to select a camera angle similar to the default position, but farther behind the bike, or a first-person camera angle, which will be viewed from slightly behind the motorcycle's handlebars.

Camera

In general, the camera will follow behind and slightly above the bike and will be aimed at the bike. In replay mode, the game will use a third-person camera.

Modes of Play

Single-Player

The single-player game offers the following play modes:

Career Mode

The player plays against a field of AI-controlled bikes in a series of progressively challenging races.

Arcade Mode

The player races against AI-controlled bikes in a predetermined or custom set up course.

Multiplayer

The multiplayer game offers the following play modes:

Career Versus

Two players each select a bike and compete against each other and AI-controlled bikes.

Arcade Versus

Two players compete against each other in a single arcade race.

Trick Mode or Free Ride

This will only be available in single- or two-player mode with the free ride track editor selection. The player will be able to compete in this area against another rider or high scores saved to the hard drive. Completion of multiple tricks will increase scoring.

Motions

Tricks and motions will be created using Maya and exported in the appropriate manner to the game engine. The motions that will be created for standard play will include:

- Ready/stopped
- Ready/riding
- Transition from stopped to riding
- Transition from riding to stopped
- Turn right/left
- Sharp right/left
- Lean forward/back
- Jump
- Crash
- Goose (wheelie)

Trick Motions

- Nac-Nac
- Cliffhanger
- Surfer/Seat Stand
- Recliner
- Gymnast/Pummel Bar Spin
- Can-Can
- Cordova
- Double Can-Can/No Can
- Seat Grab Indian Air
- Rodeo Heel Clicker
- Super Man
- Hart Attack

Level Overview

The 16 levels will be designed so that there are three progressively more difficult tracks on each level. Each circuit—amateur, semi-pro, or pro—is defined by a color. The red tracks designate the amateur circuit, the semi-pro circuit includes the amateur circuit but adds the orange track section, and the pro circuit adds the yellow track section to the semi-pro circuit. For example, as an amateur, the player will race through the red track. When the player completes the amateur circuit, then the semi-pro circuit is unlocked, and the orange track sections of the circuit are opened up. As soon as the semi-pro circuit is completed, the pro circuit is unlocked, and the yellow track sections of the circuits are added.

The following are the course designs:

Level 1: Race Around

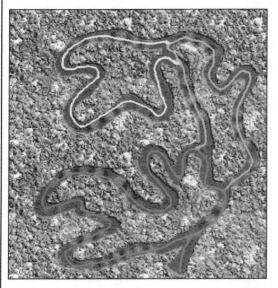

Level 2: Hillsdale

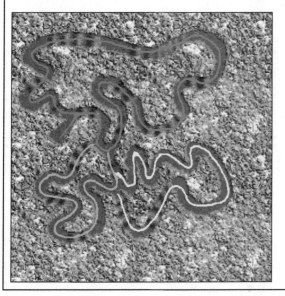

Level 3: Squirrel Tree

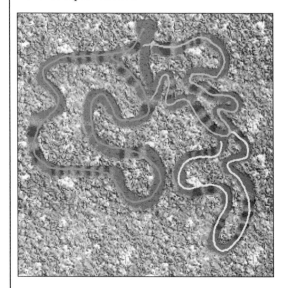

Level 4: Bear Claw

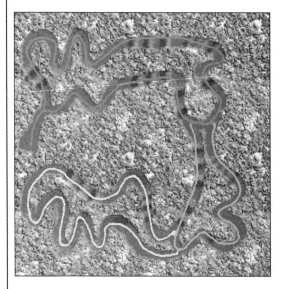

In-Game Progress, Timers, and Clocks

Textual and graphical indicators are needed to show the player's progress in each competition.

The following indicators will be used in all race competitions:

- Current position in the race, for example, second place out of eight.
- Running time for the lap and total running time for the race.
- Current and total laps to be raced, such as 2/4.

Race Replay

The game will have the ability to replay the last race, using a third-person camera. The player will have the ability to view the replay at normal speed, fast-forward speed, or slow motion.

Report Card

At the end of each race, a statistical report will be displayed. In arcade mode, the report will include each player's time and ranking. If the player is in career mode, the report will also include the player's placement based on the player's point total, the career points received based on his placement, his current career ranking, and experience points the player received.

Reward or Trophy Screens

After completion of each circuit, a trophy screen will reflect the achievement of the player if the player has placed in the top three places. Additionally, the player will be rewarded with a variety of motorcycle upgrades.

Model Production and Development

A generic model will be created for the programmers to use. This model will have a general shape, form, and textures related to motorcycles but will be a general form of no particular make. Once tested and refined, the featured bike can be developed using this generic model. The generic model is the basis for all the other models to branch from. This initial model shall be around 250 polygons. It is expected that this will take approximately one month to develop. There will be male and female characters to choose from. From there, the additional models will take 2–4 days to complete, depending upon the complexity and reference material available.

One of the best ways to collect reference material for the featured bikes will be to photograph an actual bike with a digital camera in similar lighting, background, and positions (front, side, back, and opposite side view). This information will be used to make the textures and geometry for the models. The textures can then be cut up, pasted, and blended to make realistic textures for the models.

Some bikes have strengths in one area as well as weaknesses in others, giving variety and personality to each bike. For instance, the 125cc bikes are not as fast as the 250cc bikes used in the professional circuit, nor are they as heavy.

Equipment and Upgrades

By progressing through the career mode and gaining experience points, the player will be presented with the opportunity (from sponsors) to upgrade the player's bike with different choices, depending upon the upgrade earned. Better brakes will be offered that will allow the player to slow down and/or stop more quickly; tuning the exhaust will create higher engine revolutions, thereby increasing the speed of the motorcycle; and so on.

Upgradeable bike parts will include:

Exhaust

Brakes

Tires

Engine

Chassis

Track Editor (In-Game)

The in-game track editor will use a grid, defined by approximately 100 ft. by 100 ft. increments. Each increment will be set up on the grid so that it can be rotated in the y-axis (up), placed on the grid where appropriate. The height and depth of each piece shall be scaled to give the appropriate look and play.

Preliminary pieces shall include the following:

Start

Straight

Ninety-Degree Turn

Whoops

Single Jump

Fingers

Table Top

Mound

Rhythm 1

Rhythm 2

Step Up

Finish

Triple

Turn High

Camel Hump

Ramp

Dip

Free ride track shall include:

Start

Ramp

Bowl

Dip

Four-Way Jump

Bank

Jump 1

Jump 2

Jump 3

Special Effects

Special effects shall include sparks, smoke, steam, gravel, and dust. These effects will use the existing particle engine. Smoke or steam will come out of damaged bikes, and dust will come from dirt roads or tracks.

Technical Design

Processor Use

The processor use will be similar to the Super Duper engine. The engine is expected to run about 1,500 to 2,500 Gouraud and flat-shaded polygons/second.

Main Memory Map

The main memory map will be similar to the Super Duper engine. It is expected that the memory will be used as follows:

0.5 Mbytes—code/stack

1.0 Mbytes—course track

0.4 Mbytes—vehicles

0.1 Mbytes—miscellaneous

Geometry

We will be using Maya to produce the bikes, riders, and tracks (or track pieces). We will be developing bikes and riders using approximately 250 polygons for high resolution, 190 for medium, 100 for low, and 75 for FPV model. We will have approximately 9,000 polygons split between high and low resolution worlds, explicitly built by the artists. Flat- and Gouraud-shaded polygons will be used for all the geometry.

Animation

Animation will be done also using Maya. We will update the Super Duper tools to convert the Maya output into format for use in the game.

Graphics

We will be using the So-And-So game engine (fictitious). The front-end will be high res (1024×760) and the game will also be high res (1024×760).

We will work with 24-bit textures/images, and the tools will reduce all images used by each section into 16-bit.

Audio

Audio will be installed on the hard drive during installation. Music will be streamed in real time from the hard drive. Sound effects will be loaded at the beginning of a race to allow immediate playing of sound effects.

Saving

The following will be saved to the hard drive:

Options

Careers

Stats

Bikes

User-created tracks

Physics

We will be using the same physics engine used in the Super Duper engine. Upgrades and changes of equipment will be the greatest factors in determining each motorcycle's handling. Each vehicle will handle differently according to how the player has equipped and adjusted the motorcycle during play.

AI

We will be using the same AI used in the Super Duper engine. The AI vehicles will follow nodes designated along the track. As an AI vehicle reaches the desired node, it will then track to the next node.

Art Development

The art development tools to create models and textures that will be used during development will include:

Maya Complete

Photoshop

Painter

DeBabelizer Pro

Vegas Video

The models and animations will be exported as a mesh through Maya, using the existing game engine technology in the Super Duper engine.

Potential Trouble Spots (Risk Areas)

Some of the trouble spots or potential risk areas we have identified will be in the following areas.

Player Control

The success of this game depends heavily on the playability and the ability it has to attract players and keep their interest. The playability or bike control by the player needs time to be developed and fine-tuned. It is very important that we create a playable game as early as possible in the development process. Therefore, our initial concern will be to focus on getting a controllable bike to begin analyzing the gameplay and developing this area.

Level Design

The artists need to be able to design fun levels with all objects and geometry located relative to each other in a way that facilitates wild runs as well as creating secret areas, hidden items, and so on. Each level needs to be carefully designed and tested. Again, our ability to import levels into the game engine easily to try it out is vital. We need to look into the possibility of having all data needed to define a level use the art modeling software Maya.

Texture Development

It seems to be a challenge, even with seasoned artists, to get properly balanced colors. We will create a version of the game that allows the immediate loading of art into it so the artists can make the necessary changes quickly.

Bug Type Description

Type A bug: Hard crash, unrecoverable, show stopper, reset is required.

Type B bug: Affects gameplay, but not a show stopper.

Type C bug: Minor bugs; "It would be nice if…"

Game Features

Fun

The game will appeal on two levels. For the serious racing fan, the game will have a realistic career mode. For the players who just want to have a fun race, there will be an arcade mode with high-flying tricks and power-ups.

Motorcycles

Bike performance will be a major part of the game. As players advance, they will have opportunities to custom build the best racing bike available. Bikes can be saved to the hard drive and transferred for play with friends on other PCs.

Gameplay and Rewards

The game will feature extensive gameplay in the career mode. We are currently planning to have 16 levels. Each level will contain three tracks, one for each circuit, for a total of 48 unique tracks. Players will be able to challenge the circuit in the 125 or 250 categories for 96 unique races. If the average race time is five minutes (many races will be longer), that is a total of 480 minutes of progressive racing action. The game also features a course editor, so players can build additional courses and race on them for virtually unlimited gameplay.

Obtaining bike upgrades and unlocking courses will reward players. With each race, a player is given a choice of upgrades based on his finish time and place among winners. As players advance from bracket to bracket, new courses open with more challenging course features.

Art Style

The art style will be enhanced realism. We will be using realistic models for characters, environments, and vehicles within the limitations of the game platform. Bright, vibrant colors will be used for uniforms, bikes, and environments to give the game a rich, visually exciting feel.

Art production will use both in-house and contract resources. Production tools include Maya for 3D; Photoshop, Corel, and Paint Shop Pro for 2D; DeBabelizer for file conversions; and batch operations and proprietary art tools for streamlining art implementation.

Audio Experience

Audio will consist of title tune, menu tunes, and in-game atmospheric and play sound effects. All sound and SFX will be done in-house by our resident musician/sound technician.

Game Structure

General Viewpoint

The default viewpoint will be behind and above the player's character. However, we will give the player the option of racing from other viewpoints as well.

Modes of Play

Single-Player

The single-player game offers the following play modes.

Career Mode

The player plays against a field of CPU-controlled racers in a series of progressively challenging races.

Arcade Mode

The player races and does tricks against CPU-controlled racers on a predetermined or custom course.

Multiplayer

The multiplayer game offers the following play modes.

Career Versus

The two players each select a bike and compete against each other and CPU-controlled racers.

Arcade Versus

The two players compete against each other in a single arcade race.

Player Controls
General Keystroke Controls

Steer rider left/right	Left/Right arrow keys
Lean rider forward/backward	Up/Down arrow keys
Break/hard steer	Control + Left/Right arrow keys
Look back	G
Throttle burst	B
Accelerate	Z
Camera select	A
Pause	Esc

Trick Controls

Trick Name	Keystroke(s)
Nac-Nac	D
Cliffhanger	S
Surfer Seat Stand	E
Recliner	F
Pummel Bar Spin	C
Can-Can	Shift + C
Cordova	Shift + F
Double Can-Can	Shift + S
Seat Grab Indian Air	Shift + D
Nothing	Shift + E
Rodeo Heel Clicker	Alt + C

Technical Issues

Geometry

We will be using Maya to produce the motorcycles and tracks (or track pieces).

Main Memory Map

The main memory map will be similar to the So-And-So engine. It is expected that the memory will be used as follows:

    1 MB—Code

    2 MB—Sounds

    2 MB—Front-end art

    16 MB—Bike 3D art (2 MB per bike)

    32 MB—Track

    53 MB Total

Animation

Animation will be done using Maya.

Graphics

We will start by using the game engine that was used in building *Super Duper Motocross.*

Audio

We will stream music in real time from the CD-ROM. Sound effects will need to be loaded at the beginning of a race to allow immediate playing of sound effects. The sound path will use the standard PS1 sound tools.

Saving

The following will be saved to the hard drive:

> Options
>
> Careers
>
> Stats
>
> Bikes

Physics

We will be using the same physics engine that was used in the So-And-So engine.

AI

We will be using the same AI as was used in the So-And-So engine.

Art Development

The art development tools to create models and textures that will be used during development will include:

> Maya Complete
>
> Photoshop
>
> Painter
>
> DeBabelizer Pro
>
> Video Vegas

The models and animations will be exported as a mesh through Maya plug-ins or MEL scripts that generate a compatible file that can then be used directly in the game where the models and animations can be read. The art files containing the bitmaps used to texture the object or character can be simple BMP, PNG, or TIM files.

We will update the existing tools to work with Maya instead of Alias to output an intermediate file, which is then converted into the correct output by another tool. This tool also collects together all textures used by a scene into one VRAM rectangle. It supports 24-bit TIF files and reduces all images in a scene to a single 8-bit CLUT.

Sample Art

Figure A.1
Sample motorcycle

Figure A.2
Sample motorcycle

Figure A.3
Sample main screen

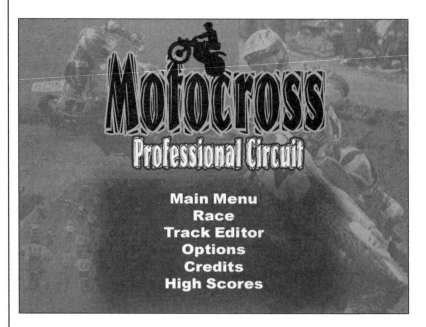

Figure A.4
Sample main screen

Figure A.5
Sample options screen

Development Team

Project Manager—LP

LP is a video game and entertainment industry veteran. He is the founder of Saffire, one of the industry's preeminent game developers. He built the company from humble beginnings in his basement to a thriving group of over 100 programmers, artists, musicians, and other creative people. In 1995, *Entrepreneur Magazine* named Saffire as one of America's hottest new companies, and in 1999, it was 32 on the Utah 100 list. LP is an active speaker at industry trade shows and conventions. He has served on the nomination committee for the Academy of Interactive Arts and Sciences awards, considered by many to be the Oscars of the interactive community. He also sits on the board of the Utah Entrepreneurial Forum and is a former trustee for UITA. He teaches marketing and entrepreneurship at BYU's Marriott School of Management. His artwork has appeared in more than 100 video game titles.

LP has overseen the development of the following games:

> NINTENDO OF AMERICA—*Nestor's Funky Bowling*—*Virtual Boy, James Bond 007*—Game Boy
>
> ELECTRONIC ARTS—*Cyber Tiger Woods Golf* –64

ACCOLADE—*Hardball 95*—*Genesis, NFL Legends 98*—PC

ACTIVISION—*Pitfall*—SNES & Genesis (Art Production)

RED STORM—*Rainbow Six*—N64, *Rogue Spear*—PSX

INFOGRAMES (GT)—*Abe's Adventures*—Game Boy, *Abe's Odyssey* II—Game Boy

HAVAS (Blizzard) *Starcraft Broodwars*—PC

SUNSOFT—*The Mask of Zorro*—Game Boy

KEMCO—*Top Gear Rally II*—N64, *RuneLords*—Game Boy

MATTEL (Mindscape)—*Kats and Dogs*—Game Boy, *Chessmaster*—Game Boy

ASC—*Animaniacs Bowling*—PSX

MIDWAY—*Bio FREAKS*—N64, PSX, PC, *Billy Bob's Huntin' and Fishin'*—Game Boy, *Serge's Heroes, Dreamcast*

TITUS—*Xena The Talisman of Fate*—N64

KONAMI OF AMERICA—*MLS Soccer*—PSX

Lead Programmer—SP

SP has been programming games for over 16 years, either as the only programmer, lead programmer, or senior programmer. He has also developed software tools for getting artwork, models, and motion into games.

Games developed include:

HardBall!—PC

Patton vs Rommel—PC

Mickey's Colors & Shapes—PC

Miracle Piano—Sega, Genesis

(English to French) *Game Boy Golf*—Game Boy

WWF Wrestlemania—PC

Space Jam—PC

WWF War Zone—N64, PSX

WWF Attitude—N64, PSX

ECW Hardcore Revolution—N64, PSX

ECW Anarchy Rulz—PSX

Started on next *ECW*—PS2

Combat Medic—PC

Motocross Mania II—PSX

Ford Truck Mania—PSX

Programmer—BI

BI graduated cum laude from Weber State University with a BS in mathematics and a French minor and then further pursued his education in the masters of mathematics department at Brigham Young University (Algebraic Topology, Adv. Linear Algebra, Adv. Ord. Differential Equation) with an emphasis in 3D computer graphics (graduate coursework). He started in Internet and Java development and became the Internet project manager and webmaster for several companies including Topjobsusa.com, topjobs.net inc., and UltimateResume.com. He was in charge of project development including the graphics for each of the sites. He joined Alpine Studios in April 2001 as a programmer to get fulfillment out of his career. He has enjoyed working on games on his own time since the first 8086's.

Games developed include:

Kublox—PC

Combat Medic—PC

Motocross Mania II—PSX

Ford Truck Mania—PSX

Art Lead—DW

Over eight years experience as director, designer, artist, and art lead for Acclaim Studios. Experience in Maya, Nichimen, 3-D Studio Max, Mirai, Photoshop, DeBabelizer, and WaveFront. Organizational skills include: setting up teams, organizing skill sets, hiring, distribution and reviewing artist and artwork, verifying completion of task and quality control, character design, storyboards, layouts, conceptual designs, logos, typography, illustration, highly motivated team player, dependable, honest, excellent teacher and communicator.

Art developed for:

Wrestlemania—PC

WWF Raw Is War—SNES

WWF Monday Night Raw—SNES

NBA Jam Extreme—Sony

NHL Breakaway '98—Sony

PC Conceptual Design, Lead Artist for *WWF Warzone*—N64, Sony

Lead Artist *Attitude*—N64, Sony, Dreamcast

Lead Artist *ECW Hardcore Revolution*—N64, Sony, Dreamcast

Artist *Anarchy Rulz*—Sony, N-64, Dreamcast

Combat Medic—PC

Motocross Mania II—PSX

Ford Truck Mania—PSX

Artist—GM

GM has over five years experience as a game artist. He is experienced in 3D and 2D applications including 3D Studio Max, Photoshop, Painter, Animation Master, DeBabelizer and Deluxe Paint. He has worked on such titles as *Marvel 2099*—PSX/PC (unpublished), *Invictus*—PC, *Rainbow Six*—N64, and *PGA Golf*—PSX.

Art developed for:

Tiger Wood's 2000—PSX

Shogun Racers

Tiger Woods 2000

FIFA Soccer 2000

Test Drive 2000

Test Drive Cycle

Test Drive 6

Test Drive Off Road

Cyber Tiger Golf

Marvel 2099

Marvel Comics Reference CD

NFL Legends 98

James Bond—Game Boy

Animaniacs Bowling—PSX

Tiger Woods 99

Atomic Bomber Man

Starcraft Broodwars

Combat Medic—PC

Motocross Mania II—PSX

Ford Truck Mania—PSX

Sound Engineer—EN

EN has been in audio/sound production for game development nearly 10 years. He is a musician himself, performing with various groups, and is currently a member of the Utah National Guard 23rd Army Band. As audio director, he oversees all audio requirements for Alpine Studios projects, from management to production.

EN has a bachelor's degree in music education from Brigham Young University, and a certificate in computer programming from Control Data Institute. Among his skills used at Alpine Studios are music composition, engineering, and sound design/recording. He has completed management-training sessions and has supervised several sound teams in the audio industry, as well as managing outside contracting and recording production.

EN's responsibilities include working with team leads, designers, and programmers in attaining the highest quality audio for each project. His duties involve sound effects design, layout and production of final effects, composition and engineering of original music, recording of musicians and voice talent(s), processing/editing and implementation of the final product.

Music created for the following games:

PSX, PS2

ESPN MLS Game Night—Konami

Tom Clancy's Rogue Spear—Red Storm Entertainment

Animaniacs at Ten Pin Alley—ASC Games

Barbarians—Titus

Motocross Mania II—Gotham Games

Ford Truck Mania—Gotham Games

Dreamcast

Army Men: Sarge's Heroes—3DO/Midway

Nintendo 64

Xena: The Talisman of Fate—Titus

Top Gear Rally 2—Kemco

Tom Clancy's Rainbow 6—Red Storm Entertainment

CyberTiger Golf—Electronic Arts

PC

Starcraft: Brood Wars—Blizzard Entertainment

Legends 98 Football—Accolade

Virtual Comics

Bionicle—LegoMedia

Combat Medic—Legacy

Kublox—Alpine Studios

Xbox

Strategic fighting game (project not yet released)

Game Boy, CGB, GBAdvance

James Bond 007—Nintendo

Billy Bob's Huntin and Fishin—Midway

The Mask of Zorro—Sunsoft

Oddworld Adventures—GT Interactive

Oddworld Adventures II—GT Interactive

Catz/Dogz—Mindscape

Microsoft Pinball

Bionicle—LegoMedia

SNES/Genesis

The Simpsons: Bart's Nightmare

Wayne Gretzky Hockey

Hardball 95

Schedule and Budget

#	Milestone Description	Date	Amount
1	Contract Signing	10/4/04	$xx,xxx
2	Design Document Approval by Publisher	10/15/04	$yy,yyy
3	Technical Design Document Approval by Publisher	10/31/04	$yy,yyy
4	Pre-production	11/22/04	$zz,zzz

Early prototype/preliminary play mechanics

Game prototype—Because a licensed engine will be used, this milestone will be a process of defining the look and feel of the game using the engine's current physics and AI routines. The prototype will include:

A. One controllable motorcycle

B. One track

C. Initial sounds

D. Initial interface screen

5	Production 1—Construction Milestone	12/20/04	$zz,zzz

Putting in the assets, race up and running, getting on a motorcycle, and riding it. This milestone will include:

A. Two complete tracks

B. Ability to race against other motorcycles

C. Scoring

D. Ability to make modifications to motorcycle such as color scheme, shocks, and brakes

6	Production 2	1/24/05	$zz,zzz

Half the tracks will be in the game with the ability to race against other riders. Game flow will be working. This milestone will include:

A. 2/3 of the tracks completed and in the game

B. 2/3 of the motorcycles will be completed and in the game

C. Sound effects for all tracks and motorcycles in the game

D. Particle system working

7	Alpha Version	2/21/05	$zz,zzz

All content is in the game. This includes all art and sound.

Gameplay should be indicative of the final product minus gameplay "tuning." Game will have bugs, including crash bugs, but all levels of the game can be played.

Feature complete. At Alpha, the game will have the features of the game but will still have bugs and may crash from time to time.

A. All art complete minus final tweaks

B. All sound complete minus final tweaks

C. All game features working and accessible

#	Milestone Description	Date	Amount
8	Beta Version	3/15/05	$zz,zzz
	All content is final and locked. No new art or sound will be added. Gameplay tuning is final. Game will have minor bugs but should be playable and have a majority of A bugs fixed.		
	All the gameplay adjustments are completed, and all known crash bugs have been eliminated.		
	Feature Freeze		
	A. All known crash bugs eliminated		
	B. All gameplay adjustments completed		
	C. All art and sound adjustments completed		
	D. Publisher standard compliant		
9	Publisher Submission	4/14/05	$zz,zzz
10	Publisher Approval and Gold Master	5/16/05	$zz,zzz
	Return of all Publisher's equipment to Publisher		
	Total		$xyz,xyz

INDEX

Gamedev.net

The most comprehensive game development resource

- The latest news in game development
- The most active forums and chatrooms anywhere, with insights and tips from experienced game developers
- Links to thousands of additional game development resources
- Thorough book and product reviews
- Over 1,000 game development articles!
  Game design
  Graphics
  DirectX
  OpenGL
  AI
  Art
  Music
  Physics
  Source Code
  Sound
  Assembly
  And More!

Gamedev.net